THE COUNTRY FORMERLY
KNOWN AS GREAT BRITAIN

Ian Jack edited the *Independent on Sunday*, of which he was a co-founder, between 1991 and 1995 and *Granta* magazine from 1995 to 2007. He began a career in journalism on local newspapers in Scotland in the 1960s and then joined the *Sunday Times*, where he worked for sixteen years as an editor, reporter and foreign correspondent. His work has appeared in many British and American publications, including the *New York Times*, the *Observer*, the *Independent* and the *London Review of Books*, and his awards include those for British journalist and reporter of the year. A non-fiction anthology, *Before the Oil Ran Out*, was published in 1987. He now writes regularly for the *Guardian* and lives with his family in London.

ALSO BY IAN JACK

Before the Oil Ran Out

IAN JACK

The Country Formerly Known as Great Britain

Writings 1989 – 2000

VINTAGE BOOKS
London

Published by Vintage 2011

2 4 6 8 10 9 7 5 3 1

Copyright © Ian Jack 2009

Ian Jack has asserted his right under the Copyright, Designs
and Patents Act 1988 to be identified as the author of this work

First published in Great Britain in 2009 by Jonathan Cape

Vintage
Random House, 20 Vauxhall Bridge Road,
London SW1V 2SA

www.vintage-books.co.uk

Addresses for companies within The Random House Group
Limited can be found at: www.randomhouse.co.uk/offices.htm

The Random House Group Limited Reg. No. 954009

A CIP catalogue record for this book
is available from the British Library

ISBN 9780099532132

The Random House Group Limited supports The Forest
Stewardship Council (FSC), the leading international forest
certification organisation. All our titles that are printed on
Greenpeace approved FSC certified paper carry the FSC logo.
Our paper procurement policy can be found at
www.rbooks.co.uk/environment

Typeset in Bembo by Palimpsest Book Production Limited,
Falkirk, Stirlingshire
Printed and bound in Great Britain by
CPI Bookmarque, Croydon CR0 4TD

For Lindy, Bella,
Alex and Harry

Everything unknown is taken as marvellous;
but now the limits of Britain are laid bare.

Tacitus

Contents

Introduction

There are the Welsh, the Scots and the English. Who wants to be British? Is there such a thing as Britishness? These are relatively new questions: in the 1950s and 1960s they would never have needed to be asked, and yet by the early years of this century the notion of a shared British identity had become so faded that a British prime minister, Gordon Brown, decided that it needed to be newly defined and invigorated if the United Kingdom was to survive in its present form and – the ulterior motive, his critics would say – under the direction of a Labour government. Hence Brown went in search of 'a British statement of values' that would provide newcomers to the country with an easily understood framework of their rights and responsibilities, repair the fraying union between England and Scotland and – again according to his critics – enhance his appeal to English voters by subsuming his Scottish identity inside a larger British one.

'Identities are not like hats. Human beings can and do put on several at a time,' wrote Linda Colley in *Britons: Forging the Nation, 1707–1837*, which when it was published in 1992 became the first book to examine, thoroughly and from an English perspective, the origins of a self-description that had satisfied most people in the island for more than two hundred years. Professor Colley argued that popular feelings of Britishness came out of the late eighteenth century, when industrialism, imperialism and the Protestant faith distinguished Britain from its European neighbours and bound the people of its various nations and regions together in a common enterprise. Today, each of these cornerstones has disappeared. First the empire went and then most of the manufacturing industry. Protestantism survives in ill-attended churches only as one faith among many, and all of them no more than little islands of religion in a sea of unbelieving materialism. There is hardly a British institution – the monarchy, the BBC, the Royal Navy – that doesn't fear for its future. In its different ways, separatist ideology flourishes among Muslims in Yorkshire as well as nationalists in Edinburgh. Most of the heavy industry that remains – steel plants, car plants, electricity generation – is owned by foreign companies. Britain believed it had secured its future by becoming one of the world's most open and lightly regulated economies, powered by London as the centre of global finance and sustained by the profits of banking, insurance, currency dealing and many other far more obscure ways of making money out of money. In 2010, that looked much less certain. Debt, it had turned out, had funded our prosperity and now the creditors were calling. In our new hair-shirt age, the hair shirts are sure to be distributed unequally. There may be many casualties. The one certain outcome is that Britain will feel a smaller place, with a rank in the world that reflects its shrinking importance.

The undertow of this book is the memory of a different country, the one that shaped my identity as both British and Scottish, and also, eventually, as a Londoner with a part-time life in Scotland. Compared to the great migrations of the past two centuries – for example, from Europe to North America, or Asia to everywhere else – this has been a small journey requiring no large adjustment, but the facts are that I was born in Lancashire of Scottish parents who returned the family to Scotland when I was seven. 'North Britain', a Victorian label that never became popular, would have fitted the cross-border territory of my childhood perfectly (the name survived in the grand North British hotels of Glasgow and Edinburgh, and in an express train, the *North Briton*, that ran between Glasgow and Leeds). This may be in part why the word 'British' has never offended me as a personal description, and also why I've never mistaken it to mean 'Greater England', which many English people have done, including someone as wise as George Orwell before he went north to Jura.

When I set out to write the pieces that follow, it never occurred to me that I was pursuing Britishness as an idea, and the word hardly features in any of them. Each arose out of contemporary places and events – the Hatfield train crash, say, or the Titanic film – and only in the course of reporting and writing did they turn into small historical studies, often drawing on the intimate experience of my family. Partly my temperament is to blame: 'What was it like before?' is a question I may be too fond of asking. Then again, the present always depends on the past, which makes the past a necessary subject of any reporter's enquiry. At any rate, many of them turned out to be journeys into odd corners of a particularly British civilisation that is vanishing, if not quite vanished. It was never, of course, confined to Britain – the empire saw to that – and in the 1980s in India and Sri Lanka it was still possible to find people and places (the jute workers of Serampur, the Anglo-Indians of McCluskiegunge) formed by the empire's social and technical legacy. These were good vantage points from which to look back and wonder.

Finally, a few details about the structure of the book. The longer essays aren't ordered by the date they were written, but the shorter pieces began life as newspaper columns and mainly appear chronologically. Many of both kinds appeared in an earlier form in *Granta* magazine and the *Guardian*. 'The White Elephant' is previously unpublished and 'The Serampur Scotch' largely so. Two others were commissioned by the *Independent* magazine and the *New Statesman*. My thanks to all the above publications and to: my agent, Gill Coleridge; my editors at Cape, Dan Franklin, Tom Avery, Alex Bowler and Alison Hennessey; my brother Harry; my former colleagues at *Granta* and my past and present editors at the *Guardian*, especially Annalena McAfee and Ian Katz; and to the generosity of Rea Hederman and Sigrid Rausing, *Granta*'s past and present publishers. I am particularly grateful to my friend Liz Jobey, a source of wise editorial advice over many years, who chose the book's pictures.

Just as great a debt, if not a greater one, is owed to the many people I've encountered and interviewed over the past two decades, in the Indian subcontinent as well as Britain, who gave patiently of their opinions, knowledge and personal history and never minded my shaping it to my own ends. For their time, indulgence and illumination, they can never be thanked enough.

THE COUNTRY FORMERLY
KNOWN AS GREAT BRITAIN

Granny Eliza Gillespie (seated second left) helping at a soup
kitchen during the miners' strike of 1921 or 1926

The White Elephant

January 2009

After my father died, my mother lived alone for twenty years in the same small flat that had once held us all as a family. My brother took the train from Edinburgh to Fife and saw her regularly. Less regularly, I'd come up from London and take her out in the car – trips that continued when she was in her nineties and which often took in the scenes of her childhood or the places she'd visited later with Dad. Until she married, her world had been very small and for that reason intimate to her. Most of the places she'd known as a child were within a morning's walk of her home in Hill of Beath, a mining village that had grown up at the foot of the hill of the same name, now a fleeting landmark to travellers on the M90 from Edinburgh to the north. Sometimes – 'on high days and holidays', as my mother would say – she'd taken the tram to the shops in Dunfermline or made her way by tram and bus to her granny's house in Kirkcaldy. But only when she left school to work in a Dunfermline linen mill – the year was 1921 – did travel other than by foot become an everyday occurrence.

It meant that nothing had rushed by her. No sight had been fleeting. On our trips by car through the same landscape eighty years later, she could attach incidents and stories to particular features: it might be a solitary house in a field or something as ordinary as a railway bridge. She would point out the place where once on a summer evening she and a group of her friends had paused to light a fire and brew up tea – and then they'd danced in the road, she said – on their way back from the beach in Aberdour. The sites of collieries were often identified: on land now occupied by saplings and smoothed hillocks had once stood the winding gear and conical waste heaps of the Lindsay, the Alice and the William pits. In Kirkcaldy, she would show me where her granny's house had been. It came just before the fields began on the road south along the coast and in its time was the last habitation before a despairing traveller reached Kirkcaldy's Poor House, a home for indigents that had been built outside the town.

'The folk going to the Poor House would knock on Granny's door and ask for a glass of water,' my mother would remember. 'They would have walked a long way. Aye, poor souls!'

I would listen in the car. Some of these scenes could be easily imagined and others could not. The water-drinkers at my great-grandmother's door might be seen as a Victorian story-painting illustrating the comradeship of the poor; householders showing charity to people not much worse off than themselves. The men would have boots and the women shawls, with perhaps the sail of a fishing yawl on the sea behind them and a small girl peering round her granny's skirts as the old woman poured water from a jug. The dancing in the middle of the road from Aberdour was more difficult. How were they dancing and to what music? Waltzes? The Gay Gordons? My mother might have mentioned an accordion or a mouth organ. I can't remember. In any case, the likelihood of my imagination matching my mother's keen memory is remote. We all have a slide show of our lives locked inside us, private scenery that nobody else will ever see, every verbalisation of its images distorting them or in some other way failing their rich significance to the rememberer.

To describe my grandfather, my mother's father, as a miner is a good example of how complexity can be so reduced. At some stage he may have worked for the Fife Coal Company down one of Hill of Beath's pits, but most of his pit-life was spent on the surface, where he loaded coal into railway wagons and trimmed it with a shovel. Later, he worked as a labourer in Burntisland shipyard. He wasn't a particularly strong man and he should have had easier work, but an early career as a door-to-door salesman for Singer sewing machines had been abandoned because he couldn't stand a job where he had to wear a bowler hat. Or that was his story, excusing the fact that he was probably too shy to make a good salesman and therefore anxious to quit the mental torment of door-knocking for any other employment, even employment that was as physically stressful as shovelling coal. The new job meant that he and his wife and young family left their house in one of Kirkcaldy's seaside lanes and moved eight miles inland to a miners' terrace in Hill of Beath. My mother could never specify the exact date but she guessed it to be about 1909 or 1910, when engineers were still sinking shafts in the Fife coalfield and mining towns and villages were expanding in a line that followed the coal seams east from Dunfermline until they reached the Firth of Forth at Methil, where new docks were being built to cope with the unprecedented tonnages of Fife coal being exported to Scandinavia and the Mediterranean. The Swedish connection was particularly strong: Sweden's state railways ran on Fife coal and Fife in return imported Swedish timber for pit props. It was also from Sweden that Fife's coal owners took one of their more progressive ideas, that pubs should use the profits from liquor sales to benefit their communities at large with improvements such as street lights and bowling greens, on cooperative principles that had first been tried in Gothenburg. The gospel of the 'Gothenburg Society' spread throughout the coal belt and almost every mining settlement built a large Gothenburg Tavern, sometimes in the Scottish baronial style that gave a misleading impression of their austere interiors (the Gothenburg Society believed comfort would encourage too much drinking). They became known as 'Goths' and even little Hill of Beath had one, just across the railway line from the Alice pit. When I drove my mother past it in the 1980s (it was demolished later), she would smile and remember its local name, the White Elephant. It was large, it was white, and, being a good distance from the village, it had perhaps never been a success.

Cowdenbeath, Kelty, Lochgelly, Glencraig, Bowhill, Cardenden: these were the bigger places, and when I first saw them as a boy in the 1950s they had a distinct way of living that separated them from the mixture of fishing, factory and farming towns in the rest of Fife. Their politics were different; from 1935 to 1950 they were represented by a Communist MP, one of only four Communists ever to be elected to parliament. Their wages were higher; a relation of ours who worked in a Cowdenbeath butcher's used to marvel at how much steak he sold to miners' wives on a Saturday. Their straggling high streets looked haphazard and unfinished, but they were brisk with trade. The furniture shops had three-piece suites and radiograms in the windows, the glass counters of bakeries were layered with pies and fruit slices, new televisions flickered in the showrooms of the cooperative stores. Public diversions, older than television but not so old, continued in the form of professional football (between 1948 and 1954, the Methil team, East Fife, won the Scottish League Cup three times), cinemas, bowling greens, dance halls, brass bands, evening classes in Soviet history at miners institutes and more career-minded study at the Fife School of Mining, where, thirty years before, my father learned the principles of heat engines. Apart from a few professionals – teachers, doctors, mine managers and ministers of religion – the middle class was invisible.

It seemed very stable; things would surely continue in the same way. In 1957 our school was lined up in Dunfermline's public park to cheer the Queen on her way to Glenrothes, there to open a new colliery where the pithead machinery was hidden inside two concrete towers. The Queen went down the shaft in a helmet and white overalls and came up again, people noticed, with the overalls unblemished by any contact with coal. Cool grey towers and white clothes combined to suggest that mining could be as modern as the making of TV sets, though it seemed a shame to me, as a drawer of things, that what seemed like an elemental part of the scenery (and one so easily depicted with a pencil – wheels and wires set at the top of a triangular frame) should vanish in the cause of looking new. The colliery, however, was not a success. 'Bad geology,' miners said. It closed in the next decade, by which time I was going out on my bike with a sketch pad to make drawings of chimneys, pits, mills, tenements and ship-breaking yards, not because I felt they would soon disappear, though some part of me may have sensed this, but because I was reading Alan Sillitoe and John Braine and other then fashionable writers from northern England, had seen the films made from their books, and wanted to draw myself, literally, into the same world. In my last year at school, I decided I would write an essay on 'Industrial Romanticism' and sat one June day on a hillside near our home writing a list of names – Émile Zola, Arnold Bennett, Charles Dickens – that I hoped would impress anyone who happened to open my notebook. But no sentences followed. I had no insights into their writing; all I knew, from the few books that I'd read by them, was that I liked what they wrote about, seeing in their subjects some part of my parents' lives that my parents never intended to be part of mine. In another place in another time, my father had threatened my brother, eleven years older than me, that if he didn't work harder at school he would 'go down the pit'. That elemental choice had seemed melodramatic even in 1950. By the 1960s it had become a joke among us, with my mother tutting and wondering how her husband could ever have made such a threat. It belonged to another age.

The mistake I made was to imagine that this age had never been new to the people who lived in it, that novelty (which in my case meant listening to the voices of the Everly Brothers in a café that sold coffee with froth on the top) was peculiar to my own generation. In fact, there had been no long unbroken past where our ancestors stepped unthinkingly into the shoes and habits of their elders, or not since the coming of the Industrial Revolution. Coal had been dug in Fife for hundreds of years, since the days of the monasteries, but the industry's boom years belonged to the same century as we did. When my mother moved to Hill of Beath aged two or three, she arrived in the village's smoke-smeared heyday, when its larger neighbour Cowdenbeath could be mentioned briefly in guidebooks as 'the Chicago of Fife' and mining families were migrating east across Scotland from Lanarkshire, where seams had been worked out and pits were closing. In the 1900s, this part of Fife witnessed spectacular change. Many of the new migrants were Catholics of Irish descent, and Fife had seen very few Catholics since the Reformation. Churches and schools were erected. A new tramway system strung electric wires over twenty miles of track that between mining villages climbed and dipped through open countryside; in darkness, sparks from a tramcar's pole would flash above the hedges and light up scampering rabbits and dozing sheep. Theatres and village halls began to show silent films, Italian families opened ice-cream parlours, the managements of football clubs built sloping earthworks where crowds of many thousands would stand on a Saturday afternoon to watch a game, Cowdenbeath v. Albion Rovers or East Fife v. Dundee. Eighty years later, my mother would talk in the car of these things. The long reach of her past tense made it easy to forget how new the society was that she had once been part of, and how recently it had come and gone.

Shortly before she died, in January 2002, my brother encouraged her to write down an account of her early life. When typed out, the result amounted to ten A4 pages. Their straightforwardness made them rewarding. She began:

My earliest memories go back to 9 Horse Wynd, Kirkcaldy, where I was born. I was about two years old. My brother Tommy had jumped over the wall to pick some flowers, [and] he cut his foot on some glass. I remember Mother bathing it in the basin and the water turning red. I also remember lots of flowers in the garden at the back of the house.

My mother was born Isabella Gillespie; 'Isa' to all who knew her. She had two older brothers – Jim as well as Tommy – and a younger brother, Lindsay, named after his father. Her younger sister, Lizzie, named after her mother, Eliza, was born two years or so after the family moved to Hill of Beath: 'I came in one day and saw Mother in bed with a baby, and I got a biscuit with pink and white icing.' There were no further additions to this particular branch and generation of the Gillespie family, though her father was one of eleven siblings and her mother one of eight. Their first house in the village lay near the White Elephant and next door to a man who kept pigs in his garden. Seeking more space, they moved twice. Eventually, just before my mother turned five, they settled in a three-roomed miner's cottage – scullery, living room and parlour – or what was then known as a room and kitchen.

We had paraffin lamps. The wicks had to be trimmed regularly or they smoked. The oil man came round with a horse and a cart with a tank and a tap – the oil was bought in gallons and half-gallons. We also had coal fires. The coal was delivered in half-tons and dropped outside the coal shed, where it had to be shovelled inside. Some of the neighbours would run short of coal and would borrow a pailful till their supply came. It was always repaid in full.

Modernity came with gas, installed by the Fife Coal Company.

There was great excitement when we got our gas lamps: no more trimming wicks or buying oil. But we had to buy gas mantels and they were delicate things, the least touch and you could put a hole in it. The lamps were in the middle of the mantelpiece with a brass tube we polished with Brasso. In the scullery the lamp was called a butterfly jet as the flare was shaped like a butterfly.

When the First World War arrived, her father joined the Royal Scots and, like his brothers, went to France.

We used to love it when he came home on leave, we all crowded round when he opened his kit bag to see the presents he brought home. I remember one time he brought a pair of brass ashtrays with Ypres' coat-of-arms in the centre.

He was wounded in France, several pieces were lodged in his arm and leg. They brought him home to a hospital near Grantham and I remember my mother and grandmother going down to see him. Then he was sent back to France and acted batman to an officer. Later he guarded German prisoners of war. He got quite friendly with some and exchanged photographs.

I used to have to go to Cowdenbeath to queue for meat and I think sugar.

I also remember the farmer letting us into the field after the potatoes had been harvested, to pick up the stray ones, and often a swede or turnip.

Jim started to work at Crossgates station [nearby]. He used to push a barrow with the parcels he had to deliver, sometimes away up to the farmhouse at the foot of the hill – a long trek.

Then there was Tommy.

Mother was looking forward to Tommy leaving school as he was nearly fourteen and would soon be able to work and bring in some money to help out, as money was pretty short. I don't know what the army pension was then. Just at that time a plague of fever broke out, scarlet fever and diphtheria: it was a common sight to see the ambulance and a nurse with the red blanket carrying her patients out of houses. Hardly a house escaped, ours among them.

Tommy went down with scarlet fever and was taken to the Fever Hospital in Dunfermline. I used to go to the shop – 'Dick's Co-operative' – to phone. The last phone call I made they told me he was sinking fast. I had just got home when the girl from the shop came to tell us he had died.

Father got home on compassionate leave and we all went to

the funeral in Kirkcaldy, where he was buried in Abbotshall church-yard. It seemed queer we all [the rest of us] escaped as in most houses two or three went down at the same time.

That all happened in 1918 [in fact Tommy died on 17 November 1917] and soon after, the war was over. I remember coming home from school and seeing sheets and blankets instead of flags strung across the road. I was young [she was eleven] and didn't take it all in, but it must have been a terrible time with all the homes that were left without fathers, brothers, etc. There were three uncles and three cousins killed in our family and others wounded.

She went to the village school, where she was 'fairly happy and managed to be around the top of the class in most subjects'. There were prizes.

I got a box of chocolates once from the teacher for being first in something, I can't remember what. What a treat that was, little round cream chocolates! I also got a prize from the Temperance Society. They used to come round and give us talks on the evils of drink; they brought models of various organs of the body – liver, kidneys and heart, etc. – and [told us] the effects of alcohol on them. The older classes had to write essays about them but us young ones had to print a card:

ALCOHOL IS A POISON AND NOT A FOOD

I got a book as a prize: 'The Pink Sash' [probably by the American children's writer Eleanor Hallowell Abbott]. When I lived in Farnworth [Lancashire, after her marriage] I loaned it to Eunice Lightbown and never got it back. I felt vexed about it but that's what happens to books you lend. Then in 1918 [her last year at primary school] for being top of the class the teacher gave me another book, 'Six Devonshire Dumplings'.

She kept that book throughout her life. Its cover had a picture of merry Edwardian children stamped into the cloth and the name of the publisher, Thomas Nelson. She must have read it, and perhaps more than once – the binding was cracked and the pages loose – though to my knowledge nobody else in the family ever did. She read a lot. In her eighties, when high blood pressure made her blind in one eye, she would persevere with newspapers, magazines and large-print editions from the library, examining them through a reading glass with such care and deliberation that when her verdicts came – 'quite good', 'not bad', 'an awfy lot of rubbish' – they seemed to carry the unarguable knock of a judge's hammer. But it wasn't books but the new experience of films that had left the more vivid memories.

We used to go to the 'Drome', a picture house in Crossgates. We used to get a penny for the pictures and a halfpenny to spend on sweets. Sometime we bought a comic. I think it was called 'Comic Cuts' – I remember Weary Willie and Tired Tim on the front page, a fat man and a thin one. The 'Drome' I think must have been short for Hippodrome, [but] it looked more like an aerodrome – a big bare hall with long wooden forms where we sat. Two or three steps up were the proper chairs for the grown-ups who paid threepence.

The screen was on a platform with a piano in front which had a light bulb in a tin box directed away from the screen [so that the player could read the music]. The keys were chipped and broken. How the girl managed a tune I don't know. Before the picture started, the kids were all over the place, running around the back of the screen chasing each other.

Then Mr Gilbert appeared [and] we knew it was time for the show to start and things quietened down. Mr Gilbert – always *Mr* Gilbert – was the owner. He always wore a trilby hat, had a very sallow complexion and must have been troubled with asthma as he wheezed a lot. The side door would open and a woman in a wheelchair was pushed in, one of those basket wheelchairs with a steering wheel at the front with a long handle. Then the show would start. There were serials which lasted for weeks: 'Exploits of Elaine' with Pearl White, 'The Clutching Hand', 'The Red Circle' . . . They ran a talent competition. I can't remember what the prize was but the children had to sing a chorus about the 'Exploits of Elaine'. It ran something like this:

Elaine, Elaine, I love you all in vain
Elaine, Elaine, you've set my heart aflame
Of all the girls you're the sweetest I've seen
– – – – – at sweet sixteen
I dream of you the live-long day
And then when I see you, you fade away
Elaine, Elaine, please come down from the screen
And be my moving-picture queen.

Sometimes Mother would take us to Slora's, the picture house in Cowdenbeath owned by a family named Slora who all looked like Japanese, though I don't think they were. They just had what we called 'ticht een' – tight eyes. That's where I saw and heard four men on the screen singing, and discovered later that a gramophone was at the back of the screen playing a record of the song, and not always keeping time. Later a new picture house was built, and all the school children had a free show the day it opened. We saw Mary Pickford in 'Daddy Longlegs' [1919]. The first time we saw an orchestra in the pit we thought it very posh.

Sundays were given over to religion and walking. The women (though not the men) in the family attended the kirk in Crossgates, until the Church of Scotland took over Hill of Beath's mission hall and made it into a more convenient place for local Presbyterian worship.

Our favourite walk on a Sunday after Sunday School was climbing the hill at the back of Hill of Beath village, quite a climb but a marvellous sight at the top, such a thrill to see the Forth Bridge. On the way up we passed a farm cottage – the couple who lived there had adopted a baby from Belgium, rescued from the Germans who killed babies and stuck their heads on bayonets, which we took as gospel truth.

In summer, we used to go to Aberdour on picnics, walking all the way and back [eight miles], two or three mothers and families with prams and pushchairs. We made fires in the wood next to the shore to boil the kettles we had brought with us. Had a great time on the sands and in the water. The sun always seemed to shine and how happy we were. Simple pleasure of the poor!

We also went on Sunday School trips on hay carts or horse-drawn lorries with forms for us to sit on. We all had to wear our tinnies [tin mugs] tied round our necks with white tape. We got milk and a bag of buns and we had races. I came second in one race and got a chain purse. One year we went to Loch Leven and it poured all the way and back. Just imagine us in open carts jogging all the way to Loch Leven, we must have looked a sorry sight as they let us into the factory canteen [there was a linen mill there]. I remember seeing the looms working dish towels.

Another linen factory eventually claimed her as an employee, but for now she was walking every weekday to her secondary school in Cowdenbeath, which took a domestic view of female education and taught lessons in laundry and cooking. There she had her lunch – threepence for mince and potatoes, tuppence for a bowl of lentil soup.

Sometimes if my mother gave me threepence for potatoes and mince, I would buy the soup and spend the penny on toffee at the shop across the road; we had a choice of treacle, fig or cream toffee sold in bars, which lasted quite a long time, sometimes aniseed balls, sherbert in little round boxes with a lid and a little tin spoon, lucky bags with soft caramels and bits of other sweets and maybe a ring or some other rubbish, liquorice straps, jube-jubes . . .

The paragraph is written with relish. This appetite for sugar – sugar as a treat – never left her and only from the perspective of a more health-conscious century does it seem remarkable or lamentable. Millions of women in her generation shared the same taste. They smoked only experimentally and rarely drank more than a sherry or, starting in the 1960s, an advocaat and lemonade. Sugar was the primary indulgence. An apprentice taste in sherbert and aniseed balls led eventually to a connoisseurship in chocolate and a stubborn preference for certain brands over others; Terry's of York becoming a kind of Chateau Rothschild for my mother and her friends, and Cadbury's a kind of plonk, whenever confectionery was discussed. They tended to be well-rounded women, often minus their original teeth, and sometimes you can still see their daughters and younger sisters hesitating at the counter of one of Scotland's few remaining sweet shops – shops dedicated purely to selling sugar with no side trade in newspapers or cigarettes – before their pointing fingers resolve the contest between a quarter of walnut creams or eight ounces of pear drops.

My mother left school at fourteen. There had been some talk of her serving in a shop in Cowdenbeath. Instead she took a tram with her mother to Dunfermline, eight miles away, where at Mathewson's linen factory she was interviewed and hired as a message girl in what was called 'the Service Room', the place where the cloth was examined after it had been brought from the looms.

My job was to go into the weaving shed and tell the weaver she was wanted if there were faults in her cloth. I was never very welcome. I had a lot of other errands – bringing up drinking water every morning in a watering can and filling up a big jar with a tinnie at the side for drinking, not very hygienic and a bit crude. The young apprentices in the Mechanic Shop used to tease me a lot when they saw me, they used to drop pieces of coal in the water and I had to go back and fill the can again. After a year of this I was promoted and had to stand at a table and look for faults. We were called cloth pickers. Sometimes I was on the folding machine, which folded the cloth into bundles to be sent to the bleachworks to be bleached white; it was cream before. They made lovely linen tablecloths and napkins and we got faulty ones quite cheap. I used to buy tablecloths for P & O line, big cloths for only 4s 6d with the name cut out, we could easily patch it with scraps of linen. We also wove tablecloths for the Lyons cafés, white with lions on the yellow border. I had plenty of linen in my bottom drawer when I got married, I never had to buy a dish towel for years.

We used to travel to work in the tramcar, quite a few of us travelled together. There was no other work then in a mining village, there was only going into service [as a domestic servant], though some girls used to work on the pithead, coarse dirty work standing at a conveyor belt picking stones and rubbish from the coal. That was dying out by the time I started work so most of the girls had to travel to Dunfermline. We could buy a weekly tram ticket in the factory, which cost us two shillings for six days.

The trams were always full and often we had to sit upstairs in the open. Fine in the summer, but bitterly cold in the winter, especially if it snowed. Sometimes the pulley which travelled along the line [the overhead electric wire] came off and swung round nearly knocking us off our seats – we had to duck fast.

We usually took sandwiches to the factory. We had a bothy there. We all had our own teapots, we put the tea in and at the dinner hour the bothy wife filled them with boiling water and put them on the hotplate ready for us coming in with our sandwiches. If it was cheese we put it on the plate to heat and melt the cheese – delicious!

The wages were seventeen shillings a week, soon reduced to ten shillings a week (because of 'some Truck Act', my mother said), with one week's unpaid holiday in the summer, which was always spent at home; excursions couldn't be afforded and visits to Kirkcaldy were rarer now that her granny had died. The one trip she recalled was with her chum Nellie Paterson, a weaver in the factory, who had a granny who lived in the fishing village of St Monans in east Fife and uncles and cousins who were fishermen there. She spent a few days in St Monans with Nellie during one New Year, saw the famous ship model hanging from the roof of the church, and had 'a nice time walking to Pittenweem, Cellardyke and Anstruther visiting relations'. It was also with Nellie that she walked every Sunday evening to and from her Bible classes at Moss Green Church. 'Two nice boys used to walk home with us. Boys and girls in our teens, we just enjoyed each other's company: when I look back, we were all very innocent compared to the young of today.' Innocent, but not always safe in their innocence.

I had a nasty experience when I was fifteen or sixteen. It happened one dark night in the winter. My chum [another friend, Jenny] and I were walking home from Cowdenbeath. When we got to Woodend, where we usually turned to go home, we decided to carry on down the main road leading to the White Elephant [and turn there instead]. It was very dark, fields on either side and no lights except for an occasional tram. Anyway, we were walking along chatting away when all of a sudden I was grabbed from behind. My chum ran away and I was left struggling with this man – he nearly had me down, but Jenny came running back. All of sudden he let go, not because Jenny came back but some miners going to work on the night shift – he must have heard them talking. A lucky escape for me as I don't know what might have happened. I certainly got a fright. I never said anything when I got home, but I was very wary after that.

The incident remained a secret. I never heard her mention it, though I often drove her past the scene of the crime, and I doubt that she told my father either. He met her three or four years later. By this time her younger brother, Lindsay, was an apprentice in the Mechanic Shop at Mathewson's, where my father had finished his own apprenticeship and now worked as a time-served mechanic. There was a seven-year difference in ages but the two young men became friends and on a Saturday afternoon or a Sunday would go out cycling together. In this way, he met my mother properly, though he must have caught sight of her often in the factory as one of the girls who sewed small pieces of red thread into flawed cloth, to show weavers where the fault lay. Then he wooed her.

I was nineteen when Dad asked me to go the Opera House in Dunfermline to see 'St Joan' by Bernard Shaw. We sat in the circle and he gave me a bag of sweets, toffee-covered Brazil nuts; after that, when we started going out regularly, it was usually chocolate gingers he gave me. But the first time he asked me out was to a whist drive and dance. I think it was run by the Cyclists' Touring Club. He didn't dance and I wasn't much good at whist. We got through somehow.

They were married on Christmas Day, 1930, after a courtship prolonged by my father's absence at sea as a junior engineer on a freighter. They left Fife the day after their wedding and spent the first twenty-two years of their married life in Lancashire, where my father had found a job. After my mother quit Mathewson's she never left home to work again, though there was a short time in my childhood when money was short and she went a few mornings a week to clean the house of a rich, or richer, woman on the better side of the Lancashire town where we lived. Then in 1952 they returned – my father to a job in one of the few linen mills that remained in Dunfermline, my mother as a house-wife. We moved to a village six miles from Dunfermline and about the same distance from Hill of Beath, and unlike either place; its population had been changed by wartime settlements of soldiers and sailors and it stood on the very edge of Fife, just across the Forth from Edinburgh. Only a small geographic distance now separated my parents from their youth; the bigger separation was the changes that time had brought. Sometimes I'd hear them talking about things that had vanished (the trams) or things that had shrunk (the mills and mines). Often they would mention 'the Factory', as though there had been only one of them, though in the course of his life my father had worked in many. They remembered and met again friends who had worked 'in the Factory' and with them wondered what had become of 'that lassie Kate' or 'thon felly Jim'.

After a few years at the village school, I was promoted to secondary education in Dunfermline. There, during our lunch hours in the late 1950s, a group of us would sometimes amuse ourselves by walking across the playing fields and following a small river, jumping from rock to rock, that ran through an echoing culvert under the railway. It emerged by the side of what had been a square reservoir, now slowly filling with mud and weeds. It had banks made of brick. Stone walls, reduced and overgrown, ran in straight lines and met at right angles. It was difficult to imagine what these were ruins *of* exactly, but eventually it occurred to me that they must have belonged to Mathewson's mill, which had closed in the early 1930s, when the demand for Dunfermline linen had slumped. The reservoir had supplied the steam boilers and the bleach-works; the broken walls were of the weaving sheds; this had been 'the Factory', placed above all other factories in my parents' talk because they had spent their young lives there and it had brought them together, the mechanic and the cloth picker.

Nettles, willowherbs, brambles: nothing suggested that ocean-going tablecloths had once been woven there or a girl's cheese sandwiches warmed on the hob. In 1959, Mathewson's end hadn't been so long ago – 1930 was closer to 1959 then than 1959 is to now – but such complete ruination, weeds replacing work, was one of the things that made my parents and so many others of that place and generation seem like survivors from a previous British age. Of course, nobody then had any idea of how much of this there was to come. In our geography class, the maps of Britain still had labels attached to towns and regions: jute against Dundee's name, ships next to Newcastle and Glasgow, coal and wool marked across the great space of Yorkshire, motor cars at Birmingham . . . and so on and on.

Last month I went to Hill of Beath, more or less accidentally. I'd hired a car at Edinburgh airport and was driving through Fife towards Glenrothes, where the Scottish Nationalists were thought likely to defeat the Labour Party in a by-election – in the event, they didn't – and I was to write a newspaper piece.

It was a fine October day. From the M90, the green lump of Hill of Beath's hill stood against a sky that was mainly blue. I turned off and began to drive along the small roads where I'd sometimes taken my mother, until I reached the site of the White Elephant, where a smaller road forked left up the slope to the village itself. There I parked in a cul-de-sac of post-war council houses where the only other vehicle was a battered American estate that had been done up as a kind of hearse. *Dead cars wanted*, said the Wild West lettering on the side. *Top prices paid.* A couple with a pushchair waited at the bus stop, but after the bus came and stopped briefly to swish its doors I saw no other person moving on the streets. Almost all the houses of my mother's childhood, the low brick terraces built by the Fife Coal Company, had been replaced by homes with gardens, brass door-knockers and satellite dishes; and sometimes simply by open ground. What was left here that she would have known? Very few things: The kirk still had a bell exposed on its belfry, but it was now a private house; a terrace on the main street looked to have survived from her era, but it now contained the Rapid Mini Market and the Peking House Takeaway, where a Happy Meal for One cost £5.50. Only the war memorial, which my mother must have seen unveiled, stood as she would have remembered it, listing the forty or so village men who had made 'the supreme sacrifice in the Great War' and happily omitting her father's name. But even the war memorial had been overshadowed by modernity, because in front of it stood a bronze statue of a footballer, poised to flick the ball that rested beside his left boot. This was Hill of Beath's most celebrated son, Jim Baxter (1939–2001), who worked in the pits as a teenager before he took up professional football to become, some would say, the finest player ever to have come out of Scotland. Gordon Brown, the local

MP and at that time Chancellor of the Exchequer, had spoken at the statue's unveiling. 'This is a man who was an inspiration to us all,' Brown told the crowd, forgetting or choosing not to remember that drinking, betting and womanising – Baxter's own version of the supreme sacrifice – had cut short his career by ruining his remarkable physical skill.

I walked about for a while and met nobody. Incredibly, there had been class warfare in these streets once. My mother would remember that in the pit strike of 1921 a colliery manager had been dragged to the brickworks pond and given a ducking. 'Poor man,' she would say, 'he'd done nobody any hairm.' Nothing of that time remained. Hill of Beath looked like a small and not very prosperous suburb, with arrowed traffic signs – this way to the recycling point, that way to Dunfermline – as its most prominent features. The southerly wind carried the sound of cars humming along the Fife Expressway, a straight, fast slash across the county that has made redundant the slow and intriguing geography of twisting roads and the branch railways that ran to the mines.

My mother was a quiet and stoic woman – I never once saw her cry – and it was always hard to know how much of the past she mourned. 'We've lost so much,' she said to me one day when we were in the car and had come by chance on the remains of a rural railway junction – hen houses and old tyres scattered across its former platforms – where she remembered flower gardens and changing trains with Dad. But that was in a prettier part of Scotland than Hill of Beath. The fact that she had once lived in such a place and time seemed, if anything, to surprise and amuse her. Its passing wasn't a great cause for regret; even as a child, perhaps, she had always been glad to get out. Her regular summer escape to Kirkcaldy is where her little memoir abruptly ends.

I used to love it, running down to the beach in our bare feet, we played there all day. Granny always said we were no trouble. If it was raining we sat and read most of the time. Jim bought the Boy's Own Paper [and the *Magnet* comic] – Billy Bunter, Bob Cherry, Harry Wharton, etc., at Greyfriars.

My other granny, my mother's mother, lived not far along the street. She was a widow with one son at home, Uncle Dave. We never stayed there but we always visited. One time we went up the stair we met a neighbour. She told my granny afterwards we didn't look like miner's bairns. We were too well dressed, I think.

Granny lived across the street from an ice cream shop, where she sent us across for ice cream wafers, sliders as we called them. Her first husband, my grandfather, died in his forties. I never knew him, but they had seven of a family. She married again to Sandy Gunn – we always called him that. I don't know how long they were married but she died during the First War when he was in the army – Sergeant Gunn. I don't know where he went after that as I never heard anything about him. He was good to us when we were young. I remember him buying us presents. There was some talk of him marrying again, that was all.

I remember my mother, Aunty Anne and Aunty Jen dismantling [clearing] the house and taking what they wanted. That's when we got the toby jug among other things. She had a nice house on a stair, four or five rooms, the kitchen facing the water. In the summer the window would be wide open. I liked to stand and look at the sun shining on the water – it was lovely, such a change from Hill of Beath.

I think of her sitting in her armchair and writing these words at the beginning of this new century. A woman of more than ninety, she has a shawl on her shoulders and her back is to the window. Beyond the window lie the woods, and beyond them, tucked in a hollow and invisible from my mother's flat, the villa where the James Mathewson of Mathewson's factory used to live and where once, as a young apprentice during the First World War, my father had been summoned the six miles from the factory to help fix the plumbing. For half a century my mother has watched these woods turn green every spring and brown every autumn, and never once remarked that the estate they grow on was bought from the profits of the linen industry. Why would she? Like so many things, Mr Mathewson went long ago to the same White Elephant's graveyard.

She sits with her ballpoint and hesitates. Her walking stick is laid carefully within reach on the sofa. Her hearing aid is turned up so she won't be surprised when her home-carer bursts in and shouts in her Fife sing-song, 'How are ye the day, Mrs Jack?' That morning's *Dundee Courier* has been read and delivered its usual ration of distant alarms: 'BOY, 12, FOUND DRUNK AND DISORDERLY', 'CRASH KILLS

THREE ON A92'. Her granny's toby jug sits on top of the bookcase, the chipped gold rim of the fat little gentleman's hat glinting in a shaft of the sun. She is remembering an idea of beauty and struggling, as we all do, to describe it

Unsteady People

October 1989

On 6 August last year a launch overturned in the River Ganges near Manihari Ghat, a remote ferry station in the Indian state of Bihar. Many people drowned, though precisely how many will never be known. The district magistrate estimated the number of dead at around 400, the launch owner at fourteen. The first estimate was reached by subtraction: 529 tickets had been sold and only a hundred passengers had swum ashore. The second estimate came from the number of bodies the launch owner said he had counted stretched out on the bank. But then the river was in flood; hundreds of bodies could have been swept far downstream; scores may still be entangled in the wreckage or buried in the silt. The launch owner had good reason to lie.

It was, in its causes and consequences, an accident which typified the hazards of navigating the River Ganges. Monsoon rains had swollen the river and changed its hydrography, cutting new channels and raising new shoals. The launch was overcrowded. Licensed to carry 160, it seems to have set out with at least three times that number, nearly all of whom were fervent Hindu pilgrims travelling from their villages in north Bihar to a shrine that lies south of the river. Devotees of Lord Siva, the destroyer, they wore saffron robes and carried pots of sacred Ganges water on their shoulders. Eyewitnesses said the launch left the north bank to the chanting of Siva's name, the chorus in Hindi, *'bol bam'*, rising from the massed saffron on the upper deck; until, hardly a hundred metres from the shore, the chants turned into screams.

According to a survivor quoted in the Calcutta newspapers, what

21

happened was this. As the launch moved off, its stern got stuck in the shallows near the bank. The skipper decided to redistribute his vessel's weight, to lighten the stern by weighing down the bow. He asked his passengers to move forward; the stern bobbed up and the launch surged forward, head down and listing badly, to run a few hundred feet into a submerged sandbank and capsize.

In Bihar a revengeful clamour arose which sought to identify the guilty and exact punishment. The Bihar government and its servants blamed the launch owner and charged him with murder. The opposition blamed government corruption and the conduct of the police. According to Ajit Kumar Sarkar, a Marxist member of the Bihar Legislative Assembly, the launch took six hours to sink, and many victims could have been saved had not the police beaten back agitated crowds of would-be rescuers on the shore. According to the police, corruption had made their job impossible; almost every Ganges ferry flouted safety legislation because the ferry owners organised 'gangs to protect their interest'. Bihar had a 'steamer mafia' whose profits had perverted the political administration. Chief among this mafia was Mr Bachcha Singh, the 'steamer tycoon of Bihar' and owner of the launch that had gone down at Manihari Ghat.

Some days after the accident another of Mr Singh's vessels approached the wreck, ostensibly with the task of dragging it off the sandbank and on to the shore. Watchers on the bank, however, saw something different. They saw the second vessel pressing down on the wreckage of the first. It seemed to them that the other ship had come to bury the launch and not to raise it, thus destroying the evidence and, in the words of the *Calcutta Telegraph*, 'obscuring the gravity of the tragedy'. In the face of public protest the second ship backed off.

Where, meanwhile, was the steamer tycoon Mr Bachcha Singh? Nobody could say. The Chief Minister of Bihar promised 'stern action', charges of murder and negligence were registered in the courts and some of Mr Singh's property was seized. But the police said they could not find Singh himself. He was, in the English of official India, 'absconding' and so the courts declared him an 'absconder'.

Thereafter public interest evaporated with the monsoon rains. Manihari Ghat became just another Ganges launch disaster. The people who had died were poor. None had relatives influential enough to secure the lasting attention of the press or the government, both of which in any case were soon preoccupied with other problems.

What was the precise truth of the affair? Nobody could say. Truth in its least elevated and most humble sense, truth as detail, truth as times and numbers, truth arrived at by observation and deduction – this kind of truth left the scene early. Like Mr Singh, it absconded. Unlike Mr Singh, it did not reappear.

Six months later I met the steamer tycoon at his house in Patna, the state capital. To European eyes, the house looked like something a Nazi cineaste might have built. It had the smooth curves of a pre-war suburban Odeon and a large tower with two large swastikas etched high up in the concrete; they were visible from my cycle rickshaw long before the mansion itself swung into view. Mr Singh had called it 'Swastika House' – the name was on the gate – but only because he was a devout Hindu and the swastika is an ancient Hindu symbol of good fortune.

Fortune had been good to Mr Singh. It was manifest in his living arrangements, the dozens of domestic servants, his house's fifty bedrooms and thirty bathrooms, the superior quality of his tipped cigarettes. All of this (and a good deal else – apartments in Calcutta, real estate in the USA) derived from Mr Singh's role as the Ganges's principal ferryman. But his person as opposed to his surroundings seemed untouched by wealth. He was a small old man with heart trouble who wore loose Indian clothes and tapped ash from his Gold Flake King Size into an old spittoon.

We sat on his terrace and drank tea from mugs. I wondered about the murder charge. What had happened to it?

Nothing, said Singh, the case would never come to court. Did I understand the caste system? In Bihar caste was the key to everything. The murder charge had been instigated by the then chief minister, who was a Brahmin. Singh belonged to the Rajput caste, and Rajputs were the Brahmins' greatest political rivals. The charge had been politically inspired.

And now?

'Now the chief minister is a Rajput. He is known to me. Case finish.'

He apologised for his English and called for his son, who, he said, would be more intelligible to me. This proved to be only partly true. The younger Singh was reading business administration at Princeton

University, ferry profits having dispatched him to the United States when he was an infant, and his English crackled with the abrasive nouns of the new capitalism. 'Cash-burn . . . acquisition and diversification . . . buy-out.' It was strange to hear these words in Bihar, still governed by ancestry and feudal law, but they completely matched the younger Singh's appearance. In T-shirt, shorts and sneakers, he might have stepped out of a college tennis game. The sight of son next to father, crouched beside his spittoon, was a testament to the transforming power of money.

The father had recalled his son to Patna soon after what both referred to, opaquely, as 'the tragedy'. The son looked at his new surroundings with cold eyes. Corruption, poverty, ignorance, tradition – they ruled life here. It was sickening. Outside the family, nobody could be trusted. Did I know, for example, that after the tragedy peasants from adjacent villages had brought newly dead relatives to the river, so that their bodies could be discreetly inserted among the launch's victims and compensation claimed?

I hadn't heard that, but maybe it was true; Bihar can sometimes be a desperate place. But what did he think had caused the accident?

'Panic and stupidity,' said the younger Singh. He thought for a moment. 'Basically these people weren't willing to make the smart move and analyse the situation.'

Of course these were ludicrous words; passengers packed on a tilting motor launch cannot be expected to plan their next five minutes like Wall Street commodity brokers. But the longer I travelled through Bihar, squashed on trains and riverboats, the more I recognised the younger Singh's detachment as an indigenous sentiment rather than an American import.

Certain facts about Bihar were undeniable. The launch owners were greedy and their craft decrepit and dangerous; the police were corrupt and tended to enforce the law of the highest bidder – the younger Singh said himself that his family had put off police enquiries with a few thousand rupees; and covert supplies of money moved through the system at every level – an honest police officer could have his orders countermanded by a corrupt district administrator; an honest district administrator could be transferred or demoted by a corrupt politician. To behave dutifully and honestly in this amoral environment involved great courage and sacrifice. It was no surprise that the safety of the travelling public, especially a public so lacking in clout, did not figure highly in the minds of their appointed guardians.

My fellow travellers would talk quite frankly about all this – humbug is not a Bihari vice – but then they also echoed the younger Singh: people in Bihar, they would say, did not know how to behave. They were 'uneducated' and 'ignorant' and, most of all, 'backward'. The populations of Western democracies hesitate – still – to describe their fellow citizens so bluntly, at least in public. But Biharis have no such inhibitions. The ancient social pyramid of caste enables those at the top to look down at those below with a dispassionate prejudice, at an inferior form of human life.

'I'm afraid we are not a *steady* people,' an old man said to me one day, and I could see exactly what he meant. Often the unsteadiness was frightening. The resources of transportation are scarce all over India; there is a continual press and scramble for tickets and seats wherever you go. But young Biharis travel on the roofs of trains even when the compartments below are empty, and rush listing ferries like a piratical horde. Even the old and lame press forward as though fleeing some imminent disaster.

Towards the end of my journey in Bihar I met another Singh, a relative of the steamer tycoon, who operated a couple of old steamboats just upriver from Manihari Ghat. In an interval between crossings he took me up on to the bridge of his ferry, which was berthed at the foot of a steep bank, glistening and slippery with unseasonal rain. At the top of the slope men with staves, Singh's employees, were restraining a crowd of waiting passengers. Then the steamer's whistle gave two hoots; the men with staves relented; and the crowd, with its bicycles and milk-churns, came rushing down the bank towards us, slithering and whooping.

Singh looked down at his customers as they milled across the gangplank and then laughed like a man in a zoo. 'Crazy people. What can you do with them?'

On 15 April this year ninety-five people were crushed to death on the terraces of a football stadium in Sheffield, northern England. Most of the dead came from Liverpool, and all of them were supporters of Liverpool football club, who that day were to play Nottingham Forest in the semi-final of English football's premier knock-out competition, the Football Association Cup. The deaths came six minutes after the kick-off. The match was then abandoned.

I read about the disaster in Delhi on my way back to London. Newspaper reports speculated on the possible causes and recalled that the behaviour of Liverpool fans had prompted the crush which killed thirty-nine people at the European Cup Final in Brussels in 1985, all of them Italian supporters of the other finalists, Juventus of Turin. It seemed something similar had happened in Sheffield. Liverpool fans had swept into the ground and pressed their fellow supporters forward until they were squashed against the barriers and fences that had been erected some years before to prevent unruly spectators rushing on to the pitch and interfering with the game.

All that winter in India I'd heard about death in Britain. Planes fell to earth and trains left the rails, and Mrs Thatcher's face appeared on Indian television talking of her sympathy and concern. There were shots of disintegrated fuselages, body bags, shattered railway coaches. Indian friends tutted at the carnage, and I recognised in their reaction the momentary interest – the shake of the head, the small ripple of fascination – that passes through a British living room when news of some distant tragedy flits before it; say, of the last typhoon to strike Bengal.

Meanwhile, the India I saw reported every day on the news – orderly, calm, soporific – looked more and more like the country I came from – or at least as I had once thought of it. Accidents such as Manihari Ghat were certainly reported, but rarely filmed. We watched the prime minister greeting foreign delegations at the airport, men in good suits addressing seminars and shaking hands, women cutting tapes and accepting bouquets. Indian news, or what India's government-controlled television judged to be news, took place indoors in an atmosphere notably free of dust, flies and mess. There was a lot of cricket. The mess – grief and ripped metal under arc lights – came from abroad, imported by satellite and shiny film cans – they were like luxury items, a new spice trade going the other way – which the makers of Indian bulletins slotted in between the handshaking and the seminars as if to prove that disaster could overtake the foreign rich as well as the native poor, and that it was not confined to terrorism in the Punjab or the chemical catastrophe at Bhopal.

There were two train crashes in the southern suburbs of London (forty dead); a Pan Am jumbo which exploded over Lockerbie (270 dead);

a Boeing forced to crash-land on a motorway (forty-seven dead). All of them had specific and identifiable causes – a bomb, signal failure, faulty engines – though the roots (what caused the cause?) led to a vaguer territory: under-investment in public utilities, 'international terrorism', the collapse of civic feeling under a political leader who has said she cannot grasp the idea of community. This kind of worry – the cause of the cause – had bobbed to the surface of British life like old wreckage ever since the Channel ferry *Herald of Free Enterprise* turned over at Zeebrugge in 1987, the first in a series of large accidents that has marked Britain out as a literally disastrous country. But from the distance of India, Sheffield looked different. It seemed to turn on the behaviour of a fervent crowd; there was, in that sense, something very Indian about it.

When my landlord in Delhi said he thought football in England must have assumed 'a religious dimension', it was difficult to resist the parallel: saffron pilgrims struggling to board their launch at Manihari Ghat, the mass of Liverpudlian red and white that surged into the stadium at Sheffield. And the parallels did not end there. In fact the nearer I got to home the closer they became.

Changing planes in Paris, I bought a newspaper and read about M. Jacques Georges, the French president of the European Football Association. An interviewer on French radio had asked M. Georges if he thought Liverpool was peculiar in some way, given its football club's recent history of violent disaster. Well, said Georges, Liverpool certainly seemed to have 'a particularly aggressive mentality'. The crowd that had stormed into the ground at Sheffield had scorned all human feeling. 'I have the impression – I am distressed to use the expression – but it was like beasts who wanted to charge into an arena.'

The English are not a steady people. Today all Europe knows that. Nonetheless, M. Georges's words had scandalised England. At Heathrow the papers were full of him, even though he had said little more than the Sheffield police. According to Mr Paul Middup, chairman of the South Yorkshire Police Federation, there was 'mass drunkenness' among the 3,000 Liverpool supporters, who turned up at the turnstiles shortly before the kick-off: 'Some of them were uncontrollable. A great number of them had obviously been drinking heavily.' According to Mr Irvine Patrick, a Sheffield MP, the police had been 'hampered, harassed, punched, kicked and urinated on'.

But then the police themselves had behaved ineptly. Seeking to relieve the crush outside the stadium, they had opened a gate and sent an excited crowd — drunks, beasts or otherwise — into a section of the terracing which was already filled to capacity. And then, for some minutes at least, they had watched the crowd's desperate attempt to escape over the fences and mistaken it for hooliganism. They had hardly made a smart move and analysed the situation.

It would have all been familiar to any citizen of Bihar. An underclass which, in the view of the overclass, did not know how to behave. 'Drunks . . . beasts . . . uneducated . . . ignorant.' An antique and ill-designed public facility. A police force which made serious mistakes. Clamorous cross-currents of blame.

At home, I watched television. The disaster excited the medium. For several days it replayed the scene at Sheffield and then moved on to Liverpool, where the football ground was carpeted with wreaths. Funeral services were recorded, football players vowed that they might never play again, and political leaders in Liverpool demanded the presence in their city of royalty — a prince, a duke — so that the scale of the 'national tragedy' might be acknowledged. When members of Liverpool's rival team turned up at a burial, the commentator spoke reverently of how the disaster had 'united football', as though the French and Germans in Flanders had stopped bombardment for a day to bury their dead. One football official said he hoped that ninety-five people had not 'died in vain'. Another said that they had 'died for football'.

Nobody in Bihar would have suggested that the dead of Manihari Ghat had made such a noble sacrifice. Nobody would have said: 'They died to expunge corruption, caste and poverty.' Whatever their other faults, Biharis are not a self-deluding people.

The Rain in the West

August 2002

Through the window I can see a narrow and almost always grey stretch of sea which is the eastern arm of the Kyles of Bute. A hill rises on the opposite shore a few hundred yards away. A white farmhouse stands some way upslope, in the middle of a pattern of trees that is said to resemble troop formations at the battle of Waterloo; the trees were planted soon after Wellington's victory. There is also a boathouse just down from the farm and the ruin of an old sawmill.

I know these things are there, but so far this morning they are, apart from the sea itself, invisible. This is the west coast of Scotland in July. Weather reports on the BBC say that the south is enduring a heatwave – thirty degrees in London, and more to come. In Bute (and in Arran and Argyll) that climate seems to belong not just to a different country but to a different continent. Here the sky sometimes rolls down and touches the sea; rain, cloud, mist are difficult to tell apart and rarely clear away. The sun is a rumour. It did appear for an hour on Sunday, but its last dawn-to-dusk showing is dated by permanent residents to two days in June. We wear anoraks. In the morning, we set the central heating going. In the evening, we light fires. Up above, God gives his wet dishcloth another squeeze.

We've come here as usual on holiday. I should know better. I've been coming to the Firth of Clyde on holiday since the 1950s, the last decade in which the population of industrial Scotland poured itself whole-heartedly downriver by train and steamer to the coasts of Cowal and Ayrshire and the island resorts of Bute, Cumbrae and Arran. Ten years or so later they were off to Spain and a fortnight of guaranteed heat and sun. This may be a story common to the whole British seaside north of Devon, but nowhere, perhaps not even Whitley Bay, has the summer desertion been more complete than in the town five miles from where I write. Rothesay, the capital of Bute, is a fine-looking place on a beautiful bay – 'Sweet Rothesay Bay', a song composed by the author of *John Halifax, Gentleman*, Mrs Craik. For a hundred years it was to Glasgow what Margate was to London or Scarborough to Leeds. Now you will be lucky to find six people walking the prom at the same time, and, if you do, all of them will have the brave look (which is perhaps also our look) that suggests they are making the best of it.

'Should we have another go at the putting?'

'Too wet. Let's have an ice cream in Zavaroni's.'

Why do I persist in coming? Hope is one reason. We might get a blue-sky day, and if that happens we and the other folk on the prom will brighten up and tell each other, as we look across to the hills above Loch Striven, 'If ye get the weather, ye cannie beat it' (so sucks to Greece and Majorca). But the deeper reason, the original reason, is the seductive power of literature. In other words, I blame a book.

I came across it in a library when I was thirteen: *The Firth of Clyde* by George Blake, bound in library brown cloth with gold titling on the spine. By this time, I had sailed on Clyde pleasure steamers and knew their names and types, which was paddle, which was turbine, which sailed where and when. I was interested in ships. An early Boyhood of Raleigh moment had come on a beach near Dunoon when my uncle identified a two-funnelled ship rounding Toward Point to the south as the 'wee *Queen Mary*' – not the Cunarder but a smaller Clyde-built turbine of the same name, which is now, ridiculously, a floating pub on the Thames. And where had it come from? 'Oh, the Kyles of Bute.' I had never been there, or to any of the unknown world past Toward Point. My uncle might have been pointing to Eldorado.

And so I took out Blake's book from the library because it contained pictures of steamers. There was plenty about steamers in it – good – but the author's main thrust was that their heyday was well in the past. Like the holiday settlements of the Clyde estuary, with their wooden piers and long lines of stone villas, they had boomed with the profits and wages of Victorian and Edwardian industry. The First World War, when, as somebody else once wrote, God died in Scotland, had marked the beginning of a long decline. The book was published in 1952, the author was mourning a vanished way of life. Its nostalgia infected me; it made me see how the Clyde had been, how interesting its history was, and what parts of it remained. Alasdair Gray once wrote words to the effect that a place couldn't properly exist in the mind until it had been imagined in fiction: Dickens for London, maybe Gray himself (though he is a modest man) for Glasgow. This is what Blake did for the Firth of Clyde, for me, and partly because its introduction is fictional.

In it, Blake imagined a well-to-do Glasgow family travelling in 1908 to their summer home in Tighnabruaich on the Kyles of Bute. It is a lyrical and, I suppose, sentimental description. Two of the family's children are twins. At last the paddle steamer *Mercury* brings them to the narrow passage through the Kyles, where the ship takes a sharp turn to reach the western Kyle. Blake writes: 'They were too young to have formulated the conception of beauty, though they knew in the dim way of boyhood that a unique loveliness of gnarled hill, thickets of small oak and hazel and moving tides in small arms of the sea lay around them . . . As he was dying of a bubbling wound in the lungs after Beaumont Hamel in 1917, the younger twin, perhaps groping in his sense of doom to envisage the nature of Heaven, had in his mind's eye that old photograph of the Kyles and, in the very core of his understanding as an individual, the sense of magic in the light of the evening that had laid the cloth of gold on distant hillsides and still but moving waters.'

Blake knew what he was writing about. His book is dedicated to his fifth-form classmates at Greenock Academy in 1910, most of whom died in the war that began four years later. Blake survived it to become a journalist on the *Manchester Guardian*, and then to edit *John O'London's Weekly* and the *Strand Magazine*. Eventually he became a full-time novelist – and at least one of his novels, *The Shipbuilders*, deserves still to be read. As a guide to the Glasgow of the slump, if nothing else, it is streets beyond *No Mean City*.

Now as I write the sky has lifted by a couple of hundred feet and I can see the farm and the trees across the water. A gannet has passed by, and also the last Clyde paddle steamer, the *Waverley*, with its raked twin funnels and rain-soaked decks. Just about now it will be turning to port in the narrows and passing an obscure memorial on the shore to two brothers who died at Gallipoli. The memorial has a water tap and a drinking cup and a basin made of a single seashell, and sits just above the tideline. The names of the brothers face away from the shore and across the island-dotted strait to the hills beyond, one of the most beautiful landscapes in Britain.

I don't know if Blake knew of this memorial; it is hidden from the road and too small to be noticed from the sea. Whenever I go there I think of him and his book, and the debt I owe them, even in the incessant rain.

Revolution on a Plate

April 2004

Thirty years ago the French writer Georges Perec tried to record everything he'd eaten and drunk over a period of twelve months. The result, when it was eventually translated by John Sturrock, was entitled 'Attempt at an Inventory of the Liquid and the Solid Foodstuffs Ingurgitated by Me in the Course of the Year Nineteen Hundred and Seventy-Four'. It is in some ways a sickening quantification, and in others an appetising one. Perec – who died in Paris eight years later, aged forty-five – had traditional French tastes. He forked his way through mounds of beef, chicken, pork, pâté, cheese, tart and cake. He ate smaller heaps of rabbit, fish and offal. He drank 141 named bottles of wine and an uncertain amount of what he called 'sundry wines', presumably meaning the stuff that just arrives slyly at the table in a carafe or the bottles that one is too drunk to remember accurately. He also drank about 150 glasses of spirits (including fifty-six Armagnacs, eight Calvadoses, and six Green Chartreuses), but only nine beers, plus two Tuborgs and four Guinnesses.

There is no mention of water other than three bottles of Vichy, nor of lemon juice, bran flakes and wholemeal bread. Salads, even side salads, come to fewer than one a week. Read Perec's list quickly so that it becomes one great stew and you may feel in need of an enema. Savour it slowly dish by dish and you can can see the daily temptations of France, or France as it was once. Among the desserts, for example: 'One apple pie, four tarts, one hot tart, ten Tarte Tatins, seven pear tarts, one pear Tarte Tatin, one lemon tart . . . two crêpes, two charlottes, three chocolate charlottes, three babas . . . nine chocolate mousses, two îles flottantes, one bilberry Kugelhupf.' Then we move on to the gateaux, the ice cream, the sorbets.

Perhaps I smack my lips over these and many other individual items on Perec's list because of a post-war childhood that was sustained by a British diet limited in its range if not meagre in its quantity. That had changed by 1974, even though the great *pax cornucopia*, the slumber of the over-fed, had yet to come. Impossible to do a Perec for that year, but I suspect fifty-two chicken bhunas, forty-nine sweet and sour porks, sixty lamb kebabs, and seventy-seven bottles of retsina might figure on my list. And ten years before? Sundry quantities of mince and potatoes and haddock and chips, forty-eight cheese omelettes, ninety-eight mutton pies, 145 lagers and lime.

This great change in British eating habits is often put down to the influential cookery books of Elizabeth David. I wonder. National Service abroad, cheap foreign holidays, higher wages, immigrants from India, China and Cyprus – these would seem larger causes. But whatever the case, here, in the same documentary spirit as Georges Perec, I shall list my own first encounters with food and drink that once seemed exotic: a brief and personal history of Britain's dietary development over the past half-century.

First banana. In a street near the Festival of Britain, 1951, when I was aged six. Previously I had had dried bananas, which were brown and sweet. The freshness of a real banana was confusing.

First tin of baked beans that also included sausages. Under a bridge and sheltering from the rain at Lanercost Priory near Hadrian's Wall, 1956. A cycling holiday – my dad had brought his Primus stove and a tin opener. 'My,' he said about the combination of beans, tomato sauce and pale little sausages, 'but this is good!'

First tinned spaghetti. On toast for tea, 1957. Delicious, though slippery. My mum said: 'You'll like it – it's just like baked beans.'

First untinned spaghetti. At the Ristorante Italiano, Parliamentary Road, Glasgow, 1966. How little like the 'original' it seemed. Hard work cutting with a knife.

First sighting of lemon as garnish. In the restaurant car of the *Flying Scotsman*, Edinburgh to London, 1959, accompanying a slice of fish as the first course (a confusion in itself). We were on a school trip. Much discussion about whether the lemon slice needed to be eaten.

First olive oil in my mother's kitchen (as opposed to bathroom) cupboard. Sometime around 1980, after I bought a bottle and put it there.

First garlic in same place. Ditto.

First sweet and sour pork. At the Hong Kong restaurant, Shaftesbury Avenue, 1961. I'd been taken there by my older brother, who lived in London. The taste and texture of the crisp little golden balls and their sauce were sensational. A Keatsian moment, never to be repeated so intensely. Then felt I like some watcher of the skies when some new planet, etc.

First curry. My dad had been at sea for a time with the British India Steam Navigation Company, which had Indian cooks, and sometimes he became nostalgic for mutton curry, which my mum would make with curry powder. While he ate appreciatively, the rest of us had scrambled eggs on toast. Other than in discouraging tastes from Dad's plate, my first curry (chicken) was dabbled with at the Taj Mahal, Park Road, Glasgow, late 1963. Astonishingly hot. Hiccups.

First sweetcorn. At a Reo Stakis steakhouse in Ingram Street, Glasgow, 1966. Served deep-fried (of course) as part of a dish called 'Chicken Maryland' – also the first hot dish I encountered which included bananas.

First untinned salmon. On the steamer *Lochfyne* between Gourock and Ardrishaig, June 1967. 'It's salmon or mince on the menu today,' said the Hebridean steward. 'It's a fine homely ship, the *Lochfyne.*'

First trout. At the Bowmore Hotel, Islay, 1967. Daringly, I'd gone there with my girlfriend and asked for a double room. At dinner, I asked the waitress about the fish we'd just eaten. A grand woman at the other end of the otherwise empty dining room said loudly to her companion: 'Imagine coming to a hotel like this and not knowing what a trout is.'

First avocado. At the Skelmorlie Hydro (now demolished), Firth of Clyde, 1968. Two of us had it and it arrived brick hard. Spoons made only small dents in the flesh. Did we complain? No, we felt the fault was ours, that we had not known how to eat it.

First artichoke. At one in the chain of Bistingo 'French' restaurants, Knightsbridge, 1970. The leaves tasted of privet and made the mouth sore. Ah, one was not supposed to eat the leaves. All dishes with 'vinaigrette' in their title (see avocado above) were obviously a minefield.

First wine. A sip of Blue Nun from a bottle my brother brought home for Christmas 1956, a few years after his National Service in Germany. Sour = bad.

First wine bought in a restaurant. A half-bottle of Sauternes to go with haddock and chips for two, my nineteenth birthday, the Royal Hotel (now defunct), West Nile Street, Glasgow, 1964. Sweet = good.

My father used to talk of his Edwardian boyhood when oranges were a treat ('We got one at Christmas') and I never entirely believed him. My own young children like olives – olives! – so it would be hard to persuade them of the idea that their father did not taste common old sweetcorn until he was twenty-one. But tomorow I am going to tell them something even more incredible: that in 1974 a French bon viveur and omnivore – 'one eel terrine . . . two young wild rabbits with plums' – could get through a whole year's eating and manage only one pizza.

The 12.10 to Leeds

March 2001

The Australian writer Murray Sayle used to remark when he worked long ago at the London Sunday Times *that a good newspaper story can be of two kinds. One: arrow points to defective part. Two: we name the guilty men. The first has always been easier than the second.*

1. Howe Dell

About sixteen miles north of central London, just before the town of Hatfield, Hertfordshire, there is a small wooded valley with a stream and a pond at the bottom: Howe Dell. This is an ancient place. Flints attributed to the Mesolithic Age have been found at the stream's bottom. Before the English Reformation the Church owned the land – it was the Hatfield Rectory's glebe land – until Henry VIII, who was between third and fourth wives at the time, 'conveyed' it along with the Manor of Hatfield to his growing list of property in 1538. Later in the sixteenth century, it was also at Hatfield, at Hatfield House, that Elizabeth Tudor received the news that she was to be queen.

This information can be read on a sign in the dell, which now has the status of 'a valuable urban wildlife site', houses having been built around three sides of it as Hatfield grew from a village to one of London's outer suburbs. Hornbeam, ash, oak and willow grow in the valley; also carpets of bluebells and dog's mercury – though of course no flowers were visible when I went there last December, nor any of the wrens, chaffinches or blue tits which the sign says haunt Howe Dell. It was a grey afternoon; bare trees, earth sodden from the wettest English autumn since 1727, the year that the keeping of records began. Men from the local housing estates walked their dogs through clinging mud. Electric trains passed close by with their windows lit – dinky little reading lights in the first-class carriages of the expresses – but they travelled slowly.

The railway forms the fourth side of Howe Dell, its eastern and most definite boundary, with a high steel fence to keep out people who might damage the railway or get themselves killed. The tracks of the main line from London King's Cross to the north of England and to Scotland curve here, perhaps because the engineers who surveyed the route in the late 1840s wanted to avoid the cost of embankments and bridges over Howe Dell, or because the landowner was stubborn, or because the Great Northern Railway wanted Hatfield's station to be located in the village rather than an inconvenient mile outside it. Whatever the cause, the four tracks coming up from London bend to the right and east – a gentle enough curve which trains had safely negotiated for 150 years, until 17 October 2000.

On that day at 12.23 p.m. the 12.10 King's Cross to Leeds express entered the curve at 115 mph – the maximum permitted speed for this stretch of track – and came off the rails. Four people died. They were:

Robert Alcorn, aged thirty-seven, a pilot from New Zealand who had been living in London and was travelling to Leeds to fly a Learjet from there to Jersey;

Steve Arthur, aged forty-six and Alcorn's employer as the owner of the Atlantic Gulf Aviation Company, married with two children aged eight and four, of Pease Pottage, West Sussex;

Leslie Gray, aged forty-three, a solicitor, of Tuxford, Nottinghamshire;

Peter Monkhouse, aged fifty, managing director of an advertising company and returning from a meeting in London, married with three children aged twenty-six, twenty-three and fifteen, of Headingley, Leeds.

All four men had been in the buffet car (coach G). Its roof was ripped off when it struck one of the steel stanchions placed regularly at the side of the track to support the line's overhead electric wires. Another seven coaches were derailed; the locomotive and the first two coaches remained on the track. If the same number of dead had been recorded in a motorway accident, it would have been a small news item. It threatened no record in recent British railway crashes (Southall, 1997, seven dead; Ladbroke Grove, 1999, thirty-one dead). Historical comparison made it almost a minor incident (the three-train Quintinshill collision, 1915, 227 dead). But no other railway accident in British history – or, I would guess, any other country's history – has led to the degree of public anger, managerial panic, political confusion, blame and counter-blame that came in the wake of the Hatfield crash. In fact, outside wars and nuclear accidents, it is hard to think of any technological failure which has had such lasting and widespread effects (to those not directly involved, those not struggling for life in the Atlantic or bereaved on land, the *Titanic* was simply a very thrilling story, a chilling entertainment; Challenger halted only a space programme). A week or so later, when overfilled rivers began to flood low-lying England and the first people were emptied from their sandbagged homes into boats, the unsettling impression grew of Britain as an unsound country, weakly equipped, under-skilled, easily made chaotic and only superficially modern; an incompetent society. 'We must be the laughing stock of Europe,' people said (and may have been correct). The reason was elementary: movement. People could not move, in an economy – the world's fourth or fifth largest – which depended on millions of everyday, necessary journeys. Few trains ran; those that did ran unreliably even to the revised schedules that sometimes doubled or trebled the normal journey times. Travellers tried other methods; motorways became impassable, domestic flights overbooked. At railway stations, even aboard a train itself, would-be passengers were advised to travel 'only if your journey is really necessary'; the train may depart, but it may not arrive – nothing could be guaranteed. In any case, what was necessity, how were we to rank it? Arriving at the office? Reaching a funeral? Getting home? The question hadn't been asked in Britain since the belt-tightening poster campaigns ('Is Your Journey Really Necessary?') of the Second World War. People old enough to remember the Second World War, its long trains packed with troops crawling through blackouts and air raids, compared that period favourably with the present. There was an enemy then; Britain was a more capable nation.

Two months after the crash, as I walked around Howe Dell, none of this had abated. Every day the newspapers reported a new crisis of trust and confidence in the railways and the businesses that own them ('New Rail Horror: My Journey to Hell'). I expected to find cut flowers at the site – the 'floral tributes' which mark the place of death by accident or murder on many British streets; bouquets tied to lamp posts and the flashing beacons at pedestrian crossings (there were 3,423 deaths on British roads and thirty-three on railways in 1999). I wanted, I suppose, some bitter monument, the names of the dead attached to a slogan – 'Killed by Stubborn Political Ideology' maybe, or 'They Died in the Cause of Profit' – something to set against the sweetness of the wild-flower information of the sign across the stream in the woods. But other than the mud churned up by the cranes and lorries that lifted the wreckage and took it away, there was no evidence that anything fatal and important had ever happened here.

What was the cause of this crash and these deaths? On the night of 17 October, various theories were aired – a terrorist bomb, vandalism, some fault with the train, driver error, signal error. By the next day, however, the immediate cause was identified and publicised: a broken rail. A 100-foot length of steel became the assassin, the Gavrilo Princip in the case, but, like the sluggish underlying causes and abrupt consequences of the First World War, how and why it came to break and why its shattering dislocated the life of Britain – these causes stretch back and out into the wider world of politics and history beyond Howe Dell.

We could begin in Babylonia.

2. The Permanent Way

When I was five or six years old, my elder brother took me for a walk one day down the hill through the cotton factories – this was Lancashire – to the place where a railway broke free of its tunnel. We scrambled down the embankment. My brother placed a penny on the line. Soon enough a train came past. Afterwards, smoke and steam hung lazily in the tunnel mouth. As the throb of the train receded into the distance, we stepped forward again and retrieved a wider, thinner penny with the head of King George VI flattened and disfigured by the pressure of many tons. (This may have been an offence against the realm as well as the trespass laws; it certainly caused a row when we got home.) That was the first time that I can remember coming close to a rail, bending over its burnished top surface and rusty sides as my brother (who was in the grip of the railway hobby) explained some technical terms: the wooden 'sleepers' – or 'ties' in North America – which hold the two lines of rail together (that day I remember their smell of pitch and creosote); the 'fishplates', which bolt the joins in place between each length of rail and the next; the iron 'chairs', which grip the rail and are bolted to each sleeper; last the 'ballast', the heaped chips of rock into which the sleepers are bedded.

An apparently simple technology and until the Hatfield crash I never thought about it. Who would? A steel rail to support and guide a powered wheel, a flange on the wheel to keep the wheel in place; result: traction. Writers and painters have been taken by the sheen of rails, their resolute straightness and smooth curves, since they became features of almost every landscape in the nineteenth century: rails by moonlight and in the morning sun, 'shining ribbons of steel', 'the romance of the Iron Road'. In film, they may make their most famous appearance in John Ford's *The Iron Horse*, when the labouring teams which are building America's first transcontinental railway from each coast meet in Utah and hammer the last spike home. In literature, the Australian writer Murray Bail has a fine description in his novel, *Eucalyptus*:

> The heavy rails went away parallel to the platform on the regularly spaced sleepers darkened by shadow and grease, and darkened further as they went away into the sunlight, the rails converging with a silver wobble in bushes, bend and mid-morning haze.

How rails look (Bail); how they could unify a nation (Ford); but how did they come to be? The whole assemblage – rails, sleepers, ballast – is known as 'the permanent way', so called to differentiate it from the temporary track which was laid to build the railway, its great earthworks, bridges and tunnels. The permanent way was first perfected in England, and in England still there is a learned and professional society, the Permanent Way Institution, founded by a group of railwaymen in Nottingham in 1884, to 'advance track knowledge and the spreading and exchanging of such knowledge among railwaymen throughout all railway systems at home and abroad'. Today it has 7,000 members – men mainly, though women were admitted in 1964 – many of them in former colonies of the British Empire or in other parts of the world, such as South America, which once imported British railway technology. The institution publishes books and monographs. One of the latter, *The Evolution of Permanent Way* by Charles E. Lee, first published in 1937 and still distributed to members, addresses the question of history – originally, one suspects, to inspire the institution's membership of permanent-way inspectors with an idea of vocation, of historical mission, in their long, often lonely, days and nights spent walking along miles of track. (My own father, a steam mechanic, an artisan, kept a commonplace book which contains, among the poems and pressed flowers, assorted references to George Stephenson and James Watt, so this idea of technological mission, of informing working men of their heroic antecedents, is believable to me.)

And so: Babylonia. According to Lee, a railway 'is merely a specialised form of road designed to meet limited needs'. According to Lee again, the earliest evidence of railways by this definition occurs in the Babylonian empire ruled by Belus, about 2245 BC. Around this time – not much after Middle Stone Age families were sitting around Howe Dell, chipping flints – Babylonian stonemasons were instructed to build certain imperial roads as two parallel lines of stone, 5 feet (or three cubits) apart, this distance measured from the centre of each stone line, so that vehicles of the same 5-foot axle width could be pulled along by mules and horses which walked down the centre of the track. This system made haulage easier, the wheels turning against smooth stone rather than rough ground, but it seems (Lee's evidence is sketchy) to have contained no means of making sure that a vehicle stayed on the track other than by the navigational instincts of its animal pullers and human drivers. Railways by their more exact definition, as prepared tracks which by their construction keep the vehicle in place and guide it independently of human or animal interference, were probably first known in Greece. When Aristophanes was alive, around 400 BC, Greek ships were pulled across the isthmus at Corinth on wheeled cradles which travelled along grooves cut into the rock. Elsewhere in Greece, images of the gods were moved to their sacrificial sites along tracks of grooved stone laid to a uniform gauge of 5 feet 4 inches, with loops – *ektropoi* – so that vehicles might pass each other. Regular and parallel grooves, all 4 feet 6 inches apart, can also be found in the streets of Pompeii, though whether they were ruts worn by chariot wheels or a form of guide-rail cut intentionally, Lee cannot be sure.

A prolonged and rail-less interval followed the collapse of Greek and Roman civilisations, until, around the twelfth century, German miners began to spread across central Europe in the search for exploitable seams of metal ore: iron, lead, silver, copper and gold. Illustrated books published in Germany in the sixteenth century have lively woodcuts of bearded men in pointed woollen headwear pushing small trucks from the mine's mouth on wooden rails, while other men, similarly bearded and hatted (mines could be high in the mountains and bitterly cold), busy themselves at the rock face with hammers and picks. These illustrations, in the book *De Re Metallica* (1556) and elsewhere, are the first to depict railways – their little trucks, mines and men eventually serving as the prototypes for the industrial hi-ho situation in Disney's *Snow White* (just as the grooves cut across Corinth are the precursor of Brio's toy track). But keeping the trucks on the wooden track – making them obey, as it were, its direction – remained a large problem when both wheel and rail were flat at their point of contact, with nothing to prevent the one leaving the other. Various methods evolved. Trucks were fitted with guide pins or secondary guide wheels which ran along the rail's inner vertical surface like castors; sometimes the rails themselves were modified with U-shaped channels to hold the wheel or an extra length of wood tacked to their outer sides to form an L shape and give them a vertical, holding edge. It seems that nobody thought of modifying the wheel rather than the rail – perhaps because the trucks needed to be versatile and run also over rough ground – until railways spread from Europe to Britain in the seventeenth century. The breakthrough was the flange, the edge which extends beyond the wheel's running surface and prevents it going astray. The first documented railway in England (Wollaton, near Nottingham, 1603) probably had trucks with flanged wheels. Like almost every railway built in Britain over the next two centuries, the Wollaton line transported coal from a pithead; and as the coal industry grew – 210,000 tons of it dug between 1551 and 1560, 10,295,000 tons between 1781 and 1790 – so railways and flanged wheels proliferated. Lines ran from collieries to ports and canals in many parts of the country; when Bonnie Prince Charlie and his Highland troops defeated the Hanoverian army at the battle of Prestonpans in 1745, they faced cannon positioned on a railway embankment built to serve a Lowland coal mine (the thought gives a jolt to romantic history). Chiefly, however, railways grew and developed on the banks of the Wear and Tyne, where the huge volumes of coal taken down steep banks to ships docked on those rivers made road transport increasingly impractical. It was here that the railway took on its modern meaning, as locomotives replaced horses as traction, and wooden rails gave way to iron. Continental Europe, when it came to import the technology of flanged wheels and iron rails from Britain in the last quarter of the eighteenth century, knew it as the *voie anglaise* or the *englischer Schienenweg* – the English railway.

And yet, among all this modernity which placed rough and unlikely stretches of Britain at the leading edge of global change, one thing remained unconsidered and immutable: the width between the parallel rails, the gauge. In Babylonia, in Greece, at Pompeii, if not in the narrow tunnels of the European metal mines, it had always measured somewhere between 4 feet and just over 5 feet. Now, in Northumberland and Durham, so many miles and years from Babylon, it measured roughly the same. The scholarship of Lee and others suggests that this was the most efficient axle width for animal haulage; narrow it, and the load wouldn't use a horse's full pulling power; widen it, and the weight of the vehicle – the deadweight – would increase disproportionately to the load the vehicle carried. On the multiplying colliery railways of north-east England, trucks began to be exchanged between coal companies with adjacent lines and it became important to regularise their gauge. By the end of the eighteenth century many of these railways were 4 feet 8 inches. The steam locomotive provided a massive increase in tractive effort over the horse and the gauge of a steam-powered railway could have been much wider. But, contrary to its name, the Industrial Revolution arrived by increments. The pioneering steam locomotives of the second decade of the nineteenth century were risky and not always successful experiments as horse-replacements; the gauge existed – there it was trailing down from the pit to the river over expensive bridges and piers; the easiest and cheapest thing was for steam locomotives to adopt it. In 1821, George Stephenson was appointed engineer to an ambitious new railway which would connect the north-eastern towns of Stockton and Darlington, the line which became the world's first public railway – not purely a coal owner's transport – when it was opened in 1825 to all kinds of freight from all kinds of businesses. To build the railway, to carry earth to and from its embankments and cuttings, he hired spoil trucks from the line that served a colliery at Hetton, a few miles off in County Durham. The trucks were of 4-feet 8-inch gauge and the temporary civil-engineering line was built to fit them; Stephenson unquestioningly followed the same width for the permanent way, though some time in the course of laying it he made a small adjustment. Previously, the right angle of the rail fitted neatly into the other right angle where the wheel joined the flange. This was too rigid for the new power and speed of steam locomotives – the constant scraping of iron against iron at this ninety-degree angle damaged both rail and wheel. Stephenson added the idea of *conicity*, curving the junction between flange and wheel and bevelling the corner of the rail to give greater play between them. Minus its sharp angles on each side, the width between the rails became 4 feet 8½ inches.

This awkward result of conservatism, happenstance and artisanship, expressed by the metric system as 1,435 mm, became one of the world's most ubiquitous measurements. When emissaries from other industrialising countries – the US, France, Prussia – came to the Stephenson factory in Newcastle, locomotives designed to that precise gauge were what they saw and sometimes purchased. A steam locomotive could still be so unreliably variable in so many ways – the difficulties and dangers of harnessing steam under pressure – that it may have been a relief to have one, constant, gauge that could be set aside as an untroubling *sine qua non*. Why worry about the rail width under the boiler, when the boiler itself might blow up? Easier, if you didn't already possess a railway, to let the locomotive determine the gauge. Later the gauge was questioned, principally by Isambard Kingdom Brunel, who built the main line from London to Bristol at 7 feet ¼ inch – a more stable and smoother railway, with a far greater carrying capacity – and countries and colonies which first built railways after the gauge question became a public debate adopted various widths: wider in Ireland, Russia and India, narrower in some parts of Australia and Africa. But Stephenson's gauge became the standard where it mattered, at the centre and not the periphery of the industrial world in the first half of the nineteenth century, and in these places Brunel lost his cause.

Of the 750,000 route miles of railway which exist in the world today, sixty per cent measure 4 feet 8½ inches from rail to rail. Across and under the Rockies, the Alps, and the Thames and the Hudson, past the cherry slopes of Mount Fujiyama, spreading into webs of freight yards, converging at junctions; shining and exact parallels, the reasons for their particular exactness lost to the mainstream of history. Trains followed this gauge to the battlefields of the American Civil War and the Somme, into the Vatican City, to the tragic little terminus under the gate at Auschwitz. On this gauge, Buster Keaton outwitted the Union army. Across it, many silent heroines were tied. Riding above it, Cary Grant kissed Eva Marie Saint and remarked: 'The train's a little unsteady.' (And in their bedroom on the Twentieth Century Limited, Eva Marie Saint replied: 'Who isn't?')

And of course on 17 October 2000 it was also the gauge that carried the 12.10 north from London, with 170 passengers including four men of middle age named Alcorn, Arthur, Monkhouse and Gray. Five minutes out of King's Cross, somewhere between Finsbury Park and Hornsey, if my frequent experience is any guide, an announcement was made from the buffet car. It was open and selling 'traditional and gourmet sandwiches, hot toasties, pastries, and hot and cold drinks'.

The four men rose and swayed down the train to coach G. The Alexandra Palace went by on its green hill. The train accelerated and bore on through the tunnels and stations of the north-London suburbs: New Southgate, Oakleigh Park, New Barnet, Potters Bar. The names of the stations became too blurred by speed to read, the tunnels no more than a momentary darkness and a change of noise and pressure that shuddered the carriage windows.

Thirteen miles out: the first countryside – cows, woods, what might still be a farmhouse. A mobile phone or two rang out its simple tune: 'Für Elise', 'British Grenadiers'. The four men were probably in the buffet car by now. Small bottles of Cabernet Sauvignon jiggled in a glass cabinet. Steam hissed from the tea and coffee machine. Hot bread filled with bubbling cheese pinged in the microwave.

Fourteen miles out: Brookmans Park. A mile and thirty seconds later: Welham Green. Some flat modern factories and warehouses appeared on the left with large and legible signs: 'Soundcraft', 'Tesco', 'Falcon for Games', 'Puzzles and Playing Cards', 'Mitsubishi'. If any of the four men looked out of the window at this point, Mitsubishi would be the last word he ever read.

3. The trouble with rails

The first rails to be made completely of metal came out of the Dowlais ironworks in South Wales in 1791. They were cast iron, much more durable than wood but also brittle; they broke. The great quest in the 210-year history of rails since then has been to find a rail that will not break – or not at least inside the parameters of the load it is expected to carry within its allotted lifespan. The answer, for a time, was wrought or malleable iron – iron beaten with hammers or pressed through rollers, rather than poured molten into casts to cool and harden. Wrought iron was more fibrous, many of the impurities had been beaten out of it; it had a greater tensile strength. In 1820, John Birkinshaw of the Bedlington Ironworks in Northumberland patented 'An Improvement in the Construction of Malleable Iron Rails . . . whereby the Expence of Repairs of broken rails [is] saved'. Each of Birkinshaw's rails had been squeezed six times between the cylinders of his rolling mill and emerged at unprecedented lengths of up to 18 feet – 'to reduce the shocks or jolts to which the carriages are subject from passing over the joints (very much to the injury of the machinery)'. Stephenson used Birkinshaw rails for the Stockton and Darlington and again later on the world's first passenger railway, the Liverpool and Manchester, where they were laid in 15-foot lengths weighing 35 pounds a yard. They also broke. By 1832, only two years after the railway opened, it was noticed that fragments of iron littered the track. New rails were ordered at steadily increasing weights, first 50 pounds a yard, then 60 pounds, then 75 pounds. By 1839, every one of the line's original rails had been replaced.

Eleven years later, when the Great Northern Railway opened its main line between London and Peterborough via Hatfield, the pattern was repeated. The trains curved past Howe Dell on 18-foot lengths of wrought-iron rail which weighed 72 pounds to the yard. They too soon began to chip and fragment under the weight of heavy coal traffic. A few miles south, at Barnet, it was judged that the life of a rail was no more than three and a half years. The Great Northern ordered new wrought-iron rails and upped their weight by 10 pounds a yard. By 1865, the entire line had been re-railed. But the new rails proved only slightly more reliable than the old. Trains ran at increasing frequency, load and speed, and the manufacture of good wrought iron depended too much on human skill, which varied from shift to shift and works to works.

Railways began to experiment with steel – a strong, supple iron alloy formed by blasting air through iron during the smelting process to remove the carbon content, the invention patented by Sir Henry Bessemer in 1855. Steel rails were a third more expensive, but trials showed that they lasted four to six times longer than wrought iron.

By the 1880s almost every main line in England, including the Great Northern's, had been relaid in steel, but that too had problems. Steel could last for years, shining brightly in the signal lights, apparently perfect, and then suddenly it would snap. Accidents were rare from this cause, but two passengers died at St Neots, thirty-five miles north of Hatfield, when broken steel rails threw a train off the line in 1895. In 1899, members of the Institution of Civil Engineers in London worried about the 'capricious' nature of steel rails and their 'remarkable vagaries'. British engineers studied the new science of metal fatigue, mainly the work of the German metallurgist, August Wohler (an early example of what became a reverse flow of railway know-how, as Britain imported new knowledge and techniques from Europe and the USA). Rails became heavier still; on the line past Howe Dell they weighed 100 pounds a yard by 1914, 109 pounds by 1950. Their shape changed. In the middle of the nineteenth century, rails had been made with the head (the top) the same as the foot (the bottom), to give two potential running surfaces, so that after one was worn out the rail could be turned upside down, doubling its life. The idea didn't work – the base plates left dents in the bottom surface – but the shape was retained for a hundred years. They were known as 'bullheads', and their replacements in the 1950s as 'flatbottoms' – the usual shape in Europe and North America. The noise made by the combination of track and train began to change around the same time. The wheels no longer ran clackety-clack over the joins ('What's the train saying?' our fathers would say. '*Peas-and-beans, peas-and-beans, peas-and-beans*? Or is it *fish-and-chips, fish-and-chips, fish-and-chips*? What's for tea?'). British engineers followed European practice and welded the lengths of rail together. The tiny gap between each rail length disappeared. Concrete sleepers replaced wood, and the rails were bolted or spiked directly to them – no intervening 'chairs' – as the US had done from the beginning. In combination, these changes made the rails more durable and saved money on repairs. When trains ran over continuously welded track the cost of their tractive energy was cut by five per cent, by the single act of removing the tiny gap or the infinitesimal difference in position between one rail and the next; the price of peas-and-beans.

Then, in 1967, forty-nine passengers died when a train derailed on unwelded track at Hither Green in south London. The cause was a rail which had fractured at its weakest point, the bolt-holes at the join.

Rails thereafter were made to a new specification, with a thicker 'web' – the spine which joins railhead to railfoot – and a new weight of 113 pounds.

This became the standard British rail, specification BS11–113A. In 1995, as part of regular repair and maintenance work, new rails of this kind were laid at Howe Dell. Like most rails in Britain, they were made by British Steel (now part of an Anglo-Dutch company, Corus) at its plant in Workington, Cumbria. They weren't quite standard. When rails are expected to carry an extra stress, they are especially hardened at the factory by quenching them with water as soon as they leave the rollers, a process called 'mill heat treatment'. These were mill-heat-treated (MHT) rails; they were to be laid on the curve. And curves bring their own problems.

4. The trouble with curves

Engineering is often easier to depict than to describe. One striking thing about engineers – apart from their disenchantment with the managerial class set above them and the trivialised culture which neglects them – is how often they want to draw things; words not being up to the work of describing the technical reality. During the research for this piece, I was handed several instant drawings. 'Give us a pen,' engineers would say. 'Look, it works like this.'

In a phenomenon known as 'the dynamics of the wheel–rail inter-face', drawing is especially useful. One day in November, I took the train from London to Peterborough – a very slow train which moved gingerly over the crash site – to meet a young engineer, Philip Haigh, who writes for the specialist magazine *Rail*. 'Give us a pen,' he said at one point, and then: 'Do you have a 5p piece?' He drew round the circumference of the coin to produce a circle with a diameter of about ¾ inch or 2 cm. That was the size of the contact area between a wheel and a rail when train and track were in perfect equilibrium. Perfection requires the straightest rail and the truest wheel; but if these ideal conditions were met, Haigh said, then only a ¾-inch strip would wear along the rail top (which is 2¾ inches wide). In an electric locomotive, 100 tons of vehicle and machinery could be shared among eight wheels and eight of these 5p contact spots. Each 5p would support a weight of 12.5 tons. Given a powerful engine, the friction caused by turning all eight wheels against two rails would easily haul a train of 1,000 tons at 115 mph.

And when the train reaches a curve? 'The contact spot shifts for both wheel and rail,' Haigh said. What happens is this: the wheels are asked to obey a new direction by the rail. That instruction, combined with centrifugal force, pushes the wheel against the rail on the outside of a curve. The shoulder between flange and wheel hits the corner of the rail. At low speed, that hardly matters, the train will scrape round. At high speed, say 125 mph, the train needs some corrective to try to restore its equilibrium. Therefore the track is 'canted' – tilted like the racing track in a velodrome, with the outside rail the higher of the two. But different kinds of train travel at different speeds and would need different levels of cant if their equilibrium was always to be perfect. Engineers reach a compromise: a cant that will work at different speeds, though not perfectly for all of them. The difference between the ideal cant for a high-speed train and the most practical cant for all trains is known as 'cant deficiency'. At high speed, the wheels still shift position and put an extra stress on the higher rail, attacking its inner corner, the corner from which the gauge is measured: the gauge corner.

Rails are made to take pressure from the top. Exposed to this different, sideways pressure from, say sixty fast trains a day, seven days a week, they can begin to crack: gauge corner cracking. Mill heat treatment prevents that; or does it? The answer seems to be yes and no. It may modify a rail's first inclination to crack, but once a crack has started, a softer rail may be the better option. Softer rails wear faster, perhaps faster than cracks can grow; a crack can be worn away before it has the chance to dive down into the heart of the rail. In Haigh's word, a softer rail can be 'self-correcting'. (Metallurgists and engineers debate this. However, the rails which replaced those destroyed in the crash at Howe Dell were not heat-treated – none of them have been laid since.)

Curves are by no means the only cause of damaged rails. The steel may contain flaws, little voids ('tache ovales') which are difficult and sometimes impossible to detect by the human eye. Wheels which are out of shape and not perfectly circular ('wheel flats') can batter and dent the rail – like gauge corner cracking this comes under the general heading of rolling-contact fatigue. The ground beneath can subside by an inch and twist the rail. The railhead can flake ('spalling'). The more I read about the subject (for example *Residual Stress in Rails* by Orringer, Orkisz and Swiderski, Kluwer Academic Publishers, volume one, 1992

– but let's not go there), the more engineers I talked to, the more I saw rails in a new light; not as simple and indestructible – the Iron Road – but as complicated and vulnerable. Railway engineers have always seen them in this way, as a technology that requires constant vigilance.

At a railway engineering exhibition in Birmingham, I met a retired permanent way engineer, Bill Armstrong, who spoke about the track as 'a living thing'. Ballast could 'develop a memory'; rails always wanted 'to go back to where they lived before'. This was in the context of track-relaying, the dangers of putting new line over old ballast furrowed by sleepers or old rails into new positions on a curve, where they would show signs of wanting to resume their original shape and need to be beaten back, with hammers. Rails were always shifting, settling, creeping this way or that. As the chief permanent-way engineer for a large part of Yorkshire, in the old coal district between Doncaster and Leeds, he'd been required to walk every mile of his track twice a year; the main line and three tributary passenger branches, several colliery lines, a large freight yard – many dozens of miles on foot, twice a year, peering at the rails. The inspectors under him walked every mile of track under their care at least once a month; in turn, the sub-inspectors under them walked it at least once a fortnight. Then there were the permanent-way gangers – labourers – who would also walk their particular stretch. In this way, every mile of line was patrolled not less than twice a week. Passenger lines were inspected no fewer than three times, usually on Mondays, Wednesdays and Fridays. 'We had a saying,' Armstrong said. 'The uninspected inevitably deteriorates.'

We were talking inside one of the bleak halls of Birmingham's National Exhibition Centre. The Hatfield crash had cast a gloom over this year's trade fair. At a couple of seminars in side rooms I'd heard speakers despair of the national culture: 'a dearth of engineers', 'a basic lack of engineering competence which is a problem across the board in the industry', 'not enough people who understand how the infrastructure works or behaves'. In the hall, videos at several stands showed pieces of machinery and stressed that 'safety is our number one priority'. The words had become the new railway mantra.

Armstrong, who was manning a stall for the Permanent Way Institution, said: 'How many folk in this country, even the ones who're interested in railways, know what happens below the wheel? With them, it's always the wheel upwards, the stuff on top, never below the wheel. Below the wheel matters. You know the trouble with England? We've never had the guts to rip things down and start again. It's all make do and mend.' He had an analogy. 'It's like having a wife who keeps asking you to paint the front door when the more important job is to get the damp seen to in the cellar.'

He spoke about an everyday garden nuisance, one apparently far removed from the dynamics of the wheel rail interface: the weed. 'In the old days you'd never see a weed on the line. That was when you had six chaps working from the same hut, looking after their bit of track. Weeds are unsightly, they're evidence of neglect, they clog the drainage in the ballast, the ballast becomes uneven, the tracks sink or twist. It's like a house, the permanent way. You get your foundations right, you get your drainage right, and you build up from there.'

And now? 'The days of a line being patrolled by a man every day have gone. But it's worse than that. Not only have the maintenance structures disappeared, but the knowledge of what the structures did has disappeared.'

The great change happened in the middle years of the 1990s, its centrepiece the Railways Act, which was passed by the Conservative government in 1993. Seven years later, at 12.23 p.m. on 17 October, the 12.10 to Leeds came off the tracks. The two events are connected.

There was a fracture on the outer high rail at the Hatfield curve. The locomotive and the train's first two coaches passed over it safely, but the shock and pressure ran through the rail like a lightning bolt. The pressure found other cracks; there were cracks everywhere. Instantly, more than a 100 feet of rail shattered into 300 pieces. The other eight coaches came off the track. Passengers fell over each other, necks hit the backs of seats. Scalding water exploded in the buffet car. Apart from the dead – Alcorn, Arthur, Monkhouse and Gray – two buffet attendants and two other passengers were seriously injured, another sixty-six passengers slightly so.

Ambulances came. Howe Dell flickered with flashing lights and the arcing sparks of acetylene torches. By 2.30 p.m., the first officers had arrived from government agencies: the Health and Safety Executive, its quaintly named subdivision Her Majesty's Railway Inspectorate, and the British Transport Police. For the next four days they bent among the ballast and the grass and picked up pieces of steel. Eventually they reconstructed the assassin, the rail, and named the assassin's weapon, gauge corner cracking. A remote technical term entered the common language. But if rail and cracks were Gavrilo Princip and his pistol, who was the Kaiser in the case? The truth is that there were several kaisers – stubborn men in love with a political idea that they imagined would fulfil the national destiny. One of them lived just down the track at Huntingdon: the former prime minister, John Major.

5. Trainspotting

Railways as an interest, a hobby like philately or butterfly collecting, began in the late nineteenth century, when English gentlemen with time on their hands (lawyers, vicars) started to see steam locomotives as fascinating objects in themselves rather than purely as the source of the most convenient means of transport. They would pursue rare types, exchange notes, lug plate cameras and tripods to the tops of cuttings, take photographs of expresses (always from a distance and head-on, to avoid too much blurring). By 1897 two magazines catered for these hobbyists. Two years later they had a club, the Railway Club, with armchaired rooms in London.

What would one of these trainspotters have seen at Howe Dell? The Great Northern Railway had been built to shorten the distance from London to Yorkshire, to compete against a longer and slower route, and in the closing decades of the nineteenth century it had a service of swift and regular trains which was said to be unrivalled in the world. In 1889, the Shah of Persia came down the 185 miles from Leeds to London in three hours forty-two minutes, and that included a fifteen-minute stop for lunch at Grantham (where Mrs Margaret, now Baroness, Thatcher's grandfather was a station cloakroom attendant). An enthusiast leaning on the fence at Howe Dell would have seen smart little green locomotives and teak-brown carriages rushing north at a mile a minute and long coal trains winding slowly south from the northern coalfields to the London depots. Gleaming paintwork and brass, the oil lamp of a signal flickering red though the smoke; superficially, the golden age of Britain's railways. Less golden, however, to the railway shareholder. Britain had a denser network of railways than any other country; travellers from London to Manchester, for example, could choose between four different routes owned by four different companies. Such extreme competition cut into profits.

The average return on railway shares between 1850 and 1875 was a modest 3.65 per cent. The most profitable lines were often small local monopolies whose main business was the transport of minerals. Many companies made no money at all. Public ownership was considered by governments as early as the First World War, but in 1923 a different solution was chosen. Britain's 120 railway companies were amalgamated into four large groups, with the government intending that each of them would become a profitable regional monoploy. The Great Northern became part of the London and North Eastern Railway, the LNER. It built more powerful locomotives and painted them a lighter green; its expresses to the north got faster; in 1938, it claimed the world-record speed for a steam locomotive, 126 mph, which has never been bettered. But profit was still difficult because by now the competition wasn't from rival railway companies but from new means of transport: cars, coaches, lorries. In the years leading up to the Second World War, the LNER paid its shareholders no dividends at all. In 1946, it managed 0.41 per cent. For a Labour government committed to the post-war reconstruction of Britain's damaged infrastructure, there could be only one solution. In 1948, as part of a pattern common throughout Europe, the railways of Britain were taken into public ownership and became British Railways, later British Rail.

Initial public investment halted their decline, but that proved temporary. Roads increasingly drew away their freight and passengers and their subsidy became unpopular in the Treasury. Golden Ageism was never far from the surface of post-war Britain and the feeling grew, especially among Conservative politicians and commentators, that things had been better arranged in the days of gleaming paintwork and brass, when porters tipped their caps as you slipped them sixpence. Over the next thirty years, the railways were 'rationalised' – lines closed, staff cut – until by the 1980s they were the most cost-effective and had the lowest level of government subsidy of any country in western Europe (still unchanged in 1996, when the figures for planned investment over the following four years, per head of population, were: France, £21; Switzerland, £40; Italy, £33; Britain, £9). There was by this time no political belief in them. Mrs Thatcher, the railwayman's granddaughter, made a point of never travelling by train and spoke of 'the great car economy'. Two other phrases began to be applied to railways in her era, 'value engineering' and 'the management of decline'. In the late

1980s, when the East Coast Main Line through Hatfield was electrified, first to Leeds and than all the way to Edinburgh, it was said to
be the cheapest such scheme in Europe, where countries such as France
and Italy copied the Japanese model and built, at great expense, new
straight railways dedicated to high-speed trains, with their rails
embedded in continuous concrete. In France, the permitted top speed
was 300 kph; in Germany, 280 kph; in Italy, 250 kph; in Britain, 200 kph
(125 mph). In Britain, the new trains through Hatfield were built at
a cost of 23,100 US dollars per seat. In Europe, nothing similar was
achieved for under 35,885 US dollars per seat (the new trains built
for the Channel Tunnel, London to Paris, cost almost 50,000 US dollars
per seat). In Britain, the overhead power lines would blow down in
high winds. Their suspension support was not robust.

Within railways, among railway people, there came an important
cultural shift. The future of subsidies was uncertain, 'profit centres' had
been created. In this climate, operators – the executives who timetabled
and managed the trains – became more important than engineers. In
the words of Michael Casebourne, the chief executive of the Institution
of Civil Engineers: 'The railways had a tremendous number of engineers, sometimes leading authorities in rail engineering worldwide or
in touch with other people who were. They were authoritarian, highly
responsible and very good at what they did, and they ran the railway
from a protective point of view. An awful lot of what they did – re-
signalling and track work – interrupted the running of the trains.
Consequently, they got a very bad name with the operators and just
before privatisation, the balance changed – it became an operators'
rather than an engineers' railway.'

Privatisation, Casebourne added, 'had the effect of reinforcing many
of these views'.

6. Ideology

During successive Conservative governments between 1979 and 1997
more than two-thirds of Britain's state-owned industry was sold to
the private sector, transferring about a million jobs and raising £65
billion for the Treasury. Mrs Thatcher wanted to 'roll back the fron-
tiers of the state'; a wider spread of shareholders would create 'popular
capitalism', and by exposing state industries to market forces they
would become more efficient and offer cheaper goods or a better

service to the consumer. The cash raised meant that the government could avoid the more electorally dangerous alternatives of raising taxes or cutting public expenditure. Harold Macmillan, a former and more patrician Conservative prime minister, called it 'selling the family silver'.

The results were uneven. Several public utilities – the gas, water and telecommunications industries – were sold off en bloc to become private monopolies, no more responsive to the market or the consumer than when they were owned by the state. There was public disenchantment. Advocates of privatisation blamed lack of competition, which in their view was the key element in raising efficiency. When the turn came for the electricity industry to be privatised, the government broke it down into more than a dozen generating and distribution companies. This seemed to work; competition between them produced efficiency – lower costs. The promotion of competition became a key element in future privatisation schemes, and the electricity industry a model for the railways.

By several accounts, Mrs Thatcher had little personal enthusiasm for privatising British Rail, realising (perhaps) that if it went wrong she risked the Conservative vote in the London commuter belt. Unlike the electricity industry, trains – more important, fares – depended on government subsidy that was running close to £1 billion a year. But two of her successive Ministers for Transport, Paul Channon and Cecil Parkinson, eventually persuaded her to include it in the Conservative agenda and in 1990 Parkinson announced to Parliament that the government was 'determined to privatise British Rail'.

Nobody had any clear idea of how, or at least no single clear idea that had unanimous appeal to Conservative think tanks, Cabinet ministers, transport economists, civil servants and British Rail itself. Ideas varied. One obvious solution was to break British Rail into several regional monopolies in a new version of the railway companies which existed between 1923 and 1948. Mrs Thatcher's successor, the English nostalgist John Major, seemed for a time to favour that and the Conservative manifesto for the 1992 general election included the hope that the new railways would 'reflect regional and local identity [and] recapture the spirit of the old regional companies'. But the trouble with this scenario of gleaming paint and polite porters – Major himself mentioned the Great Western Railway's brown and cream carriages – was that it introduced very little in the way of a new competitive element (ignoring the fact that competition against rival forms of transport, roads and airlines, already existed). A structure needed to be found which would provide competition within the railway itself – and it needed to be found quickly. Major won the 1992 election with his railway-privatisation scheme little more than a blank piece of paper (in the later words of his new Transport minister, John MacGregor); the legislation would need to be passed and the privatisation success-fully implemented by the time the next election was due in 1997. There was very little left to privatise. Major, who was aware of his mild public image, needed a privatisation of his own to demonstrate his radical credentials as Mrs Thatcher's heir.

Horizontal separation – the railways as regional monopolies – kept trains, stations, track, signalling and general infrastructure under one ownership, the way they had always been. Vertical separation was a more radical solution. It would separate trains from rails. The owner of the rails would charge the owners of the trains for access to them, on the same principle as a toll road. Different train owners could compete for passengers and freight on the same stretch of track. The idea found favour in Major's old department, the Treasury, and though the object of it has never been achieved (very few train companies compete for the same traffic over the same line), the competitive prin-ciple behind it was used to fragment Britain's railways into more than a hundred separate businesses, about the same number that had been amalgamated in 1923.

When the plan was published in a White Paper in 1992, it aroused considerable hostility. Opinion polls showed that a large majority of the public was against it, the Labour Party in opposition fought it, and even the Conservative press was sceptical. The Conservative Party itself was divided. A Conservative Member of Parliament, the late Robert Adley, interrogated ministers from his position as the chairman of Parliament's Transport select committee, and concluded that 'it seems to me that none of them, quite frankly, have a clue about how all this is going to be worked out'. Of all privatisation schemes, the railways soon became the most disliked, with few supporters outside the govern-ment and the financiers and commercial lawyers of the City of London who stood to gain. One Transport minister succeeded another – a total of six in seven years, each as uncertain as his predecessor – but Major and his government stubbornly pressed ahead with the legislation, and on 1 April 1994 the Railways Act came into effect. British Rail's assets could now be sold off, under a plan that had six broad elements and a flurry of acronyms.

The passenger trains were to be run by about twenty Train Operating Companies (TOCS) on franchises which ran from between seven and fifteen years.

The trains would be owned by three Rolling Stock Companies (ROSCOS) which would lease them to the TOCS.

The railway signalling, the permanent way, bridges, tunnels and some of the larger stations would be owned by one large infrastructure company, Railtrack.

Railtrack would contract out the maintenance and renewal of the infrastructure by competitive tender to civil-engineering companies (which had bought British Rail's engineering assets). They in turn might put out the work to subcontractors.

A new independent body, the Office of the Rail Regulator (ORR), would set the amount that Railtrack was allowed to charge the TOCS – 'the track access charges' – and in general promote competition, efficiency and safety inside Railtrack, to the eventual benefit of passengers.

Another new body, the Office of Passenger Rail Franchising (OPRAF) would decide which TOC got which franchise, adjudicate the level of public subsidy required by the TOC (this was a privatisation that actually increased public subsidy rather than ending or shrinking it), and reward or penalise train-operating performance through a system of bonuses and penalties. Later, under the Labour government, OPRAF became the Strategic Rail Authority, the SRA.

Six years later, it was hard to find anyone who would defend this structure, outside the Labour government. A paradox. In opposition the Labour Party was committed to dismantling privatisation and restoring a 'publicly owned, public-accountable railway'. On 23 March 1995, the party's new leader, Tony Blair, described the privatisation plan as 'absurd'. He said: 'They [the Conservatives] want to replace a comprehensive, coordinated national railway network with a hotchpotch of private companies linked together by a gigantic bureaucratic paperchase of contracts – overseen of course by a clutch of quangos [quasi-autonomous non-governmental organisations, then a favourite opposition target].

As the public learn more about the chaos and cost, their anger at this folly will grow.' The prediction came true in every respect. But as the 1997 election came closer, the party changed its stance. Under the influence of Gordon Brown, later the head of the Treasury as Chancellor of the Exchequer, no such commitment was included in the manifesto. Labour was anxious to be seen as 'prudent'; taking back the railways, or even just Railtrack, into public ownership would cost too much. In any case, as Brown told a colleague, 'privatisation will make the Tories unpopular and save us from having to do it'. In government, Prime Minister Blair told an early Cabinet meeting that railways were 'not a priority'.

British Rail was sold for a total of £5 billion. Government subsidies to the railway industry for the three years 1997–2000 come to roughly the same amount. The infrastructure went to Railtrack for £1.93 billion. Its market value by 2000 was just under three times as much. Thanks to stubborn political pressure, emanating from a prime minister who feared to be seen as weak, the railways had been sold off hastily, cheaply and carelessly, often to owners for whom 'the wheel–rail interface' was a term of management rather than science (if it meant anything to them at all). Of Railtrack's thirteen board members, only two had railway experience and only one was an engineer. From 1997 they were led by a chief executive, Gerald Corbett, who had previously worked as the finance director for the hotels and leisure group Grand Metropolitan. Corbett, who bears a striking resemblance to the English character actor Timothy West, became a familiar figure on television after the crash at Ladbroke Grove in 1999 and again after Hatfield. He was sincere and he was sorry, so much so that, after Hatfield, Railtrack adopted a new slogan, 'Sorry Is Not Enough', and pasted it to the windows of its London headquarters and on poster sites by the side of the track. No irony seemed intended personally against the chief executive; the poster went on to say that Railtrack was working hard to give Britain a first-class railway system. At Victoria station, some delayed passenger had seen a nice anagram. The graffiti on the poster read 'Liartrack'.

In other ways Corbett's regime at Railtrack could be seen as a success. The company made a profit, its share price rose steeply and the shares paid growing dividends (26.9p per share for the financial year 1999–2000, increased by five per cent after the Hatfield crash to keep the confidence of shareholders). Property was one source of profit. In the four years since Railtrack's flotation in 1996, the rent and sale of some of the buildings and land which the company had so cheaply acquired raised more than £500 million. In 1999–2000, about a quarter of total profit came from property sales alone. Railtrack's chief income, however, came from the track-access charges paid by the train operators – charges which were fixed in the public interest at retail-price inflation minus two per cent by the Rail Regulator. If the train operators ran more trains, the charges could be adjusted upwards very slightly; in 1995 nobody, including the Rail Regulator, expected more trains. Five years later, the figure for passenger mileage had grown by thirty per cent and for freight by forty per cent as Britain came out of economic recession, motorways got clogged and train operators adopted aggressive marketing. More people were using the railways than at any time since 1946. The rails they used took more wear, but only a fraction of the increased revenue from passengers was passed on to Railtrack. Worse, more trains meant more track congestion and more delays. The Rail Regulator had set targets for punctuality expressed in percentage points. Every percentage point missed and judged to be Railtrack's fault led to a fine of £1 million. In 2000, Railtrack faced a fine of £10 million.

So how to make a profit from the infrastructure itself, or at least keep the cost of maintaining it down? The answer lay in scrutinising the fine print of contractual obligation and putting more work out to tender, 'efficiency savings' which the Rail Regulator himself was keen on. In the aftermath of three rail disasters, this was said to be 'putting profit before safety'. On the trackside, it was rarely as simple as that.

At Hatfield, the technology of track and trains was now split among at least five different managements. Two companies ran the passenger trains, West Anglia Great Northern (WAGN) to the suburbs and Cambridge, the Great North Eastern Railway (GNER) to Leeds, Newcastle and Scotland, with trains leased from a separate rolling-stock company. Railtrack ran the signalling and owned the line. The line was maintained and repaired by the civil engineers Balfour Beatty, under contract to Railtrack. Another civil-engineering firm, Jarvis, had the contract for track replacement.

The 12.10 GNER express to Leeds was ultimately owned by a bank (the Hong Kong and Shanghai), leased by a Bermuda-registered shipping company (GNER is a subsidiary of Sea Containers) and given its green light by a Railtrack signaller. None of them was at fault. The trouble was the rail.

7. Workers

My route to work in London every morning takes me over a railway bridge. A traveller on the top deck of a bus at this point can see a junction and a single line curving off into a tunnel. Once there were two lines; once the curve was smooth. Sometime in the early 1990s, however, I noticed that one of the lines had been taken up and that the curve was really a series of angled straight rails. Bill Armstrong, the old permanent-way man, described this to me as 'a threepenny-bit curve', after the old British dodecagonal coin. The rails had probably been used elsewhere, or turned around at the same site, and wanted to assume their previous form, 'to go back,' as he said, 'to where they lived before'. Also, around the same time, I began to notice weeds here and on other lines; weeds that grew on the ballast sometimes to the size of small shrubs. Even the busy track outside Waterloo terminus had them, with their suggestion of abandoned railways in the Argentinian pampas. I imagined that the railways were obeying a new ecological stricture to ban herbicide. The cause was more straightforward.

Between 1992 and 1997, the number of people employed on Britain's railways fell from 159,000 to 92,000, at a time when the number of trains increased. Within these totals, the number of workers permanently employed to maintain and renew the infrastructure fell from 31,000 to between 15,000 and 19,000. In a rare piece of enquiring journalism on the subject, the *Guardian's* labour correspondent Keith Harper interviewed some permanent-way workers in March 1998. They were men aged between forty-five and fifty, 'the rump of what is left of British Rail's skilled workforce', as Harper described them, and they spoke scathingly of the methods of their new employers, the private contractors who worked for Railtrack. Harper kept them anonymous; speaking to the press – 'whistle-blowing' – is now usually a breach of contract. One worker said:

At least fifty per cent of the track is on its last legs. If it's not broken rails, it's broken components. If the public knew the full picture, it would be horrified. There are accidents waiting to happen and loads of speed restrictions. Some cowboy [casual worker] the other day forgot to put up a 20 mph speed restriction on a 70 mph route. How there wasn't an accident I'll never know.

Another said:

Railtrack is really responsible for seeing that the work gets done properly, but my work has never been checked by Railtrack and, in my time, I have worked on some extremely dodgy jobs that require proper inspection. It is up to the maintenance companies to do it, but they often subcontract work to many fly-by-night operators. They bring in gangs of casuals in taxis and pay them eighty pounds in hard cash for a shift.

A third said:

Railtrack is a joke. It is totally reliant on the maintenance companies and does not know what is going on. Railtrack is so pious. It wrings its hands and says that safety is paramount, yet it gets really nasty if we cannot do a job on time, usually because the time we get to do it is impossible.

In November last year, attending a session of the government inquiry into the Ladbroke Grove rail crash, which was chaired by Lord Cullen, I heard the same situation on the track described in a more academic way. Professor Christopher Baldry, head of the Department of Management and Organisation at Stirling University, was giving evidence about safety practices among permanent-way workers, based on recent research. He used the phrase 'work intensification'.

    Counsel: What is that?
    Baldry: Well, work intensification . . . can either be the same number of people producing more over a given time period, the same number of people producing the same volume over a shorter time period or a smaller number of people producing a given volume, if technology and other factors are held constant.
    Counsel: When you look at the work intensification and the

figures which support that, the conclusion which you reach is that there is a worsening safety record and a worsening trend in employee safety in the [railway] industry?

Baldry:Yes, this seemed to us [himself and his fellow researcher] to be what was indicated by the figures. Basically we took the figures for the amount of traffic in rail miles, an index of workload, we looked at the decline in direct employees of both Railtrack and the major contractors, although . . . this does not include subcontractors which is one of the defects of the official figures, but certainly the continuing downward trend in employment and the continuing upward trend in the amount of traffic carried, I think you can take as an index of work intensification: a smaller number of people are coping with a larger volume of traffic in the network.

How had this happened?

Baldry: If you are bidding for a contract on what is essentially a labour-intensive process, the only way or one of the major ways you are more likely to win the contract is through offering to do it with reduced labour costs, that is either to do the work with a smaller number of people or in a shorter timeframe.

Baldry went on to describe the long and unregulated hours that could be worked under the negligent eye of a subcontractor, the lack of communication between train crews, signallers and permanent-way men – now all employed by different companies and often new to their jobs – and the rivalry between different contractors or subcontractors.

We were given on several occasions evidence that if, for example, track workers from Scotland had been sent down to York to work on a bit of track that was unfamiliar to them, they find themselves working with other employees of a different contractor. Their instinct is to ask local people about the nature of the track. The local people may have been told by their employer, 'Don't talk to these persons because they are employed by the opposition.' In other words, there are actual obstacles put in the way of site knowledge and hazards knowledge. We encountered that in several locations.

Familiarity with the track had gone, old patterns of trust had been broken: the price of the competitive spirit. There could be so many different companies employed on the same stretch of line, Baldry said, that it would take 'a very brave person' to halt the work because of a potential hazard. He had heard reports that safety representatives had been threatened with physical violence when they suggested that work should stop. 'It takes quite a brave individual to say stop the work because of the financial penalties that then rebound back up the system if the work in progress runs over time.'

The system that Baldry mentioned was designed by commercial lawyers, in the legal belief that punishment works, and it involves confusing flows of money and paperwork between many 'interfaces' – in the managerial sense – between groups which have different and sometimes conflicting financial interests. When a contracting firm repairs a track, it 'takes possession' of it. Trains are stopped for the duration of these 'track possessions' and this may in itself cost Railtrack money, if it cannot meet its obligations to the train-operating companies and their trains are cancelled or delayed. If a track possession overruns its scheduled time, however, the penalties are fiercer. Track work usually takes place at the weekend – but say something unexpected occurs or the contractor has underestimated the time the repairs will take and the track possession runs into Monday morning? There is a schedule with tariffs. Rates differ. A delay to a train in the London morning rush hour, for example, can cost Railtrack £200 a minute at Waterloo and £147 a minute at Euston. One delayed train can cause other delayed trains for hundreds of miles down the track, with Railtrack compensating their operators for each. A bill of £250,000 is quite easy to run up. Railtrack, therefore, can penalise the contractor, gathering in money with one hand as it pays out with the other. Whatever emotion this system appeals to – fear, greed, blame, retribution – it is unlikely to inspire either trust or careful workmanship. (Imagine the following sequence of events. A man working for a contractor on the line notices that a rail has some cracks. He consults his supervisor. His supervisor consults Railtrack. How long will the rail last? A track possession will delay trains and cost money. Can a repair be done quickly? Might it be postponed? Need it be done at all? Doesn't it suit the contractor to have the rail replaced at Railtrack's cost, via another contractor? A new rail will cost the maintenance contractor less to maintain. That, a suspicious Railtrack official might think, might lead the contractor to overestimate the damage. Which person, at what rank, will decide what must be done?)

In July 1999, the government appointed a new Rail Regulator, Tom Winsor, himself a commercial lawyer. Winsor was determined to be tough. He wanted the trains to run to time. For him, Railtrack was 'a supplier not a dictator . . . it is not the king, that position belongs to the customer'. There was 'no inherent conflict between growth and performance and safety'. Still, safety began to worry both him and railway inspectors at the Health and Safety Executive. A month after Winsor became Rail Regulator, a Health and Safety report (the *Railway Safety Statistics Bulletin 1998–99*) showed an alarming increase in the number of broken rails, up by twenty-one per cent on the previous year – 937 actual breakages against a Railtrack forecast of 600. On the same day, 12 August, he wrote to Gerald Corbett at Railtrack demanding an 'action plan'. A fierce correspondence followed throughout the rest of the year and into 2000. Winsor accused Railtrack of lacking 'effective asset management'. When, on 1 September 1999, Railtrack explained that the increase in broken rails was caused partly by 'rail nearing the end of its life in high-tonnage routes', Winsor replied that the spate of rail breaks 'does not seem to suggest that the rail was *nearing* life expiry, but that it was already *at*, or even *beyond* life expiry' [his italics]. Winsor's letters demanded details of likely causes and proposed remedies and suggested that the number of broken rails was prima facie evidence that Railtrack was breaching its government licence to run the infrastructure. In July 2000, Railtrack 'categorically refuted' the allegation that the backlog of track defects had built up because resources were being diverted elsewhere. Winsor and the Health and Safety Executive then looked abroad for expert and independent advice and commissioned an investigation from the Transportation Technology Center in Colorado into Railtrack's method of managing broken rails. The Center produced a very long report, one conclusion of which was that Railtrack should inspect and replace rails more often.

It was published eight days after the Hatfield crash. When the American researchers completed their work, nobody had died because of a broken rail since 1967. But at the curve, sixteen miles up the line from the bureaucratic anger in London, the rail had continued to crack as the letters went back and forth between Winsor and Corbett. Hour after hour, day after day, expresses rode over it at 115 mph.

8. Blame

Many people knew about this cracking rail. In November 1999, four years after it had been laid, workers for Balfour Beatty, the maintenance contractor, noticed early evidence of gauge corner cracking. Their superiors knew the rail would have to be replaced eventually – the question was when. Tiny cracks may grow quickly or slowly or might not grow at all – aircraft engineers inspecting aircraft frames make similar calculations. Balfour Beatty suggested to Railtrack that 'rail-grinding' might be a temporary remedy, wearing down the surface of the rail by machine so that the cracks were ground-out before they could grow. Rail-grinding, however, had been suspended soon after the railways were privatised. There was only one operational machine in the country. Nothing came of the idea at the time. Then, at a site meeting between Balfour Beatty and Railtrack in February 2000, a decision was made to replace the rail and Balfour Beatty was invited to bid for the job. Soon after, however, Railtrack informed Balfour Beatty that the work would go instead to Jarvis, the company which had the contract for track renewal as opposed to track maintenance (the boundary between renewal and maintenance can be unclear). A twenty-seven hour 'track possession' was scheduled for 19 March. But when that date came, the replacement rail had not arrived at the site. According to John Ware, who investigated the crash for a BBC *Panorama* programme, there had been 'a cock-up in delivery' which might have stemmed in part from the confusing management of the freight wagon carrying the new rails; it was owned by Railtrack but operated by men from Jarvis. Eventually, towards the end of April, the new rails were successfully delivered and lay by the trackside. A new problem arose: in March, Railtrack and Jarvis had a track-possession slot but no new rails, now they had rails but no new track-possession slot. Could one be arranged in May? The new and busier summer timetable of trains began in that month; closing a stretch of line would cause more inconvenience and delay than in March, and incur penalty payments on Railtrack. Jarvis (again according to John Ware) said it would need five eight-hour possessions. Railtrack countered with the offer of two possessions each lasting four hours and twenty minutes. Jarvis said that to do the work in that time would be physically impossible. The re-railing was postponed until November, when Railtrack were again prepared to offer eight-hour possessions during the less crowded winter timetable. In September, a grinding-machine finally came and wore down the rail's surface, which might have been the wrong treatment at the wrong time. Grinding is meant to stop cracks growing; if the cracks have already grown beneath the surface, some engineers believe that grinding can make a cracked rail weaker.

In the meantime the rail continued to be inspected by Balfour Beatty, once a week by human eye (a man walking along the track), once every three months ultrasonically by a machine which is pushed by hand along the rail to scan its interior. This, for a high rail on a high-speed curve, was normal practice. The rail was scanned ultrasonically in April and again in July and by Railtrack's admission at least one of these scans was classified as unreadable. An unreadable ultrasonic scan suggests that either the cracking is so extensive that the machine can't register it, or that there is a fault in the machine. In either case, the rules suggest that a 20 mph speed limit should automatically be imposed. Even without ultrasonic scanning, all the available evidence suggests that the Hatfield rail had been, or should have been, recognised as a most dangerous rail which demanded the imposition of a speed limit. When the rail was reassembled, it bore obvious signs of pre-crash metal distress. Apart from the cracking its top surface had flaked up to a depth of three millimetres. A speed limit would have prevented four deaths.

On the day after the crash, Railtrack admitted that the condition of the rail was 'wholly unacceptable'. Later, before the House of Commons select committee on Transport, Gerald Corbett went further and said the rail was in an 'appalling' state. He couldn't understand why a speed limit hadn't been imposed: it was 'either incompetence or a systems failure, or . . . there might be a cultural aspect to it'. Tom Winsor, the Rail Regulator, concluded that there had been 'almost certainly a failure in the chain of command . . . between Railtrack and the organisation engaged to carry out maintenance on that piece of network'. The Commons committee concluded that it was 'clear that Railtrack's management of Balfour Beatty . . . prior to 17 October was totally inadequate'.

How much did Balfour Beatty tell Railtrack? What were Railtrack's instructions to Balfour Beatty? Which people are at fault? Who are the guilty men? As I write, in early March 2000, police investigations continue. Witnesses have been reluctant to be interviewed. There are filing cabinets of documents to be read. The evidence may support a criminal prosecution. The public mood, so far as one can tell, would like big fish in the net and the charge of corporate manslaughter. That is unlikely; as someone close to the Hatfield investigation said to me, you would need to find a piece of paper with unlikely words written on it such as: *Do not repair this track, we can't afford it. Yrs sincerely, the Fat Controller.* More likely is a charge of manslaughter – culpable homicide – made against individuals lower down the management ladder, or their prosecution for a breach of the Health and Safety at Work Act.

Corbett offered his resignation to the Railtrack board on 18 October and had it rejected. Railtrack's management was by now in a shaking fuddle. On the night of the crash, Railtrack had imposed emergency speed restrictions at eighty other high-speed curves which had gauge corner cracking, extending this later to any site where it judged the cracking to be 'severe' – that is, with cracks measuring more than 30mm long. Now the Health and Safety Executive wondered about cracks in the next category down Railtrack's scale, those defined as 'heavy' and between 20 and 29mm long. What was the scientific basis for this fine difference? Was 'heavy' cracking not just as potentially dangerous as 'severe'? Railtrack agreed that speed limits, some as low as 5 mph, should be imposed on both categories, and remain in place until the rail had been replaced or ultrasonically tested and cleared. Soon there were speed restrictions at 800 sites, and, a 'National Track Recovery Programme' which promised to replace 300 miles of rail and 860 switches and crossings by January. The implication, which Railtrack could never successfully refute, was that millions of passengers had been riding at high speed over lethally-flawed track for several years. Some important lines closed entirely; for a day or two, Glasgow was cut off from the south. The economies of large cities such as Leeds and Newcastle began to suffer. London's department stores and theatres were unusually empty. The Queen abandoned the train for an official visit to Cambridge. The Royal Mail switched its parcels and letters to chartered aircraft. Journey times doubled and trebled. On 27 November, Britain's railways established a peacetime record for slowness when passengers on the 10 p.m.

express from London to Nottingham reached their destination at 7 a.m. the next day; a journey of 126 miles had taken nine hours. Railtrack promised a normal timetable by Christmas. At Christmas, normality was postponed to Easter. A National Rail Recovery Plan was announced. The Prime Minister called 'rail summits' at which heads would be 'knocked together'. On 12 December, he conceded that it was 'absolute hell travelling on the railways' and promised that if the situation was not sorted out by January he would use 'the necessary powers . . . to issue guidance to speed this whole process up'. That was his biggest stick. The growing demand to have the railway infrastructure taken back into public ownership was firmly rejected, though it had supporters (columnists in *The Times* and *Daily Mail*, for example) who had political positions far removed from the Prime Minister's least favourite word, socialism. Railtrack: who could deny the oddity and scandal of it? It took public money and paid private dividends; it received continual instructions and interference from the government via the Rail Regulator; its revenues were fixed; it couldn't grow; it didn't work. But it was convenient for governments: in one columnist's words, it allowed 'the nationalisation of credit and the privatisation of blame'.

Corbett was interviewed on BBC television two days after the crash and the day after he'd offered to resign. He said: 'The railways were ripped apart at privatisation and the structure that was put in place was a structure designed, if we are honest, to maximise the proceeds to the Treasury. It was not a structure designed to optimise safety, optimise investment or, indeed, cope with the huge increase in the number of passengers the railway has seen.'

On 10 November he gave evidence to the Cullen inquiry.

Counsel: In statements made to the media you have indicated that, in your view, there are fundamental structural flaws in the privatised industry. You have called for a restructuring of the industry in what has been described as a personal manifesto for fundamental change. Indeed, in your own statement, at page 4, paragraph 11, you yourself quote part of an interview that you gave to BBC *Newsnight* on 19 October. On another occasion you announced publicly that we have got to think the unthinkable, that we have got to think radically.

Mr Corbett, all this appears to suggest that there has been a radical change in your view of the structure of the railway and, given that this change appeared to manifest itself post-Hatfield, that the rail at Hatfield was, if you like, a 'Road to Damascus'. What I want to explore with you is whether that is correct and the degree to which you consider that the problems currently facing the railways are of a fundamental nature, fundamental structural problems?

Corbett: Yes. I do not believe that I have ever come up with a personal manifesto and I do not believe I have ever called for restructuring. I have called attention, though, to some of the tensions and some of the difficulties with the current structure. It is not for me to try and resolve those. I think, though, it is incumbent on me in my role in the industry to draw people's attention to it. I would not describe Hatfield as a Damascene conversion because these tensions have been apparent for a while. If you would like me to develop the argument, I will.

Counsel: Please do.

Corbett: The railway as a system, under BR, was totally integrated and one person or group of people were able to balance the system. Performance, safety, efficiency, capacity, growth, it is all one system. I think that privatisation did fragment that system into over 100 different parts. That fragmentation did mean that the accountabilities were diffused and many of the different parts were set up with an economic architecture which by definition pointed them in different directions. I think it is the fragmentation and the economic incentives and the lack of clarity of accountability that actually makes it harder now to balance the system than it was then . . .

I think a month ago it was unthinkable for Railtrack to contemplate bringing its maintenance in-house. We employ 12,000 people. There are around 18,000 people employed by the maintenance contractors. I think that was an unthinkable thought given the size of the management challenge. But I think now, today, after what happened at Hatfield, we have to seriously review the new form of contract that we have and whether that is going to deliver the safety and the improvements that we all require . . .

Let us the start with the maintenance contracts. The maintenance was outsourced on privatisation. In 1995 the old British

Rail infrastructure systems' companies were broken off. The contracts agreed that they would maintain the railway to standards and they would get a lump sum of money to do that. That lump sum was based on what was spent on maintenance in the final years of BR and that lump was to decline by three per cent per annum over the next five years. Those were the contracts that we inherited.

When I arrived at Railtrack at the end of 1997 the assumption was that we had a 'competent contractor'. No one was able to answer the question: 'Which contractors are doing well, which are not?' There were no measures in place. The contractors did not have any specific targets. They had been broken off and that was the situation which we inherited . . .

Counsel: Has adherence to performance objectives adversely affected your management of safety?

Corbett: I think that answer will only be provided when we have the report on Hatfield. The tragedy at Hatfield, there was a broken rail; the rail were not in acceptable condition. I think we have to understand why speed restrictions were not put on that site. There were a number of opportunities when they could have been and they were not taken. I think when we have the answer to that we will be in a better position to be able to say whether or not the stress on performance has affected the culture at the frontline.

Lord Cullen: Mr Corbett, I have some difficulty with that answer because I would have thought that if there was genuine cause for concern on this subject, that is a challenge for management to tackle the problem [promptly], if it exists?

Corbett: Absolutely.

Seven days after Corbett gave this evidence, he was sacked by his board and went on holiday to India. His replacement, Steven Marshall, also had a previous career in the financial department of Grand Metropolitan hotels. Railtrack decided that it would not bring track maintenance and renewal work in-house – the choice that Corbett called 'thinking the unthinkable' – but on 23 November it appointed its first Technical Director, Richard Middleton, and announced that it would recruit dozens of engineers (permanent way contractors had already begun to import them from India and Romania). Until then the word 'engin-eering' had never appeared on the floor plan of Railtrack's headquar-ters in London, and only rarely in the company's annual report. Middleton, a chartered civil engineer who had worked on the rail-ways for twenty-five years, would represent engineering on the Railtrack board and report directly to the chief executive. This was a new devel-opment. Railtrack owned 10,000 route miles of track, its signalling and associated infrastructure (40,000 bridges and 750 tunnels) and yet before Hatfield it had chosen to see itself mainly as a property and contract management company, with engineering as a subdued component of the 'asset management' division. How could this be? In an interview with Nigel Harris of *Rail* magazine, Middleton said:

> We have to go back to the creation of Railtrack. Railtrack could have taken on board all of what was BR [nationalised British Rail] infrastructure, so we would have owned all the track workers, signal technicians and all overhead linesmen. But Government wanted to maximise return. It saw an opportunity by creating contracting companies that would contract with Railtrack – and they could be sold, with a revenue stream. That means you need contractual arrangements, with contracting staff overseen by a site agent and the client represented by a resident engineer – but you would have needed more engineers [in total, working for both Railtrack and its contractors] than British Rail had, it was impos-sible. So a unique form of contract emerged placing all engin-eering management — and safety responsibility — into the contracting company. Railtrack was set up as a 'light-touch' engin-eering resource to oversee that . . . But, with hindsight, it was unrealistic to expect contractors to provide network engineering resource – this is where it has all gone badly wrong.

These and other terrifying imperfections of railway privatisation may have contributed to the fatal crashes at Southall in 1997 and Ladbroke Grove in 1999; Lord Cullen's verdict will be delivered when his report into the past and future of British railway safety is published later this year. But with Hatfield, the case seems beyond doubt; the crash arose from a quagmire of divided responsibility and incompetence, inspired by an ideology that placed adversarial money bargaining over human and technical cooperation, in which 'the contract' was divine. Lawyers in their legal chambers had bent their minds to the will of a government that wanted to raise as much cash as possible from the sale of public assets; and devised a scheme driven by the crudest and most unworkable notions of the free market and its competitive benefits.

By the time of the Hatfield crash, the Labour Government, elected in May 1997, had had more than three years to abolish or modify the system that was so hastily and desperately devised by its Conservative predecessor. But its actions were mainly cosmetic. OPRAF was re-designated the Strategic Rail Authority (SRA), but it remained the *shadow* Strategic Rail Authority, waiting for the Act of Parliament which would give it legal power, until January this year. And then, despite its lengthy gestation, it turned out to be a strategic authority without a strategy. The SRA's chairman, Sir Alastair Morton, repeatedly emphasised that 'command and control' was not the authority's role. It had no specific vision of how Britain's railways should be developed; it would simply arbitrate between infrastructure schemes proposed by the private sector, subsidise those it favoured, and decide which train operating company would win which franchise. There would be no grand scheme. The SRA would not list desirable improvements to enhance a line's speed or capacity and then invite bids to meet a specification; it saw itself as a referee between rival schemes, reactive rather than pro. Its chief business would be to spend the money which had been allotted to the railways under the government's ten-year transport plan, announced in July 2000 by the Deputy Prime Minister, John Prescott, who said it would 'deliver the integrated transport system this country needs and deserves – a system fit for the new millennium and of which we can be justly proud.' Railways were to get £60 billion worth of investment out of a total of £180 billion – but these were 'headline' figures. In fact, only £26 billion of the £60 billion was guaranteed public investment, and the first figure contained about £10 billion which was already committed to two large engineering projects: the upgrade of the West Coast Main Line and the new Channel Tunnel Rail Link through Kent. The other £34 billion of the £60 billion would come – it was hoped – from private capital, which would reap its reward from increases in railway traffic which had been projected at fifty per cent for passengers and eighty per cent for freight over the years 2001 to 2011. Return on capital would depend on this growth. After Hatfield and the slump in rail travel, such growth projections began to look fantastical. Banks and financiers in the City of London spoke of railways as a very bad bet. Railtrack began to lobby the government for increased public subsidy, arguing that otherwise the railways would remain largely unimproved.

On 28 February, ten people died near Selby in Yorkshire after another Great North Eastern Railway express, this time running south from Newcastle to London at 125 mph, hit a Land Rover and a car-carrying trailer that had somehow tumbled on to the line from an adjacent motorway only a few seconds before. The derailed express, powered by the same locomotive that had survived Hatfield, then collided with a heavy coal train travelling at 60 mph in the opposite direction. It was genuine accident, a series of unforeseeable coincidences; the way the railway was run could not be held to blame.

On 2 March one of the largest train operating companies, Sir Richard Branson's Virgin Rail, threatened to sue Railtrack unless Virgin was compensated for the £100 million it had lost in revenue in passenger fares in the aftermath of Hatfield, when between October and February revenue had fallen by thirty-two per cent. Many train operating companies, including Virgin, estimated that their annual profits would be severely reduced or turned into losses. Railtrack insisted that it would not increase its total compensation to train operators from the £400 million it had already announced. All over the system, shifts of workers were still renewing cracked rails. Railtrack originally estimated the cost at £100 million, but others inside the railway industry suggested a more realistic estimate was £500 million. The total cost of Hatfield to Railtrack could therefore be close to £1 billion. Despite the likely consequences of these costs for Railtrack's profits (and some news reports mentioned bankruptcy), the company's share price remained stubbornly high. An ordinary share was worth £3.90 on flotation in 1996, peaked at £17.68 in 1998, but was still valued at £8.91 on March 6, 2001. The stockmarket expectation was that the government would always bail out the company with subsidy; it could not afford to let it fail.

Government politicians said that Hatfield had created a new atmosphere within the industry, which now – at last saw the need to 'pull together', but it is hard to find evidence to support this optimism. The world's most fragmented railway system has adversarial relationships at the heart of the philosophy which invented it, and an hour's frank conversation with most people who work in Britain's railways will eventually throw up 'mess' as their most accurate description. Animosities exist at every level: between two government departments, the Treasury and the Department of the Environment, Transport and the Regions; between two government agencies, the Rail Regulator and the Strategic Rail Authority; between a third government agency, the Health and Safety Executive, and many parts of the railway industry (the HSE was warning Railtrack about its 'weak' management of contractors as early as March 1996); between Railtrack and the train operators; and between Railtrack and its contractors.

A senior figure in the railways once told me a sad little story about the Strategic Rail Authority, then still the shadow Strategic Rail Authority. It received many foreign visitors. 'The ones from Europe come because they want to discover how *not* to privatise a railway. The ones from the Third World come to see how it should be done – because the IMF has sent them. Poor mugs.'

9. Punishment

The history of large railway accidents is filled with small human mistakes; these things happen. Signalman James Tinsley, for example. Signalman Tinsley had an arrangement with his colleague, Signalman Meakin, that allowed him to start work ten minutes after his official signing-on time of 6 a.m. In that way he could reach the signal box more conveniently by the first morning train rather than rising from his bed earlier and making the two-mile walk. It was a neat arrange- ment for a signal box in the countryside near the Scottish border; remote from inspectors and managers, a place called Quintinshill. His colleague Meakin would work the extra ten minutes, recording the train movements during those minutes on a scrap of paper which Tinsley would then copy into the official signal-box log, preserving the appearance that he had been on duty since six.

On the morning of 22 May 1915, Tinsley was preoccupied with his copying while Meakin chatted to a couple of railwaymen who had come into the box. The First World War was nine months old. The line Meakin and Tinsley controlled was the main route from England to Scotland, busy with trains of troops and naval coal. A northbound local – the train that Tinsley had arrived on – had been shunted by Meakin on to the southbound line to allow a late-running night express from London to overtake it. There it lay outside the box, forgotten. At 6.42, the next signal box to the north indicated to Tinsley that a special train was on its way south. Would Quintinshill accept it? Tinsley set the signals to green. At 6.48, the special came down the gradient at high speed carrying troops of the Royal Scots Regiment bound for Liverpool and the Dardanelles. The special hit the local, then, coming in the opposite direction and also at speed, the night express ran into the wreckage of both. All the carriages were wooden and those of the troop train lit by gas. A great fire at Quintinshill burned for twenty-four hours. Of the 227 dead, all but ten were young men of the Royal Scots.

A Scottish court found Tinsley and Meakin guilty of culpable homicide. Tinsley was sentenced to three years in jail and Meakin to eighteen months, but they were pardoned within a year. Both men had suffered severe nervous breakdowns.

The politicians and their advisers who, in Corbett's phrase, 'ripped apart' Britain's railways have never spoken publicly about the crash at Howe Dell, though sometimes their successors in the Conservative Party have admitted that 'they got some things wrong'. They have directorships, they sit on boards, they have lunch at the club. So far as we know, they sleep soundly at night. A nervous breakdown or two would be just.

Football

May 2003

There is too much football, no getting away from it. One recent morning my children told me about Beckham's broken scaphoid bone. A couple of nights earlier we watched Glasgow Celtic lose to Porto in the UEFA Cup final in Seville. I went to the loo just after half-time and my children came bouncing up two flights of stairs twice, to pound on the door and tell me of the goals I'd missed as the score changed from 1–1 to 2–1 to 2–2. Back in front of the television, I looked at the thousands of Celtic supporters in the stands, most of them dressed like the Celtic players on the pitch, in strips hooped with green and white. I remember when I first saw a man dressed like that – dressed to imitate a player in the same green and white hoops. He lived at the bottom of our street in the village. He was a Catholic. We thought he was daft. 'A grown man, did ye ever see the like . . .' and so forth.

Until I was sixteen, I knew nothing about football. In the 1950s, it was still possible to be so ignorant. Football, even in Scotland, was a discrete activity. Some people went to watch it, many others didn't. Confined to the back pages of newspapers, it had yet to metastasise. We lived in the east of Scotland and didn't have television. The sectarianism of western Scotland and the clubs it supported were just a rumour to me. Teams without some geography attached to their names were a mystery. For a long time I thought 'Rangers' must be a Highland team – the name sounded mountainous – and probably located in Fort William. When at secondary school our French teacher, trying to be pally, made Monday-morning jokes about the local team's Saturday performance, they flew over my head like the rarer verbs.

I must also admit a more intimate reason. My family were anti-football; they thought it had drugged Scottish working-class life. In what is still the best non-fiction account of Glasgow, *Glasgow in 1901*, a book published to coincide with the city's international fair of that year, James Hamilton Muir wrote: 'The best you can say for football is that it has given the working man a subject for conversation.' My father, hurrying for the bus to his class at the Workers Educational Association, would have passionately disagreed with that. As far as he was concerned, it was the *worst* you could say for football. Football was the enemy of enlightenment and decent talk. 'It was as if a fever of hate had seized that multitude, neutralising for the time everything gracious and kindly,' wrote George Blake of the crowd at a Rangers–Celtic game in his 1935 novel, *The Shipbuilders*. That was more to my father's way of thinking, perhaps because his own father had once been one of that multitude, at the Rangers end, and had never been regarded as a progressive man.

Then in 1961, Dunfermline Athletic won through to the final of the Scottish Cup. They were the local team, the subject of our French teacher's jokes, and until that year completely obscure. Now they had a new manager, Jock Stein, and started a period of unlikely success. Their progress had passed me by. On the Saturday of the final at Hampden Park in Glasgow, I did my usual Saturday things: I got the bus to Dunfermline, borrowed some books from the library, and then sat in the stalls of the Regal to see the afternoon film. Before I went in, I noticed that the High Street was so empty that the sight of tumble-weed rolling down it wouldn't have been a surprise. When I came out there were men selling special editions of the Edinburgh and Dundee evening papers. Clearly something big had happened far away – in Glasgow, as it turned out. Dunfermline had drawn with Celtic, o–o.

Schools got the afternoon off to see the replay on Wednesday and we went west on special trains which took unusual routes through the iron forges and steel mills of the Clyde valley. Inside the ground on a moist afternoon – there were no floodlights then – we stood in our school blazers among Celtic fans, men of a Glasgow type which has since disappeared: dressed with no intervening shirt between their vests and their jackets, flat caps, green and white scarves knotted as mufflers, large bottles of McEwan's pale ale to hand. They pissed where they stood – I'd never seen that before. Still, they were the metropolitans and we were the provincials: bumpkins, to be treated in a friendly way.

> 'Did youse milk the coos before ye came, son?'
> 'Did youse remember to lock the byre?'

It all went wrong for them, of course. Dunfermline won 2–0. There were scuffles on the terraces – bewildered violence at a great team's defeat – and at the trackside in Lanarkshire men cheered our trains as they steamed home. They were Rangers fans, a friend explained, and cheering on the principle that their enemy's conqueror was their friend. That night, Dunfermline's High Street was more crowded than it has ever been before or since. The team appeared to wild noise on the balcony of the council chambers with the town's provost. Whenever I watch the video (*Dunfermline Athletic: the Golden Years*) I'm always surprised to see that the provost is wearing a high wing collar and looks like Neville Chamberlain; and that I was there.

Thinking about it now, I see that my conversion to football had its equivalent in Galilee; it was my first match and I had been witness to a miracle. It was thrilling to discover that I was one of the blessed, the chosen, on account of where I came from. Later that year we got television, and soon after I saw the philosopher A. J. Ayer being interviewed about his enthusiasm for Tottenham Hotspur, pretty certainly along the lines of 'Why on earth is a clever chap like you – and posh too – interested in football?' Others may point to other historical moments when football showed the first sign that it was escaping its chains of class and gender, the flat cap and the back page. The philosopher's interview was mine.

I followed Dunfermline Athletic for several years and sometimes to the strangest places, to East Stirling, Airdrie and Stenhousemuir. For a short while I even had a job taking money at the turnstiles. But Jock Stein left to transform the fortunes of the team he and his Dunfermline side had so famously beaten. Under his management, Celtic became the first British club to win the European Cup in the final against Inter Milan in Lisbon in 1967. Last week a fact about that team was often repeated: all eleven had grown up within thirty miles of Glasgow. Much the same could be said of Dunfermline then as well: most of the team were drawn from the towns and pit villages of Fife.

In Seville the green and white masses were cheering on a highly paid team drawn from France, Belgium, Holland, Sweden, Bulgaria and England; only two were Scots. The number of Catholics in the team – though Celtic, unlike the Protestant Rangers, were never religiously exclusionist – is a question no longer worth bothering with. The Pope himself has said that Scotland can no longer be called a Christian society, and it may be that these days Rangers has as many Catholics, from Catholic Europe, on its playing staff as Celtic does. And yet Blake's 'fever of hate' still flourishes when the two teams meet – as someone wrote recently, their rivalry no longer represents 'the tip of the iceberg' of Scotland's sectarian divide, it is the iceberg itself.

My father would have seen Rangers and Celtic as a brake on social progress; many in Scotland still do. To that extent I think he was more right about football than Professor Ayer, though last week I was sorry, unlike in 1961, to see Celtic lose.

Cherries

June 2003

I have always been a nationalist about fruit. If the BNP became the BFP, the British Fruit Party, I'd be a member. Obviously, some fruits are exempted. There is no point going in quest of the English orange, the Scottish banana, the Welsh mango. But apples, pears, strawberries, raspberries, plums – I point at the boxes and ask the greengrocer, 'Are they English?' (or, in the case of raspberries, Scottish) and the greengrocer, who's been hearing my question for several years, says, 'Na, you'll be lucky, mate. Them's from Spain.'

I don't know why I do this. It may be prompted by the many pieces written on the decline of English apple varieties and some desire these arouse in me to save the British orchard from the same destination as the British shipyard, the British coal mine, the British cotton mill. Or it may be another kind of piece, which points out the waste of aviation fuel spent in flying chilled plums from the USA. More probably, though, it's to do with a stubborn belief that British fruit tastes better, 'better' meaning as I first tasted it and want to taste it again. And in no other fruit do I want this more than in the cherry – right now, in the middle of the short season of the Kentish crop.

When I first tasted one is impossible to say, but a photograph records the moment when cherryphilia took hold. My father has arranged my brother and me at the back door of our brick house in Lancashire. It's a sunny day. My brother is in his new RAF uniform – aged eighteen, he's just been called up, a Brylcreem Boy. I'm standing on a ladder beside him. He's smiling firmly. I seem to be laughing. But what's that small blurred object between my mouth and the ground? Answer: a cherry stone, inadequately caught by a Box Brownie with a shutter speed of one twenty-fifth of a second. The year must be 1952 – pinpointed by the the the new RAF recruit and the location; we left this house and moved back to Scotland a few months later. The month must be either June or July, when cherries came and went from the shops in a blink. I remember the juicy sharpness of them and how you could crowd two or three in your mouth at once, and how easily your tongue slid the stones free, and how easily they could be spat, which is what I've just done in the picture.

It seemed impossible then, and for a few years after, ever to eat enough cherries. A pound of them in a brown paper bag, smudged purple with juice at the bottom, went nowhere. The best, not too ripe, had what is now known in the food industry as 'mouth feel'; a skin firm enough to offer a slight resistance to the bite, then a spurt of juice from the flesh. As their short season wore on, they changed from light red to almost black, and then, in a kind of late-flowering miracle, you sometimes got the white ones mottled with pink: White Hearts or 'Naps' (Napoleons). I write this in the past tense, slightly untruthfully because you can still buy English cherries if you look hard enough, but truthfully enough in the sense that they are rarely available in the places where people buy most food, supermarkets. This week, wandering through Marks & Spencer and Sainsbury's, I found cherries from Turkey, Spain and the USA ('Biggest, sweetest, juiciest: keep refrigerated,' said their plastic wrapper) but none at all from the Kentish orchards, only thirty miles away.

What happened? Margaret Burns of the Brogdale Horticultural Trust in Faversham, Kent, told me a little of the cherry's history. Brogdale has the world's largest collection of edible plants, including more than 200 varieties of cherry. The cherry, she said, was recorded by Pliny the Elder (who noted three varieties; red, black, hard) and probably came from Greece to Rome and from Rome to southern Britain (cherry stones have been found in the excavations at Silchester). The Normans brought more. Contemporary writers observed cherry orchards at Tower Hill, London, in 1295, and in the vineyard of the monastery at Ely in 1302. Many of the varieties we have now were planted by England's first serious cherry man, Richard Harris, fruiterer to Henry VIII, who established orchards at Teynham, also in Kent. For centuries the English cherry went from strength to strength; to test its cultural signifance, I looked in the *Collins Dictionary of Quotations* and discovered it to be number three in the list of fruit references (apples, twenty-five; grapes, thirteen; cherries, ten; oranges, nine; kiwi fruit, zero,). Then, in the years after the Second World War, farmers began to find it more trouble than it was worth, too sensitive, too tricky a plant. An April frost could ruin its early blossom; rain split the fruit; birds gorged on it; successful pollination among so many varieties needed large orchards. Worse, there was the danger and expense of picking the crop, finding casual labour willing to mount ladders up sixty-foot trees.

Recently a lot of that has changed. Kent orchards now have new breeds of smaller, self-pollinating trees, which can be covered with nets (against birds) and polythene (against rain), and the word is that this has been a good season. You can expect the English black variety – Van, Colney, Sunburst, Lapin – in shops, maybe even in supermarkets, in a few weeks' time, when the Spanish, French, Turkish and Italian supplies run out. But will they be sharp on the tongue?

It's the sharpness that I miss. Only once have I had too much of it – a surfeit, a sickening. In 1959, my school organised a summer trip to Bavaria, funded by parental payments of ten bob a week. We came down from Scotland to London on the train, and then by another train from Cannon Street to Dover in green carriages pulled by a steam locomotive named after a public school (Oundle, or maybe Repton – one of the two). It was an England I had never seen before. Lush suburbs and green country rolled past the window. At Orpington a woman with pink-blonde hair waited on the platform (unprecedented; I wrote a postcard home, 'Saw strawberry blonde at Orpington!'). We coasted down the Weald in a rich evening light: orchards, oast houses, men with bowler hats further down the train, England as in books. At Dover, we went in a crocodile to a boarding house. Dover is in Kent. Kent was full of cherries. They were cheap.

The next morning I bought two or three pounds and ate and ate, and then around lunchtime felt foreboding. There was a stiff wind and the Channel was rough. I would surely be sick. Had I been, my passion for cherries might have ended. But I wasn't – force of will, probably, scared by the prospect of public shame – and soon the bile at the back of my throat was tempered by egg sandwiches as we crossed on our steamer to Ostend.

Hugh MacDiarmid wrote in one of his more readily quotable poems about 'the little white rose of Scotland / That smells sharp and sweet

85

– and breaks the heart'. This is about troubled nationhood. I don't say that it means nothing to me, but the English cherry, with its own sweet-sharpness and its summer brevity, means, for the usual Proustian reasons, so much more.

Blitz Spirit

July 2005

Generalisations about the national psyche – supposing there is one – must always be treated with suspicion. In 1997, the great crowds who mourned the death of the Princess of Wales with their tears, flowers and candles were taken as evidence that British behaviour had utterly changed. We were at last in touch with our feelings, prepared to show them, to hug strangers, to weep and tear our hair. We would never be the same again. Eight years later, in July this year, our alleged conversion to the open emotions of (say) Brazil had been forgotten. The traditional strengths of stoicism, resilience and understatement hadn't, after all, died with the princess in her Paris car crash. They were merely sleeping, to spring awake when three terrorist bombs went off in London tube trains and a fourth on a London bus, killing fifty-six people including the four bombers and injuring hundreds of others. London's response to the bombs showed what Londoners were made of; we would be cheerful, we would not be cowed, we would carry on as usual. We showed 'the spirit of London', the same spirit of our citizen forebears during their bombing by the Luftwaffe – 'the Blitz' – in 1940 and 1941.

How such conclusions are reached, from what evidence, it is always difficult to know, but on 7 July they were reached very quickly, perhaps with the understanding that the wish can be father of the fact. Speeches by politicians, messages on websites, pieces to camera by television reporters, columnists in the next day's newspapers – all of them spoke of the calm and quiet resolution of Londoners. One commentator daringly ascribed it to the domestic, unthreatening scale of London's

architecture; many others saw it exemplified by the sight of hundreds
of thousands of Londoners walking quietly home that evening in the
complete absence of buses and tubes (and those crowded pavements of
one-way human traffic certainly were a striking sight, unknown even
in the Blitz, though caused by pure necessity rather than feelings of
communal solidarity).

For the sociological record, my own very commonplace experience
was this. That morning I got to the bus stop much later than usual,
around 10.30. For that time of day there was a surprisingly big crowd
– the orderly London bus queue disintegrated years ago – and very
few buses, all of them full. My mobile phone wouldn't work. I got a
taxi and the driver pushed his window back and asked me if I had
heard the news, and I thought for a second that the Queen must have
died, and then he told me about the bombs – three or four buses hit,
an unknown number of tubes, no casualty figures, lots of rumour. 'I'd
fucking hang the fuckers, no questions asked,' he said. 'I'd fucking hang
them, whoever did it.' Even for a man in an England football shirt, he
was a champion swearer and ranter and I was glad to step out of his
cab. In the office, people were listening to the radio and looking at the
BBC website. On a landline – the mobile phone networks were still
down – I checked that my wife and children were safe at work and in
school. They had no reason to be on the number 30 bus or on the
Piccadilly or Circle lines, but we use all of them sometimes and their
routes and stations are very close; King's Cross under a mile away. And
then I worked as usual and in the evening walked home to watch the
continuous news on television, following the same pattern the next day.
Many kind emails arrived hoping that we were safe and well. It was
only then, perhaps, that I understood that seen from far away (Tel Aviv,
Delhi, New York) I was at the centre rather than the fringe of a global
drama. On Friday night, my wife told me of the passenger on the
number 30 who, before he got impatient with the bus's slow progress
and got off, had noticed a young man next to him who kept fiddling
with something in his backpack. I had a nightmare in which I saw a
similar thing but couldn't leave the bus. Then, in Saturday's newspaper,
I read an account of one policeman's experience working underground
in the narrow tunnel of the Piccadilly line, in the carriage where so
many had died. Blood, oppressive heat, a multitude of body parts (the
blast had nowhere to go). When the policeman reached the surface after

his day's brave work he said that he had 'never felt so lonely'. I nearly cried at that, and for most of the day I felt sad and fearful, 'unhinged' might be the word. The attack on London had inevitably come; others would follow – would they ever end? – and, much though I like London (my home for thirty-five adult years), there are safer places to live.

The mood passed. The next day, Sunday, I took a friend from Chicago who is interested in railways to have a look at the civil engineering works at St Pancras station, where the new fast line to Paris will start, stopping on its way at the site for the London Olympics in 2012, which were announced the day before the bombs. We walked around new embankments and looked at the cranes and the earth-movers. A forgotten swathe of London, once occupied by freight yards and more recently by crack addicts, is being redeveloped and spruced up. This is London as an advertising agency might see it – confident, multicultural, new and yet old, the fancy Victorian Gothic of the old terminus surviving among undercorated concrete and glass. Then, more or less by accident, my friend and I got to King's Cross. Outside the station, relatives had pinned up pictures of men and women who could only be described as 'missing' because they were not yet confirmed dead. There were flowers, messages of support, and television crews. It was a hot, sunny day. As we stood on the pavement across the road, I realised that a hundred feet or so under my feet, men were still working in the tunnel to retrieve pieces of the bomb, and of the tissue and bone of the people, the ex-people, whose friends and relatives hoped against hope were still alive.

How can we stand such a thought, such proximity? I don't know, but we do. Later in the day my children passed though King's Cross on the Victoria line and were interested to see that the train slowed at the station but didn't stop. Nothing much more was said about it.

In this, there is nothing special about London. New York, Madrid, Jerusalem, Baghdad; people there have suffered equal or far greater terrors and carried on. That London has a special spirit must be a myth. But myths can be helpful – their point isn't their trueness – and to imagine that you are part of some resilient tradition – that you are resilient simply because of where you live – may help rather than harm you, so long as you don't buy it completely, remembering that you are only flesh and blood.

★   ★   ★

The myth came out of the last months of 1940. Just like this year's terrorist attack, the German bombing of London had been long awaited, and with an even greater fatalism. As the historian and anthropologist Tom Harrisson wrote thirty-five years later, 'the idea that attack from overhead would become the final, totally devastating stage in coming wars grew [to] near-obsession – comparable, say, to the one-time belief of strict Christian sects in a burning hell for the unredeemed.' The first big raid occurred on 'Black Saturday', 7 September, a fine day towards the end of a fine summer. Another writer, Ritchie Calder, watched it from his garden on the Surrey Downs 'with a detachment which surprised and rather shocked me' – until the sight of London, apparently on fire from end to end, filled him with 'dread and horror'. As more German planes came in from the coast, the family took a break from its cricket game and had tea. 'How silly that sounds! How callous and inconsequential! Yet how much in keeping with the strange unreality of it all!'

Calder wrote that in a small book, *The Lesson of London*, published in 1941 as one of a series called the Searchlight Books, which were edited by T. R. Fyvel and George Orwell and also included Orwell's famous essay 'The Lion and the Unicorn: Socialism and the English Genius'. Calder's book is very good – a mixture of eye-witness reporting from ruined east London and a castigation of poor planning by the authorities – and in it he notes that 'the old standards of courage disappeared in the common and unconscious heroism of ordinary individuals', often meaning people who did no more than continue to come to work. Very early on in the war the celebration of quiet 'ordinariness' became a dominant theme – the thinking British patriot's weapon of choice – which was a kind of miracle given that Britain then was a class-conscious country with the largest empire the world had ever seen, and quite literally pompous. But it was lucky in its writers, its radio producers and its film-makers, men such as Harrisson, Calder, Orwell and Humphrey Jennings who had in the 1930s made journeys from backgrounds of relative privilege to discover and document the working class. Their commitment to a certain demotic idea of Britain, at war or at peace, gave British propaganda the ring of modest truth, and an appeal to the egalitarian instincts of Roosevelt's America.

The key contribution was made by Humphrey Jennings and another documentary director, Harry Watt, in a ten-minute film called, for foreign audiences, *London Can Take It* and for British audiences, *Britain Can Take It* (presumably to prevent resentment of the capital in other British cities which were also being bombed). As Kevin Jackson writes in his biography of Jennings, the film was 'perhaps the most influential work he ever made – one of the few films that have played some small part in changing the course of history'. It was shot in September 1940, soon after the night bombing started and when the outcome of both the Blitz and the war was far from clear. The British army had been evacuated from Dunkirk only months before; France was occupied; the Soviet Union and the USA still neutral. In Britain, a terrorised population and defeat were strong possibilities, though not ones countenanced by *London Can Take It*. The film showed ordinary people coping – old people asleep in air-raid shelters, a woman kicking broken glass aside as she collects milk from the doorstep, commuters continuing to commute across the rubble – as on the soundtrack the American journalist and broadcaster Quentin Reynolds delivers his fiercely optimistic commentary. 'I am a neutral reporter. I have watched the people of London live and die . . . I can assure you, there is no panic, no fear, no despair in London town.'

It was finished in ten days, and Reynolds took it immediately to the USA, where a special screening was arranged for Roosevelt. Soon afterwards – by 25 October – it had taken enough at the American box office to be judged 'a wild success' by the British Ministry of Information. 'The Spirit of the Blitz' had been born.

The film was not untrue to its subject; many diaries and records from the period attest to a remarkably matter-of-fact reaction to being bombed. But like any piece of art it was highly selective in its truths: no body parts, no grief in a city where, between September 1940 and May 1941, about 20,000 civilians died from the detonation of 18,800 tons of high explosives dropped from above. Other British towns did not react so stoically. After severe raids on Plymouth and Clydebank, smaller targets than London where the effects of bombing were more obvious, many in their populations took to camping in the nearby hills. And it is also fair to wonder how long London would have continued to 'take it' had the bombing gone on at the rate of the first few months. A film called *Dresden Can Take It* would seem unlikely, though *Falluja Can Take It* must never be ruled out.

*   *   *

About a mile away from my house there is a cemetery, the Abney Park Cemetery, which was laid out by a private company in the nineteenth century to accommodate the growing number of the London dead who failed to qualify for burial in the graveyards of Anglican parish churches – that is for Jews, atheists, Nonconformists, and I imagine Muslims too, had any of their bereaved come knocking. It has some large and well-tended memorials, including those to the Booth family, who founded the Salvation Army, but mostly it is overgrown and tumble-down. Nicely so: it looks like a wood rather than a cemetery, with rambling paths through the trees, crazily tipped gravestones, and cracked monuments in the shrubbery.

One now neglected memorial was erected by the Metropolitan Borough of Stoke Newington to those people in the borough who died in the wartime bombing. A lot of the lead has been picked from the stone, but it's still possible to read the inscription: 'Death is but crossing the world as friends do the seas, they live in one another still.' Underneath, the dead are listed beneath the names of the streets they lived and died in. The street that suffered most grievously was Coronation Avenue, where on 13 October 1940 a bomb (more probably a stick of bombs) landed and killed ninety-five people. The names suggest it was quite a Jewish street: two Coopersteins, three Edelsteins, one Katz, two Danzigers, two Krakowskys, etc. Perhaps one of them was the man described by Ritchie Calder in his chapter 'The Courage of London': 'the little German Jew who looked up at a dogfight over the East End, his tattered beard quivering with excitement, and cried, "Our Spitfire boys are *wunderbar*."'

I've never seen flowers at this memorial, or any other sign of care. It all seems so long ago. What most remains is a folk memory of that time, the stoicism that has been so beautifully enshrined in films and literature.

Two Sheds

November 2003

My mother outlived my father by more than twenty years and died in 2002. In all those years, and in the many months since my mother's death, two outlying provinces of the household remained undisturbed: the garden shed and the coal shed, both of them arranged and ruled by my father in his role as gardener, repairer of domestic goods, coal-drawer, shoe-mender, and, long ago, hen-keeper to the family and toymaker to his children. The coal shed occupies the hollow space beneath the outside stair. It last kept coal in 1979, when the local authority installed central heating and 'modernised' every flat in the street, chucking out a lot of fine old panelled doors and 1920s tiled fireplaces while they were at it. The garden shed dates from the 1930s, when my parents got their first house with a bathroom and a garden. They took the shed with them when they moved from Lancashire back to Fife and it has stood in the same spot behind the hedge for fifty years, slowly getting shakier and leakier.

It was the condition of the garden shed that made me decide last month to sort its contents and transfer those worth keeping to the coal shed, while we decided what to do with the flat. But first we would need to sort and discard the contents of the coal shed, to make room. Both places were crowded with things. My father wasn't a man who easily threw them away. Sometimes I felt like one of his heroes, Howard Carter, whose discovery of Tutankhamun's tomb had thrilled my father as a young man. A Carter, in this instance, who not only rescued Tutankhamun for history but miraculously remembered how he had been when alive.

'There's a funny thing right at the back like a barrel with two bulges,' my wife said when we'd cleared a path through the coal shed. I went to look. Not one barrel, but two, stacked one above the other. They were metal but surprisingly light. Zinc was the material. The date 1930 was stamped on their bottoms. Each had a small oblong shelf protruding from a part of the rim. Dolly tubs! I remembered how a brick of red soap would lie on the small shelf when not actually in my mother's hand as she scrubbed clothes on a Monday. But why two dolly tubs? I tried to reconstruct the process. One filled with hot water for washing, the other with cold for rinsing; a pole to press down and stir the clothes, its wood furred below a certain level due to its frequent immersion; a washboard to scrub with; a mangle to squeeze; on dry days clothes poles to stretch the rope on the drying green; on wet days a clothes horse suspended from the ceiling on pulleys.

But why the name 'dolly tub'? Why that powder – starch, possibly – that came in a packet labelled Dolly Blue? Because, according to my later consultation of the *Shorter Oxford*, from about 1790 'dolly' became a pet name for a child's doll and was then further applied to 'contrivances fancied to resemble a doll', hence (*dialect*) 'a wooden appliance with two arms, and legs or feet, used to stir clothes in wash tub, called a *d. tub*'.

I told my brother about our find. He remembered wash days with a shudder in his voice. 'All that steam and the smell of damp cloth, and the food not being quite up to scratch on Mondays because Mum had no time – a couple of boiled potatoes and a bit of bacon, that kind of thing.' I remembered that too, but also the light-green cabbage that came on the same plate: a combination that preceded the tastier era of tinned spaghetti and which I'd happily now sit down to, anytime.

We dug further around the coal shed and discovered evidence of its original purpose: a sack, the fragments of a small shovel. Coal had landed here once a week with a thud and then a dull rattle as it escaped its hundredweight sack, upended by the men who brought it down the path from the Co-op coal lorry, men who wore leather vests with steel studs on the back. Had they really shouted 'Small c-o-a-l and brick-ettes' in the street? I guess they must have done, because that's what my parents sang whenever they heard Mario Lanza or David Whitfield on the radio, their voices being judged to be about as good as the coalman's.

The coal then came up two flights of stairs in buckets, carried by my father and sometimes by me. I don't want to bring Orwell into this, to add grandeur to the ordinary, but his passage in *The Road to Wigan Pier* about the essentialness of coal to the comfort of British life – to the nancy-boy poets, and so on – remained absolutely true long after he wrote it. Without coal – and coal in the kitchen cupboard, not at some distant power station – no heat. Without heat, no hot water. Without hot water, far less frequent washing of the person, armpits and groins, and none at all of clothes. The first noise I heard every morning as I drowsed in bed was the scraping of the grate and the curling of newspaper, the scratch of a match. Without coal we would have been cold and dirty. Even with it, I am sorry to say, baths were weekly. More often, in the words of Jimmy Edwards playing Mr Glum, there was 'a good all-over in the sink'.

When the wind got up, we would hear the quick clatter of the whirler on the chimney pot, which was meant to promote the up-draught and which for some reason (the *Shorter Oxford* is no help here) we called a 'granny'. On the streets, many women far younger than grannies had legs mottled pink and red though the habit of pushing up their skirts and warming themselves by the fire. We called this 'fire tartan'. All this, you might say, was part of the departed culture of coal, and the coal shed.

The garden shed was even fuller. Some items stood out: my mother's heavy cast-iron griddle for scone-making, an antique blowtorch, the cobbler's last on which my father had resoled the family's shoes, the vice that had once gripped the wood that became my lovely model yacht and the wooden railway engine made from factory leftovers. We passed through layers of biscuit, toffee and tobacco tins (Huntley and Palmer, Sharp's – 'The Word for Toffee' – Bulwark, Walnut Plug) that contained neatly categorised screws, nails, tacks, bolts, hammers, files. Eventually we got down to my father's three toolboxes – he had been a fitter all his life – which were locked and had to be crowbarred open to reveal many spanners, many chisels, many bolts, and spirit levels and steel rulers.

When the shed was emptied I saw something I hadn't seen for fifty years. A tiny door at the bottom of one of its sides, where the hens had come and gone. My father's favourite was called Betty. Aged six, I had watched him try to twist Betty's neck in the kitchen, hen-keeping having come to an end. 'I can't do it, I can't do it,' he had said, but eventually he managed to. My mother couldn't face eating her. I don't think any of us did.

We took most of the stuff to the dump, though I kept a dolly tub back with the idea that it might be a plant-plot. Recycling is the thing. A man showed us the various skips: this one for household refuse, this one for metal, this one for wood. In they went, the shoe-last, the griddle, the files, the chisels, the tobacco tins, with banging finality. It took several trips. I thought: how strong my parents must have been, how physically strong, to have used so many things to make and maintain so many things, including us.

The Vivid Present

March 2004

At a dinner during the London Book Fair, I was surprised to find that we were all talking about writing. Not writers: 'She's just so marvellous.' Not books: 'I heard it went for £250,000.' Not sackings: 'Has he found a job yet?' But about how things were written. Perhaps this was because the people I was with were from Spain and in one case Argentina. Gossip wasn't an option. The publisher from Buenos Aires and I were talking about tenses, when he suddenly said: 'My daughter talks entirely in the present.'

I knew exactly what he meant. I don't know how it sounds in Spanish, but in the English of my own daughter, aged eleven, it goes something like this:

> We're on the *train*? and Tom's like Give me my mobile back and she's like No go away and he's like No please Rache I really need it and then this *man*? comes up and he's like looking for a *seat?* and Rache throws the phone at Tom and it *hits?* this man and he's like angry and the train is coming into Potter's *Bar?* and . . .

This would have happened in the morning on the train to school, ten hours before. The italicised words with question marks attached are meant to suggest the strange, questioning stresses that settle on random words, not necessarily at the ends of sentences (if any sentences happen to be hanging around, that is). Where this speech tic comes from is a question in itself – Australian soaps, television news readers, New Zealand barmen?

– but it almost certainly does not come from me, because although I grew up in Fife, among the high endnotes of the Fife sentence, my accent was later flattened out by several years in Glasgow.

Half a century earlier my grandfather made a smaller move, the ten miles inland from Kirkcaldy to the mining village of Hill of Beath. Some years later, on a day out to the Kirkcaldy sands with his children, he overheard a Kirkcaldy family on a nearby bench conversationally skirling away like a pipe band. 'My Goad,' he said, 'tae think we used to speak like that!'

My mother always delighted in that story and always told it in the past tense, just as I've done above. My daughter might tell it differently. 'Like they're sitting on this *bench?* and they're like Noo pet wid ye like a read o' the morning pipper? and he's handing over the *Dundee Courier* and . . .' so on. Where does it come from, this new love of the present tense? I can make only guesses. Hip-hop, rap, stand-up comics ('This man walks into a bar'), voice-overs for film documentaries (all the way from 'This is the Night Mail crossing the border' to my daughter's favourites such as 'Meanwhile, the dolphin is still searching for krill' or 'Meanwhile, back at the check-in desk, Ken has an angry passenger bound for Palma'). It adds drama, just as the word 'like' suggests the attitude of the speaker as well as a rough idea of the words spoken. Perhaps it encourages us to see the scene.

Actually, I doubt it. Or rather I doubt that it encourages us to see the scene more accurately than the past tense whatever it may do for vividness. The worst tense used in print journalism, in my view, is the present. 'We're having lunch and Renee Zellweger is picking at her lettuce', 'Our cruise ship slips down the river and into the night', 'Blair comes bounding through the door.' It is so obviously mutton dressed as lamb. We can see through its artifice. The events so described have happened, to be replaced by another event, a writer picking away anxiously at his or her keyboard. It is impossible – and dangerous – to proclaim iron rules about writing, but I would say that the same hold good for most narrative non-fiction books and essays. A step into the dramatic (or false) present is nearly always a mistake; it tends to break our belief in the reality that the writer is trying to describe.

The past tense is simply the more truthful tense, and in this way it conveys a precision and conviction that the present tense lacks. V. S. Naipaul is masterly in his use of the pluperfect past – the city *had* come about in this way – which suggests not just precision but a kind of grave omniscience. True, Jonathan Bate opens his recent biography of the poet John Clare in the present tense, but that's because he is partially inventing a scene and by borrowing the tricks of fiction he is tipping us off about its partial inventedness. And in fiction all things are possible, because fiction invents it own reality. If good, we accept it unquestioningly. Molly Bloom's soliloquy needs to be in the present, obviously, but I was surprised when a friend told me this week that all 1,500 pages of John Updike's Rabbit novels were written in the present tense, which (such was my pleasure in the books) I had never noticed.

So should I worry about my children and their addiction to the present tense? I don't think so. In writing, they are more fluent, more articulate and more expressive than I was at their age. They are even better spellers. One went to an inner-London state primary and the other still goes there. I went to a Scottish village school in the 1950s – chalk, blackboards, the belt for wrongdoing. Narrow institutional conclusions may be drawn from that, but perhaps too easily. All I know is that, at least in writing, I was a cramped – perhaps the word is occluded – little chap. I know this because I recently unearthed some pocket diaries (Letts *Wolf Club Diary* for 1956, for example) and the longest sentence in them is 'Chicken for tea.'

I was thinking, rather sadly, of the brevity and bad spelling of these diary entries last Saturday when, in the *Guardian*, I came across John Updike's fan letter to the cartoonist Harold Gray, written when Updike was fifteen. My sadness increased. His letter was so clever and fluent and winning. The only thing that cheered me up was his misanthropy: 'Contrary to comic-strip tradition, the people [in Gray's strip, *Little Orphan Annie*] are not pleasantly benign, but gossiping, sadistic, and stupid, which is just as it really is.' Then I remembered a sentence from a diary (not the pocket ones, but a bigger notebook) that I kept for a while when I was sixteen: 'One almost wishes de Sica had never made *Bicycle Thieves*.'

Dearie, dearie me. Had I ever seen *Bicycle Thieves*? Did I know anything about Italian neo-realism? I don't think so, but I can't remember the context of the sentence because I read it a few years ago and vowed never to open that notebook again. What a little prick I had been. Perhaps that is the one thing Updike and I (and thousands of other pretentious and prematurely worldly-wise fifteen-year-olds) had in common. Certainly – alas – we have had little in common since, not even tenses.

Women and Children First

July 1999

1.

My son was three and my daughter five. It was the summer of 1997. James Cameron's film had not yet appeared, but a great human tragedy was unfolding on our living-room carpet.

'Here it comes!' said my son to his sister, and began to push a small toy ship across the floor from the direction of the television set. 'Here it comes, *brm, brm, brm,*' (the noise of marine steam engines, as a three-year-old thinks of them). My daughter moved a scrunched-up ball of white paper towards the course of the toy ship. They would meet; there would be an accident. My son swung his boat to the left, but the paper ball was too quick for him.

'Bang! Crash!' my son said, tilting his toy up and turning it over. 'Glug, glug, glug.'

'Let's get the passengers into the lifeboats,' his more humanitarian sister said. 'Look at all the people in the sea.'

We needed to imagine them, just as we needed to imagine the carpet as the North Atlantic, the paper ball as the iceberg, the toy boat as the *Titanic*.

'Don't worry,' my son said. 'Here comes the *Carpathia*.' Another toy was being pushed across the carpet to the rescue.

They played the game on many afternoons, but there were dissatisfactions. No detachable lifeboats; a funnelling discrepancy. The model ship had three funnels (it was based on the *Queen Mary*), whereas the *Titanic* had four. I explained to my son that the *Titanic* didn't need four to suck the smoke from its boiler furnaces – one funnel was a dummy – but that there was a fashion for over-funnelling in the Edwardian age – 'a long time ago,' I said – when numerous funnels implied grandness, size and speed; the more funnels the better the ship. Of course, this was just an impression, the equivalent of go-faster stripes and spoilers on family saloons at the other end of the century, but for about twenty years (like many other fashions, it died with the First World War) it held sway among the public and the premier passenger lines of the North Atlantic. Germany's Norddeutscher Lloyd line started the trend with the *Kaiser Wilhelm der Grosse* in 1897. Britain's Cunard Line followed after the turn of the century with the *Mauretania* and *Lusitania*. When the White Star company came to order their trio of *Titanic*-class ships from Harland and Wolff's yard in Belfast in 1909, four funnels were the only way to go.

'Doesn't matter. We'll just pretend it has four funnels,' said my son of his toy. But I could see that it was niggling him and when, a few months later, I spotted a model *Titanic* in a junk-shop window in Lancashire, I went in and bought it for £9.95. It was new – the Hollywood film was out by then and *Titanic* souvenirs were everywhere – and, oddly, made of coal, or at least a sort of coal-based resin. 'British coal' said the label on the back with its Union Jack. The same shop window had coal railway locomotives, coal vintage cars and coal English country cottages – all a dull black, like Victorian memento mori. Coal had fuelled Britain and its industrial revolution; when the *Titanic* was at speed, the ship's 196 stokers had shovelled up to 100 tons of it through 159 furnace doors during each of their four-hour shifts. Now, to judge from the display in the window, it had dwindled from the country's leading power source to a raw material for folk art. Further back in the shop, I could see shiny brass coal miner's lamps, equally new, which people could put on their mantelpieces above their 'coal-effect' gas fires.

The shop was in a back street of an old cotton town, Nelson, which is high in the Pennines and close to the border with Yorkshire. Nelson had been a considerable town, growing in the last half of the nineteenth century from a crossroads with a pub (the Lord Nelson, from which first a railway halt and then the town had taken its name) to an industrial settlement of 30,000 people, twenty mills and 26,000 steam-driven looms weaving specialist cottons for the clothing trade: flannelettes, poplins, ginghams, twills. But that Nelson had gone. A few old weaving-sheds and their mill chimneys still stood; terraced houses of the local millstone grit still ran straight up the hillside towards the moors; there were still a few Nonconformist chapels, churches and municipal buildings in the centre (though many more had been demolished and replaced by roads and a sad concrete shopping mall).

The shop, like many other shops in small English towns where trade in essentials has been drawn away by supermarkets, sold ornaments – strange and sometimes florid objects in porcelain, clay, wood, imitation bronze, and (in this case) coal, which could be placed on a domestic flat surface and regularly dusted. Many were old, or imitation-old. 'Vic-toariana,' said the elderly Lancashire man who ran the shop, deliberating over the word, 'they're very keen on it round here.' He was happy to see a customer and even happier to sell me the *Titanic*. A hunch had been proved right. 'I ordered a few of these,' he said as he placed the ship in its cardboard box. 'I thought it would be topical, like.'

At home in London, the coal *Titanic* steamed across the carpet on many voyages, all of them fatal. So many sinkings took their toll on its most vulnerable parts: the funnels. One by one, they split from the upper works. When there were three, my son sometimes imagined his toy as the *Queen Mary*; when there were two, it became the *Queen Elizabeth*; when there was one, it stood in for the *Carpathia*, the single-funnelled Cunarder which had picked up the *Titanic*'s survivors and sailed with them to New York in April 1912. It could be all these ships to my son and still, when required, be imagined as the *Titanic*. Then the last funnel came off. A ship without funnels was . . . a wreck. This was the coal *Titanic*'s final form, as a discard buried deep in our cellar, a tiny replica of the funnel-less, broken hull that Dr Robert Ballard and his expedition eventually discovered 13,000 feet down on the seabed of the North Atlantic in September 1985.

In 1998 in our house – in millions of houses and thousands of cinemas, wherever the sea rushed in, the stern tilted vertically, and Rose called to Jack from the screen or the video recorder – art continued to imitate death.

2.

The film *Titanic*, directed by James Cameron and funded by Twentieth Century Fox, is said to be the most commercially successful film of all time. This is a questionable claim; when American receipts are adjusted for inflation, *Gone With the Wind* comes first and *Titanic* fourth. But at least in the span of the 1990s, no other film comes near it. By the end of June 1999, it had earned more than $1,835 million at box offices worldwide and repaid its costs ten times over. Other large sums came from the video release, compact discs, books and general merchandising which ran the gamut from *Titanic* champagne flutes to *Titanic* yo-yos. It won eleven Oscars – only *Ben-Hur* forty years before won as many and no film has won more. Young adolescent girls formed a large part of its audience; newspaper reports from several countries – India, Australia, Japan, the United Kingdom and the US – said that some had watched the film scores of times, mainly to see its young lead actor, Leonardo DiCaprio.

But its phenomenal appeal was more than hormonal. According to the London *Evening Standard* (27 April 1998), the Chinese president, Jiang Zemin, saw in the film a parable of the class war, in which 'the third-class passengers (the proletariat) struggle valiantly against the ship's crew (craven capitalist lapdogs and stooges)'. In a statement published in Beijing, the president applauded the film's 'vivid descriptions of the relationship between money and love, rich and poor' and urged all fellow socialists to see it. The French also considered *Titanic* in political terms. Serge July, the editor of *Libération*, wrote: 'The subject of the film is not – this is obvious – the sinking of a famous ship, but the suicide in the middle of the Atlantic of a society divided in classes.' In Germany, according to the *New York Times* (26 April 1998), 'heady articles . . . with no discernible tongue in cheek, have spoken of the movie as an emblem of the zeitgeist, an allegory that provides catharsis for all, a surrogate myth in a trivialized era, an icon at the end of history'. In *Die Zeit*, Andreas Kilb, the paper's cultural critic, wrote that the key to the film's appeal lay in its representation of a 'lost wholeness'. Hans Magnus Enzensberger, again in the *New York Times*, compared the durability of the *Titanic* myth with the transience of modern catastrophes, and wondered if the contrast demonstrated that we were losing a proper sense of history. (My son also became a critic. Owing to a lapse in parental attention, he watched the video. We worried that he might have been affected by the disaster and death which Cameron had so realistically evoked, as well as – though this, I admit, was ridiculous – the sight of Kate Winslet's bared breasts. But he was chuckling on the sofa. 'They had smoke coming from the fourth funnel. What a mistake!')

James Cameron's own gloss on his film was similarly myth-driven.

He wrote in the 'production information' (the press pack for critics and other journalists): 'April 10, 1912. Technology had been delivering a steady stream of miracles for the better part of two decades and people were beginning to take this never-ending spiral of progress for granted. What better demonstration of humanity's mastery over nature than the launch of *Titanic* [the missing definite article was important to the film's marketing; 'the', presumably, carried too nautical and traditional a ring], the largest and most luxurious moving object ever built by the hand of man. But four and a half days later, the world had changed. The maiden voyage of the "ship of dreams" ended in a nightmare beyond comprehension and mankind's faith in his own indomitable power was forever destroyed by uniquely human shortcomings: arrogance, complacency and greed.'

Then, perhaps aware that public chastisement had not made good box office since the time of Savonarola and John Knox, the director added that his film was also 'a story of faith, courage, sacrifice and, above all else, love'.

Most of those latter qualities enter the film through its fictional story: a shipboard romance. Briefly: Rose DeWitt Bukater (Kate Winslet) is a seventeen-year-old, upper-class American girl, 'suffocating under the rigid confines and expectations of Edwardian society' according to the press pack, who meets a free-spirited young American from the Midwest called Jack Dawson (Leonardo DiCaprio). Rose is travelling first class and Jack steerage. They fall in love, have sex, and then, when the ship begins to sink, help each other to survive a villainous subplot. In the sea, Jack urges Rose to hold on to life and the wreckage. Jack drowns, but his love and her freshly discovered will-power enable Rose's survival. The story is framed by the present or the near-present. Rose, rediscovered in her hundredth year, narrates the events of the voyage from a perspective which suggests that both experiences – forbidden love across the class boundaries, the awakening of a tougher, unladylike strength – have turned her into a prototype of modern, independent womanhood. The title song, 'My Heart Will Go On', is sung by Celine Dion, but the same sentiments, to better music, can be heard in Edith Piaf.

I saw the film twice at the cinema. There were many things to admire in it. The ship was wonderfully and faithfully recreated (the fourth funnel, in fact, carried the fumes from the kitchen fires; smoke was therefore a possibility). Some scenes had a painterly touch. The *Titanic* overtaking a tiny yawl as the liner leaves Southampton; an officer in a lifeboat casting a torch beam on the sea to scan it for survivors – scenes such as these could have come from an Edwardian easel. The cleverest aspect of the film, however, depended neither on computer-created images, nor on expensively researched historical detail, nor even on the ninety per cent scale replica of the ship itself, with the stern that tilted almost to the vertical – people falling screaming from it, bouncing from the propellers – before it slid under the sea. Its cleverest aspect, I thought, was how it had taken a previously masculine story – male blunder, male heroism, male sacrifice in that most male of environments, the sea – and feminised it as a monument not to the dead but to a modern notion of . . . 'girl power' is probably the phrase.

The true opposition was not between classes (*pace* the president of China), just as the film's true subject was not the 'suicide' of the society that produced these classes (*pace* the editor of *Libération*). In Cameron's film, the armies that clashed on that calm North Atlantic night represented youth and age, the new and old. To be young and new (to be, in a sense, now) was to smoke and spit and wear a flat cap and no tie like Jack; to be creative, an artist, like Jack; to be free and resourceful like Jack; to have heard, improbably, of Picasso and Freud like Rose; to make love in the back of a car, part of the ship's cargo, like Rose and Jack; to drink and dance Irish jigs in steerage; to be Irish or Italian or Scandinavian or American (though not clipped, rich, East Coast American – Anglo-American). To be young and new was to have, as your soundtrack, the ghastly Celtic-twilight pastiche of James Horner's music.

And to be old? That was to lose, to be part of dying things, an *ancien régime*; to be repressed and repressive; not to have heard of Freud; to have as your soundtrack the hymn 'Nearer, My God, To Thee', like Captain Smith (Bernard Hill) as he stood stoically, purposelessly, in the wheelhouse and saw the sea come crashing through its windows; to be smug and autocratic like the ship's officers and owner before the disaster, and then to be weak, brittle and cowardly after it; or to be weak and servile like the crew, before and after.

In other, shorter words: to be old, to be the enemy, was to be British.

I watched the film and felt a slight sense of ancestral, racial injury, and eventually took the train to Lancashire.

3.

Four days out from Southampton on its maiden voyage to New York, the *Titanic* hit the iceberg at 11.40 p.m. on Sunday 14 April, and sank at 2.20 a.m. on 15 April. Its last known position was 41° 46' N, 50° 14' W; about 350 miles south-east of Newfoundland and 1,000 miles and three days away from New York. According to the British Board of Trade inquiry, 1,503 passengers and crew died and 703 were saved. The *Titanic* had steamed into an ice field at twenty-two and a half knots; it had ignored ice-warnings tapped out in Morse from other ships; its lifeboats had room for only 1,178 people; its watertight bulkheads did not rise high enough in the hull. But these reckless errors of navigation and flaws in ship design were largely ignored in the immediate British coverage of the disaster. Tragedies needed heroes. *Titanic*'s band supplied them. To preserve order and calm, they had started to play soon after the iceberg was hit and had gone on playing until the very end, insouciantly, stoically and, finally, religiously and comfortingly. Their last number was said to have been the hymn, 'Nearer, My God, To Thee'.

'Why is it,' George Bernard Shaw wrote in the *Daily News and Leader* one month later, 'that the effect of a sensational catastrophe on a modern nation is to cast it into transports, not of weeping, not of prayer, not of sympathy with the bereaved ... but of ... an explosion of outrageous romantic lying?' Shaw listed what he called the 'romantic demands' of a British shipwreck. The first was the cry 'Women and Children First' and the second that all the men aboard ('except the foreigners') should be heroes and the captain a superhero. Finally, Shaw wrote, British romance demanded that 'everybody should face death without a tremor; and the band, according to the *Birkenhead* precedent, must play "Nearer, My God, To Thee".' The *Birkenhead* was a troopship which foundered off the South African coast in 1852. While the women and children were got off in the boats, the troops were held in ranks at attention on deck. In Victorian Britain the story had a powerful effect.

The evidence from the *Titanic*, according to Shaw, ran in the opposite direction. 'The captain and officers were so afraid of panic that, though they knew the ship was sinking, they did not dare tell the passengers so – especially the third-class passengers – and the band played Rag Times [*sic*] to reassure the passengers, who, therefore, did not get into the boats, and did not realise their situation until the boats were gone and the ship was standing on her head before plunging to the bottom.'

Sir Arthur Conan Doyle replied to Shaw's attack in the *Daily News* of 20 May.

'Mr Shaw tries to defile the beautiful incident of the band by alleging that it was the result of orders issued to avert panic. But if it were, how does that detract either from the wisdom of the orders or from the heroism of the musicians? It was right to avert panic, and it was wonderful that men could do it in such a way.'

Shaw, as usual, was being controversial; he was England's leading controversialist. But he was also being brave, because in the middle of this still familiar London newspaper phenomenon, the columnar spat, the body of its chief subject, the leader of the *Titanic*'s band, had been unloaded from a ship in Liverpool and taken by hearse inland across Lancashire, up past the noisy weaving-sheds of Preston and Blackburn, Burnley and Nelson, to the town of Colne. If disasters need heroes, heroes need burials, and burials need bodies. The body of Wallace Henry Hartley, violinist and bandmaster, had been retrieved from the sea and brought to Halifax, Nova Scotia, on 30 April. In Halifax it had been coffined and taken by train to Boston, and from there shipped by the White Star's *Arabic* to Liverpool, where it arrived at South Canada Dock on 17 May.

Even before his body had been found, Hartley was a hero. Reports of the band's behaviour, how they had continued to play, first appeared in the *New York Times* on 19 April, the morning after that newspaper's reporters interviewed survivors who disembarked from the *Carpathia*. Newspapers in Britain magnified these reports – Shaw was right about 'outrageous romantic lying' – until Hartley became the man who not only went on playing his violin when the ship began to settle by the bows, but continued playing even when he was waist-deep in water.

On 18 May, Hartley was buried in Colne. About 26,000 people then lived in the town. The local newspaper, the *Colne and Nelson Times*, estimated that a crowd of about 40,000 attended the funeral, drawn from across northern England by trains and trams. The crowd's size made Hartley's funeral the largest single solemnisation of the *Titanic* disaster on either side of the Atlantic. The *Colne and Nelson Times* reported that the town had reached 'the highest eminence of its character and tradition . . . The whole world has been at the feet of Wallace Hartley; then why wonder at the jealous pride of Colne?'

4.

In Lancashire, I went first to Liverpool to consult the newspaper archive and look at the *Titanic* monuments. The city has two of them; the ship, like all of White Star's fleet, was registered here (when the last of the hull slips under in Cameron's film, the sight of the word 'Liverpool' on the stern jolted me into remembering that this was once a city of global importance). Many Liverpudlians were in the crew, especially as firemen and coal trimmers in the stokeholds, and it was a Liverpool musical agency that recruited the band. One monument stands at the Pierhead, originally intended for the ship's engineers (no engineering officer survived) but later modified before its unveiling in 1916 to take account of the First World War and 'honour all heroes of the marine engine room'. In the bas-reliefs, stokers with bare chests stand with rags and shovels in hand while an officer in a naval cap and jacket holds a spanner. They stare out at an empty river – a process of desertion which began when White Star moved their finest transatlantic liners to Southampton, so that they could cross the Channel to Cherbourg and embark the rich passenger trade from continental Europe. The legend beside them reads: 'The brave do not die / their deeds live for ever / and call upon us / to emulate their courage / and devotion to duty.'

Inside the city, away from the waterfront, a bronze plaque to the *Titanic's* musicians is fixed to the wall in the foyer of the Philharmonic Hall. There were eight of them: Wallace Hartley, violin and bandmaster; Theodore Brailey, piano, of Ladbroke Grove, London; Roger Bricoux, cello, of Lille, France; Fred Clarke, bass, of Liverpool; John 'Jock' Hume, violin, of Dumfries, Scotland; George Krins, viola, of Brixton, London; Percy Taylor, cello, of Clapham, London; Jack Woodward, piano, of Headington, Oxfordshire. They performed in two groups, as a trio and a quintet, in different saloons of the ship. All of them died. The legend in art-nouveau lettering said they had 'continued playing to soothe the anguish of their fellow passengers', followed by the words: 'Courage and compassion joined / make the hero and the man complete.'

According to the *Liverpool Daily Post and Mercury* (18 May 1912), 'scenes of a very affecting character' had been witnessed in South Canada Dock when Hartley's coffin came ashore. His father, Albion Hartley, had come from Colne to Liverpool and paced the floor of the dock shed as he waited for the casket to be swung from the ship's hold to the quay. He was, said the *Daily Post*'s report, 'a pathetic figure . . . suffering from intense mental agony . . . as he signed the receipt for the delivery of the body his hands quivered with emotion . . . his eyes filled with tears, and he walked away broken with grief'. Before he left, however, Mr Hartley 'communicated a few particulars with respect to his son's personal history'. These included: that his son had been engaged to be married (Miss Maria Robinson of Leeds); that his son had regretted moving from one of the Cunard Line's bands because the switch to White Star meant that his home port became Southampton rather than Liverpool, taking him further from his parents' home; and that a gentleman who regularly travelled by Cunard had told him, Albion Hartley, that he had heard his son play 'Nearer, My God, To Thee' several times on board the *Lusitania*. (The last seemed to be offered as evidence to doubters. Already there were doubts.)

Then the hearse's two horses began the slow fifty-nine-mile pull to Colne, where the coffin with Hartley's bruised body inside arrived at one o'clock the next morning.

5.

It was dark when I got there; two changes of train, then a long ride up a bumpy single line which ended at a bare platform. The terminus: Colne. I walked across to the Crown Hotel – Victorian, built soon after the railway came in 1848 – where I'd booked a room for the night. Two women were propped against the hotel wall, pawing each other.

'You're a bitch, you're a bitch,' one woman was saying.

'And you're a right cow,' said the other.

In the hallway, a man in a white shirt and black tie ran past me with blood dribbling from his cheek. In the bar, several men, also in black ties, were talking softly and urgently to their womenfolk.

'Now love, just shut it . . . have another drink and then we'll get a minicab.'

All the men were small and dark, as though they belonged to the same large family. A life-size model of Laurel and Hardy stood in one corner of the bar, and next to it (or next to Hardy at least) these men looked like angry jockeys.

'He's coming back in,' said one man, who was watching the door.

'Nay, he'd never, he wouldn't dare,' said another.

Eventually the Crown Hotel's manager appeared and took me upstairs to my room. 'It's not usually like this,' he said, by way of apology.

Outside the window I could hear a woman shouting: 'Don't give me that shite. You wanted to shag him, didn't you, you bitch.'

The manager smiled and said: 'It's a funeral. Drinking and that. I think it got a bit out of hand.'

6.

Wallace Hartley's funeral began a few hundred yards from the Crown Hotel at the Bethel Independent Methodist Chapel. 18 May was a Saturday. The next week's *Colne and Nelson Times* spared no detail; the idea that Britain, and especially northern Britain, shied away from emotional display at that time, that crying began with the Princess of Wales in 1997, is confounded by this single report. A thousand people crowded into pews which had been built to hold 700. Before undertakers screwed down the coffin lid – 'a coffin of an unfamiliar American make, polished to appear like rosewood' – Hartley's parents and sisters came to take a last look at the body. The body is described; 'somewhat discoloured by a blow he had evidently received and by the embalming process'. Then the congregation stood and began to sing in an atmosphere of 'fervid emotion'. Hartley's mother, who remained seated in the front pew, wept bitterly at one point and almost choked with suppressed grief at another. Hartley's two sisters and his fiancée, Miss Robinson, 'shook visibly'; and when 'Nearer, My God, To Thee' was sung (for the second time) almost the entire congregation was in tears: 'Girls had not the heart to sing . . . men and women broke under the strain . . . voices shook with emotion.'

Mr T. Worthington, an Independent Methodist preacher who had sailed with Hartley on the *Mauretania*, gave the address. Reading it in Colne library almost ninety years later, I was struck by how vividly it had been phrased. 'She [the *Titanic*] had been only a few days out . . . when she comes into contact with another force, designed in no engineer's office, constructed in no dockyard, possessed by no compass and guided by no rudder, giving off no steam, nor driven by any machinery; but a force with which man's latest and noblest construction coming into contact bolts, shakes, reels, sinks . . .' Worthington concluded: 'The traditional British character was magnificently shown . . . Yes, it is brave to be British. It is both brave and noble to be Christian. In fact, it is easier to be British when we are Christian.'

People stepped up to the catafalque to place wreaths on the coffin. 'To Uncle Wallace', from his sister's children; 'Teach me from my heart to say, Thy will be done', from Miss Robinson. Then the cortège set out for the cemetery. The procession was half a mile long. Five brass bands came first, followed by a battalion of the East Lancashire Regiment, buglers from the Boy Scouts, the town's ambulance brigade, the congregation of the Bethel Chapel, the Colne Orchestra, the Bethel Choir, the representatives of Colne town council and, at last, the carriages with coffin, wreaths and mourners. The bands took it in turns to play the Dead March from *Saul* with muffled drums: 'The subdued tones of the bands thrilled one with the immense tragedy of the proceedings.' Great whispering crowds lined the route; men doffed their hats as the coffin passed; flags floated at half mast; blinds were drawn in every house. And, unusually, no large amount of coal smoke blew across the town; the town's mills had shut for the morning shift. According to that day's *Manchester Evening News*, 'workmen and masters assembled together in awed silence on the tramless streets'.

At the cemetery gates, twelve men, all cousins of Hartley, took the coffin. Worthington read the last rites. The reporter from the *Colne and Nelson Times* noticed a lark singing overhead. The hillsides all around were dotted with groups of men who stood silent and bareheaded.

In 1912, it was the most impressive scene Colne had ever witnessed, and – my guess – most probably ever will. But were there no sceptics, people who wondered about the fuss? A week later a letter appeared in the *Colne and Nelson Times*. There were plans for a civic memorial to Wallace Hartley. The annoymous writer hoped, drily, that it would not be a drinking fountain: 'Surely there has been enough water in this sad affair.'

7.

I left the Crown Hotel that night and went to look at Hartley's memorial, not a fountain but a bust on a pedestal, flanked by two carved figures representing Music (with a lyre) and Valour (with a laurel wreath). The people of Colne had subscribed £265 to its cost, but when the mayor unveiled it, in 1915, Hartley's death was no longer so remarkable and the mayor took care to connect him with thousands of other young men 'who were giving their lives freely'. In 1992 the bust had been vandalised and four years later repaired. Now, because of the film, in which Hartley makes a fleeting appearance, people had recently begun to bring flowers.

I walked higher up the main street, inspecting the prices of houses in estate agents' windows. There were few people about. I went to a pub – a large saloon with only three drinkers – and heard a middle-aged woman who was slightly tight sing 'Once I Had a Secret Love' to the karaoke machine. The wallpaper and the lamps, like the Crown Hotel's, were new-Victorian. Original Victoriana lined the streets: there were several handsome buildings, but most of them adapted to purposes other than their original. In the ground floor of the old Colne Co-operative Society headquarters I ate spaghetti at Carlo's Pizzeria in a room that pretended to be a red-tiled Tuscan cottage.

Colne and this part of Lancashire once had a singular culture – a way of thinking and being, which, though many parts of it were common to northern Britain, had special twists and peculiarities. Even Nelson, just down the hill, was different, and Colne people still – a cultural relic – spoke of it disparagingly. Nelson was an upstart, a pure nineteenth-century invention. Once Colne people had called Nelson 'Little Moscow' because of its socialism; on my visit I heard an old man call it 'Little Calcutta' because so many South Asian families lived there. Colne had very few Asians; also it was a much older town; also it was higher, 600 feet up and surrounded by moorland which rose another 1,000 feet still.

Did Hartley's stoicism and nobility – if he had been stoic and noble – depend on Colne, grow in Colne? That would be absurd, though in Colne in 1912 the claim was often made. On the other hand, two Colne specialisms had placed him on the *Titanic*, had given him the chance to behave like a Christian gentleman, if that is what he had been. Without cotton and Methodism, he would never have learned to play the violin and, consequently, never have gone to sea.

8.

Cotton came later to Colne than the rest of Lancashire. From the fifteenth century it developed a thriving woollen business, then, after the narrow canal from Liverpool reached Colne in the late eighteenth century, cotton began to be imported from the United States and India.

By 1824, there were only three manufacturers of wool in Colne but twenty-two of cotton. By 1843, seven of these mills were driven by steam. More cotton, coal and supplies of Welsh roofing slate came with the railway. Over the next sixty years, Colne changed from a riotous little town with bad sanitation, smallpox and public stocks, into a model of municipal enterprise and self-improvement, with electric trams, reservoirs, good drains, and libraries. Express trains from Colne ran all the way to London, as well as to Leeds and Manchester and Liverpool.

The Hartley family improved with the town. Their addresses and occupations were listed in each ten-year census, and with every entry there was change. Wallace's grandfather Henry was a weaver of woollen worsted in 1841 but a weaver of cotton twenty years later. Henry's son Albion was a cotton 'sizer' in 1871 but a cotton-mill manager ten years later. By 1891 Albion had become an insurance agent, about as far away as could be got then, in Colne, from physical work, smoke and machinery. And so Wallace, born in 1878, grew up in the middle stages of his family's social progress. Unlike his grandfather, his father, his uncles and aunts, he never went to work in a mill. He had an education and got a job in a bank.

The education came courtesy of Methodism, which arrived in Colne when John Wesley preached at the opening of the town's first Methodist chapel in 1777. By the middle of the next century it was rampant, evangelising and schismatic. Wesleyan Methodism became identified with the new middle class of manufacturers and shopkeepers and was seen as autocratic. More radical preachers, anxious to proselytise and uplift the new working class, broke away into new groups: the Bible Christians, the Kilhamites, the Primitives. The Primitives set to work in the poorest and most squalid parts of the town, but they too split into conservatives and radicals, the radicals favouring volunteer rather than paid preachers and renaming themselves the Provident Independent Methodists.

In 1857, the Providents decided to evangelise the growing working-class quarter of Primet Bridge, close to Albion Hartley's house and Wallace Hartley's birthplace. They built a chapel there: the Bethel Independent Methodist Church. Albion Hartley became its choirmaster and the superintendent of its Sunday school and sent his son to Colne's Methodist day school, which existed to educate the children of the poor but self-improving. In Colne, the Methodists stimulated many improving activities – elocution lessons, temperance groups, evening lectures for adults – but music was their special strength: glee clubs, brass bands, choirs, the Colne Orchestra. Sometimes rival choirs would combine to sing a great oratorio: the *Messiah* or *Elijah*. Sometimes a musically gifted mill worker left the town and became a professional singer or player. One or two had careers at Covent Garden. At school, Wallace Hartley learned to play the violin. After a few years in the bank, he left Colne for a middling career as a violinist with tea-room trios in department stores and touring opera companies. He played at Bridlington, Harrogate, Leeds, and for the operas put on by Carl Rosa and Moody Manners. Then he joined Cunard.

That is really all that is known about him. There are no family memoirs or (so far as I could find) surviving members of the Hartley family. In his last letter home, written on board the *Titanic* and collected from the ship at its final port of call, Queenstown, Ireland, he wrote: 'This is a fine ship and there ought to be plenty of money around . . . We have a fine band and the boys seem very nice.' At his funeral, he was recalled as 'tall, handsome, and of a pleasant disposition – he was popular with passengers and proved a merry companion.'

There are no more clues to his character. And the particular society of Colne that might have influenced it, one way or another, has gone; or almost.

9.

Jack Greenwood took me to see the tombstone. Greenwood was an old Colne man, a retired bus driver, a local historian who specialised in the history of Colne's most famous figure, Wallace Henry Hartley. Like the shopkeeper who sold me the coal *Titanic*, he spoke in the broad, deliberating accent which, in the valleys of Colne Water, the Calder and the Ribble, takes on a special peculiarity, as though vowels were warm beer twisting down a plughole. He said 'thee' for 'you', 'nowt' for 'nothing', and 'brew' for 'hill'. It would be useless to try to reproduce it.

We met at the library and walked west through the town. It was a grey winter's day with cloud on the hills and a dampness in the air that would later settle into steady, unremitting rain. Eventually we came to a gate. Through the gate, Colne's cemetery ran down a steep hill. 'It's down theer on the left,' Greenwood said. 'I'll stay at the top. That brew's too steep for me.'

I went down on my own. Hartley's tomb was more monumental than the rest and included the names of his father, mother and infant brothers. It was topped by a broken pillar covered in a shroud while at the base a stone violin reposed on its side next to the first words and musical bars of 'Nearer, My God, To Thee'. It was here, at Hartley's funeral, that the Bethel Chapel choir sang the hymn for the third and last time that day to the accompaniment of the Trawden silver band, and here, as Hartley's coffin was lowered into the earth, that buglers from Colne's Boy Scouts blew the 'Last Post'. Their notes, said the *Colne and Nelson Times*, 'went rolling through the valley and came back again, loath to be done'.

A few old flowers lay at the foot of the monument. Those apart, there was no sign of pilgrimage or a continuing memory. I went back up the hill and asked Greenwood if he thought the grave had the right hymn to the right tune – one of the most vexing questions in the historiography of the *Titanic*. Greenwood didn't doubt it. He'd done his work in the local archives. It was Albion Hartley who had introduced Colne to 'Nearer, My God, To Thee' in the musical arrangement by Sir Arthur Sullivan when he was the Bethel choirmaster; it had been regularly sung during Whitsuntide processions. The tune is called 'Propior Deo' and its first notes were those on the tomb. Furthermore, Greenwood added, a Mr Ellwand Moody of Farnley, Leeds, had made twenty-two trips on the *Mauretania* with Wallace and had once asked him, as one cheerful North Country man to another: 'What would you do if you were on a sinking ship?' And Wallace, according to Moody, according to Greenwood, had replied: 'I don't think I could do better than play "O God Our Help in Ages Past" or "Nearer, My God, To Thee".'

We walked back through the centre of Colne and started down the hill which runs towards Nelson. It was raining hard now; in the fading light, the town was wet and black; at the foot of the streets that went off steeply to each side, there were patches of wasteland where the mills had been. I remember feeling how good it would be to take the small, slow train down to the junction at Preston and then sit in a much faster one to London. Or to sign up as a violinist with the White Star Line.

Instead, we went to Greenwood's terraced house and his wife made tea and biscuits. I asked her about 'Nearer, My God, To Thee'. Not many people these days, I said, believed that this was the last tune Wallace Hartley had played on the *Titanic*. Mrs Greenwood said firmly: 'Well, we believe it in Colne, don't we, Jack? Look at the last verse

– "Out of my stony griefs, Bethel I'll raise." Bethel, you see. That would have reminded him of the Bethel Chapel, his father, this town, everything he'd grown up with and loved.'

10.

The hymn 'Nearer, My God, To Thee' was written by an Englishwoman, Sarah Flower Adams, and first appeared in a hymnal compiled in 1840 and 1841 by the Reverend William Johnston Fox for use by the congregation at his Unitarian chapel in Finsbury, London. The first two verses – there are four in all – go:

> *Nearer, my God, to Thee*
> *Nearer to Thee!*
> *E'en though it be a cross*
> *That raiseth me.*
> *Still all my song would be,*
> *Nearer, my God, to Thee,*
> *Nearer to Thee.*

> *Though, like the wanderer,*
> *The sun gone down,*
> *Darkness comes over me,*
> *My rest a stone;*
> *Yet in my dreams I'd be*
> *Nearer, my God, to Thee,*
> *Nearer to Thee.*

Mrs Adams died (childless and 'of decline' according to the *Dictionary of National Biography*) in 1848 at the age of forty-three. To try to learn a little of her life is to face one of the great problems of the modern secular imagination: how to imagine a time when God was a powerful idea, when biblical tags and stories were a part of everyday life, when hymns were as familiar and meaningful to most of the population as advertising slogans are now. Mrs Adams might easily be imagined as a Christian sop, disappointed on earth and pining for heaven. In fact, so far as one can tell, she was a spirited woman, a friend of the poet Robert Browning, with whom she corresponded about her religious doubts and difficulties. But perhaps the most surprising thing to discover about her is that she was not, in the strictest sense, a Christian; as a Unitarian she did not accept the Holy Trinity or the divinity of Christ. Neither is her hymn about Christ. It tells, elliptically, the story of Jacob who, fleeing the wrath of his brother Esau, falls asleep on a pillow of stone in the wilderness and dreams of a ladder lined with angels that descends from heaven. God stands at the top. Jacob erects a monument of stones at the site of his dream and calls it Bethel, which in Hebrew means 'the House of God'. According to the Reverend James Hodson's *Hymn Studies*, 'it is a song of the soul in a lonely and gloomy place'.

For many years after it was published, it remained problematic as a Christian hymn. It lacked any mention of Christ; the 'cross' in the first verse is simply a metaphor for human suffering. Various churches tried to amend it, but none of the new versions caught on, until, in 1855, Henry Ward Beecher included it in a general, non-Unitarian collection of hymns (his sister, Harriet Beecher Stowe, published *Uncle Tom's Cabin* four years before and was sometimes miscredited with the words of the hymn). In 1856 another American, the prolific hymnographer Lowell Mason, replaced the original setting, composed by Mrs Adams's sister, Eliza, with a tune called 'Bethany', in 4/4 time, that was altogether more stirring and affecting.

By the time of the Civil War it seems to have reached most corners of North America. One Bishop Martin, fleeing Union troops in Arkansas, heard its tune as he stumbled through backwoods country; located the source as a log cabin; found in the log cabin a poor old woman singing lustily; felt therefore 'an unreserved trust in God, thus ridding him of his fears'.

The books I looked at – old, unvisited books in church libraries, books of earnest, pre-First World War Christian sincerity, books that it now seemed inconceivable that anyone had ever read – told many similar stories. The late Queen Victoria had expressed her love for the hymn. It was the favourite of the late President McKinley, who had repeated it frequently on his deathbed. It was the absolute favourite of His Majesty, King Edward VII, who considered it as 'dear to the peasant as the prince'; and also of the Australian Antarctic Expedition who had sung it 'amid blizzards, in ice caves and at the end of the day's toil'.

A Reverend Dr Moulton, for thirty years a missionary to the Tonga Islands in the South Seas, recounted how he had visited the hut of an old and now dying convert and there met 'a curious sight'. Two friends had propped the old man up so that he could hang from a beam in the roof. 'Judge of my astonishment,' wrote the Reverend Dr Moulton, 'when I heard these words uttered over and over again – in Tongan of course – "Nearer, O God, to Thee! Nearer to Thee".'

The tune, however, was not always the same. North America sang it to Mason's 'Bethany', while British Christians were divided by denomination; Anglicans favoured a tune called 'Horbury' by John Bacchus Dykes, while Methodists chose Sir Arthur Sullivan's 'Propior Deo'. However they were sung, the words were a hit throughout the English-speaking world. According to the Reverend Canon Duncan in his *Popular Hymns* (1910), the hymn was ranked at number seven in 'The Sunday at Home List' of the hundred best and most popular hymn tunes. He wrote: 'The testimonies are many and from all quarters as to the comfort and help this hymn has been to the souls of men, women and children, even in some of the most depressing circumstances of life.'

Could there be a more depressing circumstance than to stand in a fearful crowd on a slowly tilting deck with a child in your arms, waiting to die in a near-freezing sea? In the early morning of 15 April 1912, the hymn's greatest hour had arrived. Wallace Hartley tapped his violin (the moment is in James Cameron's film) and his band struck up its last tune: 'Nearer, My God, To Thee'. So it was said, so it was reported in the newspapers, so it was widely believed. Within days of the *Titanic's* loss, the words were on memorial postcards, within weeks they were in instant books and the dialogue titles of silent films. By 12 May, according to Reuters news agency, 55,000 copies of a French translation had been sold in one week at the equivalent of a penny each: 'The hymn is even being sung by groups at street corners after the manner of popular songs.'

But which of the three possible tunes had they heard, Dykes's, Mason's or Sullivan's? On 24 May, at a concert for the *Titanic* Relief Fund in the Albert Hall, conducted by Sir Edward Elgar, Sir Henry Wood and Thomas Beecham, London's massed orchestras played Dykes's tune, 'Horbury'. Hartley's grave uses Sullivan's. Cameron's film uses Mason's.

Then again, had anyone aboard heard any of them? As the *Titanic's* story moved through its various revivals in the century, a new and secular orthodoxy was slowly established.

II.

Mrs Vera Dick, a first-class passenger from Alberta, was the origin of the story. Fresh off the *Carpathia*, she told the *New York Times* (19 April): 'What I remember best was that as the ship sunk [*sic*] we could hear the band playing "Nearer, My God, To Thee". We looked back and could see the men standing on deck absolutely quiet and waiting for the end. Their conduct was splendid, splendid.'

Almost all of the *Titanic's* many historians over the past fifty years have chosen to disbelieve her. Mrs Dick was among the first to leave in the boats, at 1 a.m., and she was probably at least a quarter of a mile away when the ship went under. On the other hand, it was an unusually still night (everybody attests to that) and on a quiet day the noise of a cello and a couple of violins will carry half a mile across a London park. There is also the private testimony of Mrs Charlotte Collyer, second-class and also in a lifeboat when the *Titanic* sank, whose husband did not survive. She wrote to her parents-in-law in England from Brooklyn in a letter dated 21 April: 'I feel I shall go mad sometimes but, dear, as much my heart aches it aches for you, too, for he is your son and the best that ever lived . . . But mother we shall meet in heaven. When that band played "Nearer, My God, To Thee" I know he thought of you and me for we both loved that hymn . . .'

Other witnesses had different memories. A. H. Barkworth, first-class, from Yorkshire, wrote: 'I do not wish to detract from the bravery of anybody but I might mention that when I first came on deck the band was playing a waltz. The next time I passed . . . the members of the band had thrown down their instruments and were not to be seen.' Second Officer Charles Lightoller remembered the band playing 'a cheery sort of music . . . I think it helped us all.' Archibald Gracie, a retired US Army colonel, recalled that the band stopped playing half an hour before the ship sank. 'I did not recognise any of the tunes, but I know they were cheerful and were not hymns. If, as has been reported, "Nearer, My God, To Thee" was one of the selections, I assuredly should have noticed and regarded it as tactless warning of immediate death to us all and one likely to create a panic that our special efforts were directed towards avoiding.'

Lightoller and Gracie, unlike Mrs Collyer and Mrs Dick, were among the last to leave, swept overboard by the wave that came rushing up the deck. Harold Bride, the ship's second wireless operator, went into the sea at the same time. Like Mrs Dick he was interviewed by the *New York Times* on 18 April and was quoted as saying: 'The ship was gradually turning on her nose – just like a duck that goes down for a dive . . . the band was still playing. I guess all the band went down. They were heroes. They were still playing "Autumn". Then I swam with all my might.'

Bride did not specify 'Autumn' as a hymn, and some versions of his interview include an earlier reference to 'the ragtime tune'. But when Walter Lord came to write his book *A Night to Remember*, published in 1955, he decided that 'Autumn' and not 'Nearer, My God, To Thee' was the hymn that had been played. Lord's book, an early example of quick, episodic, narrative history, became a bestseller, the most influential retelling of the story that has ever been published. Three years later, in the British-made film of the book, 'Autumn' is the tune the band plays.

The British hymnologist Sir Richard Johnson decided that the *New York Times* reporter had misheard 'Autumn' for 'Aughton', an American Episcopal hymn and tune written by a pupil of Lowell Mason's. The English composer Gavin Bryars accepted the idea and incorporated 'Aughton' in his orchestral piece *The Sinking of the Titanic*, first performed in 1969. In the meantime, Lord had discovered something he did not disclose until he published his follow-up book on the *Titanic* in 1986. In 1957, a former Cunard Line bandmaster wrote to him remembering that '*Songe d'Automne*', a waltz composed by Archibald Joyce, had been a big hit in London in 1912. The waltz is on the playlist of the White Star Line's bands for that year. Books began to reproduce the playlist.

By 1998, God and his comforts were in full retreat.

12.

The Bethel Chapel in Colne was demolished in the early 1980s – dry rot – but Independent Methodist services still take place in a smaller outbuilding that used to be the Sunday school. I had told Jack Greenwood I would like to attend one, and somehow the word got round. On the Sunday morning, as I was walking across the waste ground where the chapel used to be, a elderly man came forward to greet me. They were going to sing The Hymn in my honour.

There were eight or nine people inside, all of them, save the woman organist and a couple in their fifties, at least sixty-five years old. We sat on metal chairs and sang several hymns, including 'Nearer, My God, To

Thee' to Mason's tune. A woman preacher addressed us on St Paul's letter to the Ephesians. Communion wine and bread – small, torn pieces of sliced brown – went between us. Outside, Colne people were doing whatever they now do on a Sunday in March. Waking up, driving to the superstores, looking out from their kitchen windows at bare gardens and wondering when spring will come.

Eric Lambert, the caretaker, took me to see Wallace Hartley's birthplace. On the way I asked about the communion wine, it seemed sweet. 'Vimto,' Lambert said. 'We don't hold with alcohol.'

We walked across a bridge over Colne Water, and then over a motorway sliproad. We were now on the very edge of Colne, among fields. Hartley's birthplace was down a track in a lonely terrace of millstone grit houses: 92 Greenfield Road. 'Don't look in,' Lambert said as we passed the house. 'They don't like folk looking.'

We walked on. 'You know what did for the churches?' he said. 'It was the First World War.' He remembered an old preacher at Bethel, a Mr Diggins, telling him what people had said in 1917: 'There can't be a God or he wouldn't allow this sort of stuff.'

It had made Mr Diggins despair.

I went back up the hill to look at Hartley's bust and now considered the war memorial next to it. There are eight columns of the dead from the First World War and about ninety names to each column. More than 700 young men from a community of about 25,000 people had died in four years, mainly in Flanders. Twenty-one of them were called Hartley: there were even three W. Hartleys. Who in Colne could now remember where, how, and for what they had died? If, at the age of thirty-three, there is ever a right time to die – a time to be remembered for the act – Wallace Hartley had chosen it.

13.

The little train took me down the valley. Two drunk youngish men got on at Accrington. They had no tickets. The ticket inspector and the driver were women. They said the train wouldn't move until the men paid. 'Away ye go to fuck,' said one of the men; they were travelling to Glasgow. Eventually the women gave up and the train moved on. The rest of us studied our newspapers.

One of the questions Cameron's *Titanic* plants in our imagination is:

how would we, the modern audience, behave on the deck of a slowly sinking liner without enough lifeboats, surrounded by a freezing sea? Worse, better, the same? The question implies that we know how people behaved then, and that Cameron's film portrays it accurately. These things are difficult to know. Perhaps Hartley and his men continued playing because it occupied them in what they slowly realised was a hopeless predicament. Perhaps they threw down their instruments long before the end and tried to paddle off on deckchairs, or anything else that would float. The fact is that all eight of them died and many of the people who survived were thankful to them. As to general good behaviour – good in the sense that men hung back and allowed women and children to fill the boats – there are many testimonies and one interesting statistic, which comes from the percentage of passengers saved, arranged by age, gender and class. These are the British Board of Trade Inquiry figures for survivors:

In the first class: thirty-four per cent of the men, ninety-seven per cent of the women, a hundred per cent of the children.

In the second class: eight per cent of men, eighty-four per cent of women, a hundred per cent of the children.

In the third class: twelve per cent of men, fifty-five per cent of women, thirty per cent of the children.

The usual juxtaposition is to compare the percentages of the first- to third-class children, or of first-class men and third-class children. These are shameful – by the principle of equity and the code of women and children first. But the interesting statistic in the context of 'good behaviour' is for the second-class men: eight per cent. Unlike the third class, they had easy and early access to the boat deck, and yet only thirteen survived out of 160. Could it be that this class, which on the *Titanic* was largely drawn from the middling tradesmen and professionals of Britain and North America, behaved more nobly and stoically than the men above and below them?

Hartley came from such a class. It may have been a heroic class or a foolish one. 'The old Lie,' Wilfred Owen wrote six years later, '*Dulce et decorum est pro patria mori*.' But it is hard to dismiss the thought that a way of thinking, of being, in Colne and in Britain, must have affected the way people behaved, and that they behaved differently then.

14.

Still hunting for scraps of Hartley's life, I followed his passage back to Halifax, Nova Scotia. It was from Halifax on 17 April 1912 that a Canadian cable ship, the *Mackay-Bennett*, was dispatched under hire to the White Star Line. It sailed towards the *Titanic's* last known position with a cargo that included one hundred coffins, several tons of ice, and embalming tools and fluid for use by the professional embalmers who were also on board. By the time the ship returned to Halifax on 30 April, it had recovered 306 bodies. They were often found in clusters; a member of the crew counted more than a hundred floating together in their white life jackets 'like a flock of seagulls'. Some had drowned in the immediate turmoil of the sinking; others had floated off and frozen to death. As each body was hauled on board, it was given a number before clothes and personal effects were removed and put into a bag with the same number. Bodies that were too damaged or decomposed – though decomposition was not much of a problem in such near-freezing water – were returned to the sea weighted with iron, which had been brought for that purpose. One hundred and sixteen bodies from the *Mackay-Bennett's* haul went back into the Atlantic, but that still left 190 for the voyage home to Halifax.

On board, the bodies, or the identifiable majority of them, were divided in death as in life. The dead from the *Titanic's* crew were stacked unembalmed on the foredeck or in the ice-filled hold. Second- and third-class passengers were sewn up in canvas bags. First-class passengers were embalmed and encoffined and placed at the stern. All of this last class had been successfully identified, perhaps because they carried so many valuables and inscribed memorabilia. When the bodies reached port, some were claimed by relatives and taken for burial at final destinations across North America and in Europe. Halifax undertakers buried the rest: 150 in all, sixty of them never identified.

Of the band, only three were found. John 'Jock' Hume, the violinist, was body number 193; and Fred Clarke, the bassist, body number 202. Hartley's body was found soon after, perhaps in the same group; body number 224. His details were in the Nova Scotia Archives. Reading through them I cleared up one small mystery. In several accounts of the *Titanic* disaster, Hartley was said to have been found with his music case strapped to his body – as though he had died to save the muse as represented on his memorials. The original handwritten entry for him reads:

sex: male. est age 25. hair brown. clothing – uniform (green facing), brown overcoat, black boots, *green box* [my italics]. effects – gold fountain pen, WHH diamond solitaire ring, silver cigarette case, letter, silver match box marked to WHH from Collingson's staff, Leeds, telegram to Hotley [*sic*], Bandmaster, Titanic, watch, gold chain, gold cigar holder, stud, scissors, sixteen shillings, 16 cents in coins.

A later typed entry amends the 'green box' to 'green socks', which were part of a White Star bandman's uniform. Box/socks. I thought I could imagine the confusion: the undertaker's clerk with his nib-pen scurrying across the page, a colleague opening each of 190 bags and identifying their contents, shouting his list in a noisy warehouse filled with bodies and ice.

That accounted for the music case. I decided I would pay my respects to the grave of John 'Jock' Hume of Dumfries.

The bodies which were buried in Halifax lie in three groups. The identifiably Catholic (such as the bassist, Clarke) were taken to the Mount Olivet cemetery. The identifiably Jewish to the Baron de Hirsch cemetery, from where some of them were quickly removed after an undignified squabble with the local rabbi, who was accused of being too eager to use debatable evidence (circumcision, probably) to call a body Jewish. But by far the largest number went to Halifax's non-denominational cemetery, the Fairview, which is spread across a slope at the head of one of Halifax's inlets from the Atlantic. It was a fine breezy afternoon, with a sparkle from the blue chop in the sound and the rippling green of the cemetery grass. Halifax now advertised itself as a chief port of call on the *Titanic*'s new tourist trail, and a big new sign had been erected: 'The *Titanic* Graves'. A path, newly worn, led through the grass to a large oval of small uniform headstones, like those to the dead in Flanders. I bent among them, looking at this name and that, remembering the stories attached to some of them. Here (body 313) was Luigi Gatti, maître d' of the ship's French restaurant, who was found clutching the teddy bear his small daughter had given him before he left home in Southampton. And here (number 193) was 'Jock' Hume, whose parents in Scotland were later asked to stump up for an unpaid uniform bill – it became a small scandal.

There were 121 of these stones, some engraved only with numbers, and other than the occasional flower, very little sign that any of them had recently been remembered.

Then, further down the slope, I came across a grave which was heaped with tributes. Before the headstone to J. Dawson (number 227) candles had been lit and artificial flowers arranged. There were also several keys, some sweets, a crayon or two, a piece of chewing gum still in its wrapper, cinema tickets, and (the most striking thing) a large plastic model of a transatlantic liner – not the *Titanic*, but a three-funnelled ship that could have been the *Queen Mary*.

Someone had written a note: 'Dear James Dawson, I feel sorry about your life. They should have built the *Titanic* stronger. Paula.'

This was the grave of Leonardo DiCaprio.

Keys, flowers, candles: all had been taken to the grave by the young people – girls mostly – whom, I was told in Halifax, had towed their parents here from as far away as France and California. Most of the tributes I could understand, but the keys were a puzzle until I remembered that at one point in the film Dawson/DiCaprio is handcuffed to a pipe deep inside the sinking ship, the water rises to his neck, and, despite a frantic search, no keys can be found. (Can he be rescued? Yes! Enter Kate Winslet with an axe.)

But who was the J. Dawson under the headstone? According to the Novia Scotia Archives, he was a fireman, a stoker of coal. His body had been found unmarked and dressed in dungarees with a grey shirt. His estimated age was thirty. He had light hair and a moustache. The only item found on him was a card showing his membership (number 35638) of the National Seamen's Union. There was some confusion over his address, originally given as 17 Bolton Street, Southampton, then changed to 17 Briton Street, Dublin. Nothing else, so far as I can tell, is known about him, though we have some idea of how he worked.

Terry Coleman describes it well in his book *The Liners* (1976). Here was the life of a fireman on a four-funnelled, coal-burning Atlantic liner:

> At sea, they worked two four-hour spells in each twenty-four, lifting five tons of coal each a day . . . They worked in twenty-one-minute spells. There were seven minutes to feed coals into furnaces whose heat scorched them, then seven minutes for cutting and clearing clinkers with long slicers, and then another seven for raking over. A man who was behind in any seven minutes could

not escape being seen by his fellows to be weaker, and so the weak drove themselves to keep up with the strong. After three periods of seven minutes there was a short pause, and then a gong announced the beginning of another twenty-one minutes. This was the fireman's work for four hours on end, scorched by furnaces and choked by coal dust and by gases from white-hot clinkers and ashes. When they had finished their watches they often took the air with chests open to the cold Atlantic wind. They worked, ate, and then slept exhausted. They could not obtain drink aboard, so when they did get ashore they made up for this by getting and staying drunk. As firemen, only the Hungarians were as good as the Liverpool Irish.

It doesn't seem, from this, that one of them would have had time to teach Kate Winslet to spit.

15.

Flying home from Nova Scotia, the *Titanic's* wreck somewhere in the sea beneath me, I thought: the *Titanic* story is so barnacled with metaphor and myth that it hardly matters whether Wallace Hartley played his hymn or not (for the sake of Colne, I hoped he had). There are much bigger lies. The first is that the ship was billed as 'unsinkable'. The great paradox of the *Titanic* is that it became unsinkable only after it sank, when White Star officials were anxious to counter early reports of the disaster. Previously the only reference in the company's publicity to 'unsinkability' was a cautiously worded sentence in a 1910 brochure for the *Olympic* and the *Titanic* which said that 'as far as it is possible to do so, these two wonderful vessels are designed to be unsinkable'.

Nor was the *Titanic* a particularly fast ship – her older Cunard and German rivals were three or four knots faster. Nor, though she was briefly the largest ship afloat, was the *Titanic* staggeringly huge; only one foot longer than her earlier sister, the *Olympic*, and significantly smaller than the German *Imperator*, which went into Atlantic service later in the year the *Titanic* went down.

But perhaps the largest untruth is in the hubris metaphor – in James Cameron's words, that 'mankind's faith in his own indomitable power was forever destroyed by uniquely human shortcomings: arrogance, complacency and greed'. What in fact happened was that the lifeboat regulations were redrafted; ice patrols were introduced; hulls given a double lining of steel. Otherwise, Atlantic liners went on growing more luxurious, larger and swifter.

Hubris, if it had ever existed, was killed with the millions of names on the thousands of war memorials like the one in Colne. If it had ever existed, and − I thought, watching *Titanic*'s director holding his final Oscar aloft and calling out 'King of the World!' − if it has ever died.

16.

On 20 May 1999, a cruise liner, the *Sun Vista*, caught fire in the Strait of Malacca and slowly began to sink. More than 1,100 passengers and crew were taken off in lifeboats and other small craft. Ram Yalamanchi, a businessman from India, said: 'It was a true nightmare. I thought we were all going to die. We were on one of the last lifeboats; we watched her [the ship] slip into the water. People were screaming and praying.'

Many passengers sang to keep their spirits up. According to an Australian, Greg Haywood: 'We were singing the Celine Dion song, "My Heart Will Go On".'

Deluge

August 2004

Three weeks ago, the wind was very warm on the Firth of Clyde. We remarked on its untypical heat as it bent the bracken and rhododendrons on the Argyll coast; a fancy, foreign wind coming up from the south, where it had been brewed (so the papers said) by a hurricane in the Caribbean. None of us could remember such a warm wind in Scotland before. When we swam, we came out of the sea and pretty well immediately stopped shuddering. In the evening, we went to a hotel and asked if we could take our drinks outside to the garden. 'You'll need to be quick,' the barman said, because by that time the sky had changed from blue to purple-black, with showers tugging down delicate fronds of cloud to the hills in Kintyre.

Then the wind died and it began to rain properly. A couple of hours later the road was like a river on the hills and a pond in the hollows, and the car headlights picked out thousands of frogs who were seizing their chance to explore this unexpected new wetland. We drove further north through the rain the next day and came across sights which were at first merely exciting: a familiar glen had been suddenly converted into a long loch, with sheep and cattle perched on its freshly created islands; swollen burns and rivers and risen above their bridgeworks and spread earth and rock across the road; patches of sea had turned into milky coffee and uprooted trees drifted helplessly among the foam. Towards the head of Loch Fyne, we began to see fresh brown scars on the steep green hillside, where the earth, which had rested snug and content there for many centuries, had found a life of its own and slipped away.

It was only at Cairndow, at the loch's end, that we changed from interested spectators to concerned travellers. A landslip had torn through a cottage and spread mud and rubble across the main road to Inveraray and Kintyre. There was no way forward and only a complicated way back through the private lane of a Highland estate, because other landslides had blocked the roads to Glasgow and Dunoon. The pub was filled with mystified drivers, wondering what to do next. Older people remembered the newspaper pictures of Aberfan, but not even the oldest could remember anything of this sort happening in Argyll before, at least in summer. We talked about the weather and for how many hours or days the roads would be closed. But we didn't blame ourselves, our prosperity, our cars, our planes, our central heating, our reckless burning of coal and oil; a way of living that you could argue had its origins very close to here, James Watt being a Greenock man and the world's first sea-going steamships coming up the loch well before the battle of Waterloo (and, up there in the early nineteenth-century stratosphere, the hydrocarbon from the world's first industrial nation starting a process whose effects would remain unknown for almost two hundred years).

Nobody said as they debated the immediate future of the A82, 'That's it. No more cars for me. How do I join the Green Party?' Nobody promised to be a better dweller on and for this earth. No connections were made between the atmosphere's behaviour and our own.

'Global warming' is a phrase that a dozen years ago implied unpleasant things happening to faraway people – a rising sea drowning Pacific atolls and large parts of Bangladesh – while in Britain we imagined vineyards in the Pennines and Mediterranean summers. Few of us realised that climate change would mean 'extreme weather' – extreme not just in heat, but in wind and rain and unpredictability. The consequences are too late to stop but not too late to modify, so that perhaps in fifty or a hundred years' time the glaciers and the ice caps could end their retreat and the climate begin to stabilise. Science (most of it) agrees that we need to change the way we live, but we refuse to do it. We like cars, motorways, cheap flights, untaxed aviation fuel. Increasingly, our lives are built around them. Hen parties fly from Dublin for a night out in Edinburgh, town centres surrender themselves to the 'evening economy' (the drinking young), while superstores and multi-screens sit soberly next to their out-of-town car parks. Governments, even when not as wilfully blind to the future as the present American regime, are fearful of their electorates and our consuming desires. In any case, what about the growing economies of India and China? Who will deny their populations' ambition to enjoy the consumables that historically have been mainly the preserve of Europe and North America?

It seems that we have made our fate and feel helpless before it. Driving back, I thought of Gandhi and his anti-industrialism, every village its own government, every person to his own spinning wheel and a diet of goat's milk and vegetables. He had asked people to renounce things, including the popular, material idea of betterment, but even in a country used to the idea of renunciation, where the simple life and the spiritual life are often confused, where the poor with nothing to lose were much more numerous than the rich, it had found few takers. That today's world could embrace a similar movement, restricting human need and desire, husbanding and more equally sharing finite resources, seems close to impossible.

At home, the rain still plinking against the windows, I read more of my proof copy of Jeremy Treglown's excellent biography of V. S. Pritchett, which will be published next month. In it that night I came across a passage about a celebrated symposium published by the *Left Review* in 1937 called 'Authors Take Sides on the Spanish War'. Many writers, most on the Republican side, contributed (the names include W. H. Auden, Samuel Beckett, Aldous Huxley and Arthur Koestler) and the idea has been reprised many times since. The *Guardian* itself sometimes does it, most recently on Iraq. What side writers privately take in current public arguments is always interesting to know and even, improbably and very occasionally, influential.

But wars in other countries are easy stuff, involving personal opinion (easy to give) rather than a change in personal behaviour (harder to make). And yet climate change is, we are told, a far bigger threat to the world's civilised future than terrorism (though it will undoubtedly promote various kinds of armed struggle in itself).

Which writers will stand up and be counted on global warming if the symposium were entitled 'Authors Take Sides on Their Volvo, Their Second Home, Their EasyJet Flights to Tuscany and Their Weekly Drive to Waitrose'? I hope not be asked.

Fat

September 2005

As usual, I spent most of August on the Firth of Clyde, and one
Sunday I sailed by steamer all the way upriver from Rothesay to
Glasgow. The trip took almost four hours. It was a beautiful evening,
the sky turning pink over the Cowal hills, the firth a blue and gold
and silver mirror – so lovely that it was possible to forget (for those
of us old enough to remember) how busy this river had once been
with shipyards, cranes, freighters and liners; so still and warm that we
could sit on the topmost deck without shivering inside an anorak,
and look with less than the usual melancholy on the supermarkets
and weeds that have replaced the slipways where until the 1970s thousands of men used to work.

It was on the stairs to this top deck that accidents number one and
two happened. In the first, which occurred somewhere between Rothesay
and Largs, an excitable fat boy tumbled down and for a few moments
lay still on the deck below, until a concerned crowd helped him to his
feet. He was holding a couple of bags of crisps. In the second, somewhere between Largs and Greenock, another, unrelated fat boy did the
same thing, this time clutching several Twix bars. I didn't see accident
number three – it occurred somewhere below deck – but at Greenock
the ship was delayed while three paramedics came aboard and stretchered
off a woman to an ambulance on the quayside. She seemed to have
broken her ankle. She was also, it must be said, very large.

In all my days aboard Clyde steamers, in summers that go back fifty
years, I'd never been on such an accident-prone voyage. Perhaps people

were both nimbler and more cautious in my childhood, and knew that ships contained all sorts of hazards and kept their eyes peeled. Perhaps they were also thinner. As I stared over the rail at the high-rise flats of Greenock, I thought about the official anxiety over the Scottish diet (too much fat, too much sugar) and Greenock's historical role in its alteration. Greenock was the first Scottish port to import sugar in bulk from the West Indies and a great refining industry grew up there. In the same century, the eighteenth, it was the birthplace of the great inventor James Watt, whose improved steam technology changed the face of the world. In the late twentieth – *O tempora o mores!*, etc. – the same town was the birthplace, or so it is said, of the deep-fried Mars Bar. (For a long time I thought this heart-stopping combination of sugar and fat, nestling in its warming compartment next to its elder cousin, the deep-fried mutton pie, was a myth created by stand-up comedians. But then at my mother's funeral I met a Port Glasgow cousin who said he'd eaten and enjoyed one – they were freely available. And Port Glasgow is Greenock's neighbour. The case rests.)

Drink and drugs are staples of Scottish fiction. With the recent exception of Andrew O'Hagan's novel *Personality*, where the heroine lives in the world of the deep-fryer before dramatically (though understandably, you might feel) rejecting it in favour of anorexia, Scottish literature has not dwelt much on Scottish food. The occasional description of food – healthier food it must have been – in old Scottish novels gave this child reader the Dr Johnson shivers. At the beginning of *Kidnapped*, young David Balfour is given some porridge by his mean and evil old relation at the House of Shaws. 'They're grand food, parritch,' says Uncle Ebenezer, and with the plural subject of the sentence I could see all too easily the plurality of the lumps. When, later in the novel, David is marooned on a small Hebridean island, it seemed to me that the prospect of a raw limpet dinner was delicious in comparison. In other books there are mentions of herring and oatmeal, none of them appealing to the childhood appetite, which feasted on stories composed south of the border by Enid Blyton and their picnics of sandwiches, cakes and lemonade.

A hundred years and more ago, working-class Scotland began to exchange this plain fare for food that was, from its perspective, tastier and often easier to prepare. Sidney Mintz, in his excellent history of sugar, *Sweetness and Power*, records how Dundee's women jute workers stopped the time-consuming business of making soup in the morning to carry to the factory for lunch, and made jam sandwiches instead. Then dawned the age of the deep-fried potato. My father, who grew up in Edwardian Scotland largely (to hear him talk distastefully of it) on a diet of porridge and boiled fish and potatoes, and a few other dull things made by boiling water in pots, was a living testament to the seductive power of sugar, fat and the frying pan. Not in his size – he wasn't particularly big – but in his preference for chips above mash, for fried eggs rather than boiled, for toast above bread, for his pay-day quarter pounds of Duncan's walnut whirls, and for the occasional Sunday-morning treat of a hot roll with a Fry's Cream Bar as the filling. But even he, I suspect, could never have guessed that sugar and fat would cease being delicacies, exceptional food to be savoured, to become what many people ate all the time. A study published this month by the West of Scotland Food Group revealed that a new dish called a 'hoagie' (chips, cheese and doner kebab meat) had become a firm lunchtime favourite among school pupils who had handy access to takeaway shops. An average hoagie contains 1,224 calories, 136 grams of fat and 9.6 grams of salt. Jamie Oliver's famous enemy, the turkey twizzler, limps like an old lettuce leaf in its shade.

Fat has more than one way to kill you. Two weeks after the steamer trip, we went as a family to Bute Highland Games, where my daughter came back from a tour around the pipe bands, dancers and caber tossers to ask if I'd seen 'the Chip Pan Blaze Competition'. She was only teasing: it wasn't a competition ('Mrs Flora Smith from Falkirk is wearing the McGregor tartan and wielding a five-pound pan') but a public-safety demonstration by the fire brigade. Two firemen heated a pan of fat so that it caught fire and then poured a cup of water over it, *which you must not do*. Whoosh! The flames leapt thirty feet. It was the most exciting event at the games and it happened every hour.

The firemen said that Scotland had 12,000 chip-pan blazes every year, in which an average of fifty people died. They said the primary cause had once been absent-minded housewives; now it was drunk or drugged men. As making chips is a complicated art even when sober – the peeling, the cutting, the drying, the waiting for the first whisps of smoke from the pan – the determination of the drunk man to do it may show the hold that deep-frying has over the Scottish imagination. Forget 'A Drunk Man Looks at the Thistle'; 'A Drunk Man

Forgets to Look at the Chip Pan' may be the poem that Hugh MacDiarmid should have written.

Of course, I am my father's son and my own frame fits this fat landscape rather well. In the writing of this column a sugary doughnut and a crumpet from Rothesay's Electric Bakery have helped the composition. Half a dozen potato scones still lie innocently in the bread bin, unaware of their teatime fate.

Signals at Red

November 2000

Somewhere in that mainly flat stretch of country between Doncaster and Grantham the train stopped again – unwontedly, as the Georgian poem has it. Through the carriage window I could see fields of water and, on a higher stretch of green pasture that had become an island, a couple of cows bending into the grass and chewing blankly. The cows were pretty, black and brown and white, and there was a touch of blue in the sky; the water in the fields shone. No human beings and no houses could be seen. The train's engine idled. As the poem also has it, no one left and no one came.

I imagined this scene as one of those mysterious Victorian story-paintings – *The Scapegoat* or a new version of *The Last of England* – in which every superficially attractive feature suggests something ominous. Stopped train, flooded fields, a couple of marooned survivors from the recent bovine holocaust. I have travelled this way on the East Coast Main Line many times – by my calculation (there being not much else to do at this point) hundreds of times – and this bit of England has always seemed unknowable to me. One part looks much like the next. I continue to confuse Retford and Newark and not be quite certain that the large river, brimming and rippling when we passed it a few minutes back, is the Trent. To the east lies Lincolnshire (Skegness, Cleethorpes), where I have never been; to the west, Nottingham, where I have almost never been. Perhaps this is the real Middle England. Never before had it seemed so fragile and undependable, or so threatened by the biblical punishments of plague and flood.

Eventually the train moved on. We passed a few broken trees which were straddled across the opposite line. There were workers in bright orange coats. One of them was furling a yellow flag – proceed with caution. This was a pioneer train, so far as I could tell, the first sent south from Doncaster on that day, Monday 30 October, though the time was after two in the afternoon.

At Newark, the last stop, passengers for Grantham had been told to get off and on to a special bus. But then, strangely, the train went on to stop at Grantham. I remembered a remark of an older colleague on a newspaper fifteen or twenty years ago. Didn't I think that the people of Britain were becoming 'thick'? He'd noticed that they bumped into each other more, stupidly, like dodgem cars. This seemed an odd and even offensive remark at the time, but in Grantham I wondered if he hadn't caught some Naipaulian splinter of the truth. I turned the page of my newspaper and read that the railways are so short of skill that a contracting firm in Scotland is recruiting fourteen engineers from Romania.

A red signal light shone brightly at the platform's end. When it turned green, we moved down the plain towards the capital. We would get through.

Last weekend I spent fourteen hours on trains. I don't want to describe this as 'a nightmare'; that word, along with 'cattle trucks', properly belongs with troops trains and transports bound for destinations in central Europe sixty years ago. I travelled from London to Fife via Edinburgh late on Friday and back again early on Monday. Perhaps I was lucky, but it didn't even reach the standards of a bad dream. I had no urgent business. I saw my mother. All that happened along the way was that I was stuck on trains or stood waiting for them far longer than I should have been. So what did I feel? I suppose a kind of irritable melancholy.

I am interested in railways. It is a sad thing these days to be inter-ested in railways. I don't mean by this that a railway interest indicates a sad personality, repression, infantilism and so on (though it may do); rather that to be interested in railways, to believe in them as an effect-ive, reliable and environmentally necessary mode of transport, is to be made sad by the lethal muddle they have become. I used to be angry. How could politicians (Tories) have got away with such a crazy privatisation, such a careless and perverse scheme? How could politicians (Labour, and contrary to their pledges) have persevered with the scheme intact? But on Friday as I made my way to King's Cross I hoped I would be shielded by the iron of fatalism – adjustment to new conditions. There may be a train, or there may not. If not, then I would try to behave with the dignity of a poor man on a platform in, say, Bihar. I would walk away with my bundle and try again another day.

I'd booked a seat on the four o'clock to Edinburgh. I collected my standard saver return (£77) at the ticket office and then went to consult the departures board. The four o'clock was listed with a revised arrival time in Edinburgh of 21.19 rather than 20.20, the extra time to allow for a detour to avoid the Hatfield crash site and the consequent speed restrictions further up the line. There were queues in the concourse, marked with small signs at their head: queues D and C and E for Newcastle, Edinburgh and Leeds. The 3.30 to Newcastle has been cancelled. Queue D joined queue C. No platform had been announced. At four o'clock the train to take us out still hadn't come in. The good behaviour of the people queuing was completely admirable and also, in a survival-of-the-fittest sense, foolish. At King's Cross, you might say that the queue is for herbivores. Less obedient people who know the ropes hang around the entrance to the likeliest platform and become the front of the queue if they've guessed rightly. By the time platform number three was announced, the crowd around its end was so big that passengers leaving the train were blocked by those trying to get on.

Porters, if they are still called porters, came and cleared a way. And then we began to run down the platform. A voice over the tannoy said we were not to run – it was dangerous; there would be room on other trains – but still we ran. 'Thick' as my old colleague might have said; after all, most of us had booked seats. Or perhaps not so thick, given the capricious booking arrangements. I had seat 38 in coach B, but the seats in coach B were all ticketed for coach A. And, a thrilling double layer of confusion, the seat numbers on the tickets didn't correspond to the numbers on the seats to which they were attached. Seat B40 had a ticket for A38, going only as far as York.

Somehow we made do without too many arguments, remarking to each other as passengers do in a country such as India that no public system can be relied on, nothing bloody works. The train left late and got later, three hours later than its original time, two later than its revised time. The staff on the train were helpful and informative; there were many apologies – this country has become brilliant at apology. I was at my mother's home by midnight. She is ninety-three. 'I wonder,' she said, 'why trains have to travel so fast. A hundred miles an hour! That's surely dangerous.'

On my way back I thought about her question. The little train from Fife was late and crowded, standing room only. On board the nine o'clock to London at Edinburgh, we were advised to get off unless our journey was 'really necessary' because the train might get no further than Doncaster. At Newcastle, we were told it would advance no further than York. 'Deteriorating' or sometimes just 'adverse' weather conditions had cut off southern England from the north. At York, we got off, only to be told that the train would in fact go to London. Back on, we were told it would go only to Doncaster. At Doncaster, we waited on a windy platform where pleasant officials of the Great North Eastern Railway Company (the best of the new railway companies in my experience, though perhaps I've been seduced by the olde-worlde hokum of the name) told us that they were as much in the dark as we were, but with any luck we could expect a train from Leeds. After an hour, one came, and nearly empty.

We reached London at half past five, a journey of eight and a half hours from Edinburgh rather than the advertised four. My mother would have approved, and the truth is that I didn't mind too much. A warm and empty carriage, work to do, some compensatory free coffee, and time enough to look at the cows. In 1910 – according to the *Bradshaw* of that year – the journey time would have been thought satisfactory. Even in the 1960s, the fastest trains took six hours and there were far fewer of them: five a day, slow or fast, from Edinburgh to London, whereas now there are more than twenty. Or would be, were it not for broken rails.

But, *pace* my old mother's question, we think we live in a modern European country. We expect trains to travel fast, motorways to be clear, schools to educate, hospitals to care and cure, safe food. This isn't so much of a problem of rising as of risen expectation. It may be no more than a brief illusion – this country is brilliant at illusions (new uniforms for the Underground but escalators that crack). All of us, even the thickest, surely now know that the underfunded ice we skate on is very, very thin.

Quitting

October 2005

First voice: 'We must quit Iraq immediately.' Second voice: 'No, we can't quit now – we must set a timetable for quitting.' Third voice: 'No, a timetable would make quitting even more dangerous – there must be no mention of timetables. We must build the democratic institutions of Iraq and only then quit.'

Listening the other day to these opinions ping-ponging their way around a radio studio, far removed from the blood and sand, I thought of poor Lord Wavell, the penultimate viceroy of India, struggling in Delhi to divine the desires of his political masters in London. Churchill not for quitting India, Attlee for quitting (but how, and how soon?). Historical analogies are dangerous: leaving the Indian empire after a couple of centuries and removing 8,000 troops from a province in Iraq after a couple of years are not the same thing. And yet there are similarities. There is the feeling shared by most of the British population, apart from the Churchillians/Blairites, that getting out double-quick is a very good idea. And there is the fractious and fracturing nature of Iraq, a country poised on the brink of division into three parts, just as India was divided into two.

Wavell devised a plan for the British evacuation of India and called it 'Operation Madhouse' (with, I think, an alternative strategy called 'Operation Bedlam'). Military rather than political plotting was really his forte. He was a field marshal who in 1943 got the viceroy's job almost by accident after Anthony Eden turned it down. His biographers describe him as taciturn, awkward, cautious, shy, stoic and hopeless in company. He lost an eye while serving with the Black Watch in 1916. Churchill, with whom he never got along, said that meeting him was like being 'in the presence of the chairman of a golf club'. As both a military and a political bureaucrat he was unlucky, a manager of retreat in the first years of the Second World War and absent from its later victories. Lying didn't come easily to him and, unlike Montgomery or Mountbatten, his successor as viceroy, he cut no dash. His great love and solace was poetry, the reading and reciting and not the writing of it, and it's for one book of poetry that, outside the realm of military history, he will be mainly remembered.

Jonathan Cape published *Other Men's Flowers*, an anthology of Wavell's favourite poems, in 1944. It became a large and unlikely success: it has been rarely out of print since and by 1979 had sold almost 130,000 copies (my wife's edition is a Pimlico paperback, 1992). The idea for its publication came not so much from Wavell himself as from the traveller and writer Peter Fleming, who was on Wavell's staff in Delhi during his pre-viceregal days as the army's commander-in-chief in India. Fleming's day job was the concoction of intelligence stunts that it was hoped would deceive the advancing Japanese: 'Operation Error', for example, in which a crashed car had been apparently abandoned on a jungle road complete with Wavell's despatch case containing bogus documents that fictitiously implied reinforcements and secret weapons. (One can imagine the verdict at intelligence headquarters in Tokyo from men holding paper up to the light: 'Ah, Mr Fleming again – very clever, but not clever enough!')

In the evening, under a ceiling fan and over a drink, Fleming would listen to his boss recite and talk about Browning and Kipling, and eventually suggested that Wavell compile an anthology and send it to Cape, who had published Fleming's pre-war travel accounts. Cape wasn't impressed. Wavell, far from home and a good library, had quoted many of the poems from his formidable memory. There were frequent mistakes. Cape sent a humiliating letter of rejection in which the general's choice was described as 'familiar school recitations advancing in close formation'. The situation was retrieved only after Fleming lobbied a Cape director, Rupert Hart-Davis, who reproved the publisher by telling him his letter was 'tantamount to a sock on the jaw' to a shy man who had delivered 'the complete bones of a tremendously saleable book'.

What accounted for its success? My guess is that it made poetry respectable for manly men – Wavell's section on war is called 'Good Fighting' but his section on love a tongue-tied 'Love and All That' – in an age when reciteable poetry still had a popular appeal. Looking at it again this week, my wife remembered how her father could speak all of the 'Rubaiyat of Omar Khayyam' and Hilaire Belloc's 'Do you remember an Inn, Miranda? / Do you remember an Inn?' My own father could do as well with a lot of the included Burns and Coleridge. Both our fathers left school at fourteen. They had uneducated memories compared to Wavell's, who wrote in his introduction that while, nearing sixty, he couldn't claim that he could repeat by heart all the 260 or so poems in the anthology, he thought he could safely claim that he once could.

Wavell was clearly an awkward customer. In his introduction, he apologises for his notes on the poems, saying, 'The Notes are not altogether my fault, the publisher asked for them.' But he was far from a bluff fool who kept himself going on the march with a few verses of Kipling. He knew that a key to poetry's success – you might say its departed success – was its memorability, but he also knew that that wasn't its only quality. In 1961, eleven years after his death, T. S. Eliot wrote, 'I do not pretend to be a judge of Wavell as a soldier . . . What I do know from personal acquaintance with the man, is that he was a great man. This is not a term I use easily . . .'

As it turned out, 'Operation Madhouse' was a good term for the British departure from India, the operation supervised to a very quick timetable by Mountbatten after Wavell was prematurely sacked. At least half a million people died in the slaughter following Partition. Perhaps it could have been done better; perhaps it could have been done worse. When the time comes – soon – the same will be said of Iraq.

Bus Conductors I Have Known

October 2005

There are no more Routemaster buses on route 38 from Victoria to Clapton Pond. The last one ran last night. As of today, only one Routemaster route still runs in London – the 159 from Marble Arch to Streatham. When that ends on 9 December, there will be no more buses with conductors as well as drivers, and with open rear platforms that you can jump on and off. The London bus conductor will join the crossing-sweeper and the old-iron collector as a defunct personality. Just as I have never heard the cry 'Cherry ripe, who'll buy my sweet cherries?', my grandchildren will never hear 'This stop for the British Museum!', 'Room on top!', or (my favourite) 'Highbury Corner for Highbury Tube and all international destinations!'

London was the last preserve of the bus conductor in Britain, and, for all I know, the world. I suspect that Blackpool trams may still have conductors, but buses everywhere ditched them long ago. In the early 1980s, a London woman once gave me her definition of provincial cities: 'They're all Chelsea Girl boutiques and one-man-operated buses.' That was before provincial cities turned their disused mills into art galleries, and also before a few canny enterpreneurs saw money in the government's deregulation of bus services and set old London buses to work in places such as Paisley and Perth: an Indian summer of bus conducting, which came quickly to an end when 'competition' proved really to mean private rather than municipal monopolies. No need to pay two wages when you can get away with paying one.

Conductors, or rather conductresses, were a memorable feature of my youth. The bus map of Lowland Scotland was then divided like Gaul into three parts. The blue and cream buses of William Alexander held the land north of the Forth–Clyde valley, while the green and cream of the Eastern SMT (the Scottish Motor Traction Company) brightened the roads south of the Forth, and the red and cream of the Western SMT lit up those south of the Clyde. Ours was blue-bus territory. A big blue double-decker came to our village every half-hour, where, helped by the conductress blowing a whistle, it did a reverse next to the Albert Hotel and then stood with its engine switched off before the journey back to town. Driver and conductress would sit on the back seats that ran parallel to the passageway and share a flask of tea. This being Fife and not Sicily, the conversation was quiet and understated – what I remember is the silence of a stilled bus and the illegal drift of cigarette smoke on the bottom deck – and what little animation there was usually came from the conductress who, being a woman and having to deal with the public, had been given a licence to talk.

We knew their names: Big Ella, Sadie, Maggie. Ella was probably my father's favourite. He was a big confectionery man and Ella, too, liked her sweets. She would dip into the offered bag and dig out a Callard & Bowser treacle toffee, heedless of the results on a body that was already doing battle with her thick uniform and the straps that held her leather money bag and the ticket machine. She had a big voice. Before the stop near the pier, her call of 'Ferryboat!' would ring up the stairs, right to the front seats on the top deck. Once, she told us, she'd opened her back door at home to call the cat in and shouted 'Ferryboat!' by mistake. The bottom deck laughed at that.

Sadie was different: thinner, huskier, smokier. I was reminded of Eartha Kitt. After I left school, I saw her once at the Aberdour Palais, for the first time as a woman in civvies, holding on to a sailor as they whirled about to the music of trumpet, saxophone and drums. Like many conductresses, she came from what were then the mining villages of central Fife – Kelty, Lochgelly, Lochore, Cardenden – which seemed to breed tough women who could tell Saturday-night drunks where, in both senses, to get off. The Fife folk singer and composer John Watt wrote his most famous song about them, 'The Kelty Clippie' who 'hasnae got nae culture' and reads the *People's Friend*. 'Oh she's just a Kelty clippie / She'll no tak nae advice / It's ach drap deid or I'll bile your heid / Or I'll punch your ticket twice.'

Watt recorded the song in 1976, but I first heard it only a few years ago, and when I did I was grateful to Watt for preserving as art something so specific and local; something that might so easily have vanished from the public memory. I never expected to hear the word 'Kelty' in a modern lyric – modern lyrics assenting mainly to American geography. Has anyone done the same for the London bus conductor? According to Travis Elborough's book on the Routemaster, *The Bus We Loved*, the sad fact is that the unfunny ITV series *On the Buses* may be our best fictional record of the conductor–passenger–driver relationship. It was certainly popular – the film version was the biggest earner at British cinemas in 1971 – but its London characteristics were questionable, its buses being green and operated by the Luxton and District Traction Company.

I shall miss London conductors and their Routemasters, which are such well-designed and beautiful objects. Riding with my son on the number 38 to Clapton Pond last weekend – a farewell trip – I couldn't help thinking how both belonged to a more civilised and orderly metropolitan era, before the disintegration of the bus queue and the coming of the CCTV camera and the warnings about unattended objects. Earlier this year on another of my local buses, the 43, a man on the upper deck was stabbed to death when he objected to a fellow passenger throwing take-away chips at his girlfriend. No wonder, then, that the drivers-cum-faretakers are protected from their passengers by a strong screen, with help available by two-way radio. In my memory, the most that Big Ella and Sadie had to worry them was a man who had stayed too long in the Volunteer Arms singing 'The Yellow Rose of Texas' on the last bus home.

My Father's Bookcase

November 2005

How best to serve the memory of the dead? A year or so ago I wrote about my father's tools — his chisels, hammers, awls, drills and files — which my mother had kept untouched in the garden shed for twenty years after his death in 1981. Then she too died and my brother and I inherited the tools and I threw most of them away. Many readers wrote to chastise me for this, some pointing out that the tools could have gone to tool-hungry countries in Africa, but what was done was done. What I didn't know when I wrote was that I would preserve, almost by accident, another anthology of things that is a better memorial to him and to others of his kind (a very good kind, in my view). I mean self-improvers: autodidacts if you must. I mean his bookcase.

The case itself has had many adjustments. When my parents bought it second-hand, sometime in the 1930s, it was the upper portion of a good dining-room dresser, glass-fronted above with drawers and cupboards below, the whole in varnished light oak and probably late Victorian. It was far too tall for the ceilings of a council house, so my father sawed the bottom from the top and made a sideboard of one and a bookcase of the other. This was before my time. What I do remember, though vaguely, is how he replaced the brass handles with Bakelite ones — very smart in 1952 — and how twenty-five years later my brother reversed the process to replace the Bakelite — hopelessly unsmart in 1977 — with brass. A Toby jug perched on top at one end and a family photograph at the other. The top itself could be lifted off to reveal a useable space, a sort of hidden compartment. A Box Brownie was concealed there for many years until it was replaced by an Agfa Isolette, and then, after my mother was widowed, with envelopes containing insurance documents and ten-pound notes. She was on the state pension, but, as she often said, she had never been so rich in her life.

_ What changed very little were the books themselves, or at least those on the four shelves of the left-hand side (the four shelves on the right made way for new additions by the relegation of old stock to the cupboard). These same books have remained in the same place for as long as I can remember and may have assumed their final arrangement around 1944. I say 'final' because I now never want to change it. For a while I certainly intended to; when I moved the bookcase from one house to another, I imagined filling its shelves with my own books. But entropy set in, and then a respect for what already existed. I like to think now of these four left-hand shelves as the pattern of my father's life and thoughts, and as a key to the aspirations of his generation.

The top shelf contains the smallest books and the predominant colours are black, buff and brown. Here God is at war with no-God. There is a hymnary for use in the Church of Scotland, a tiny New Testament given to my mother's father during his service in the First World War, and two Bibles, one inscribed by his mother to my father in 1912 and the other inscribed by my father to my mother for Christmas 1928, when they were courting. 'Be guided only by the healer of the sick, the raiser of the dead, the friend of all who are afraid and forlorn', my father has written on the endpapers. The injunction sits oddly with the rest of the books on the shelf, which are mainly the buff volumes of the Thinker's Library, published by Watts and Company and the Rationalist Press, with a motif adapted from Rodin's statue on their spines. Their authors – Wells, Bradlaugh, Haldane, Anatole France – preach scepticism if not downright atheism. What this shelf shows is that my father gave up on God sometime in the 1930s, even if he persisted for a time with some Independent Labour Party version of Jesus Christ.

The second shelf is mainly green, nine novels by Dickens in a nice edition by Macmillan, purchased second-hand on 7 September 1930. He loved Dickens and around this time, in his first marital home, kept a small bust of the author on the mantelpiece. The green bindings were a problem, however. It was a colour his mother detested for superstitious and political reasons (she would pronounce the Irish republican de Valera as 'Devil-Era'). My mother said that when her mother-in-law came to visit, the books would have to be taken off their shelf and hidden. My own memory is of searching for a Christmas card for my grandmother without any green in it (difficult, given the colour of holly and fir trees) and of a Christmas tree my father made at his workbench, with wire branches interwined with sweeping-brush hairs as the tree's needles – dyed blue. What this shelf shows is that my father's love of literature overcame his fear of his mother, most of the time.

The third shelf was my childhood favourite. Large books, mainly red, among them Shaw's collected plays, the poetry of Burns, and a giant of a book called *The Wonders of the Past* published by the Amalgamated Press, which reflected my father's appetite for ancient civilisations, whetted by the discovery of Tutankhamun's tomb in 1925. The chief glory of the shelf, however, is the five volumes of *The World's Library of Best Books*, published by George Newnes and containing extracts ranging from Homer to Wodehouse. 'Lavishly illustrated' would be the phrase for them, with their woodcuts and stage stills and colour plates. The one accompanying Pepys is F. W. Topham's *An incident in the great plague of London*, which shows a naked young girl being passed down from the window of a plague house. Everybody else is clothed. There is no reason for her nakedness, other than the Victorian taste for mild pornography. I used to look at this picture a lot though I never read a line of Pepys. It was my introduction to the erotic.

The bottom shelf is a mixture of green and blue spines: eight volumes of *The Textile Industries: A Practical Guide to Fibres, Yarns and Fabrics* by the Gresham Publishing Company, with covers in an art nouveau style that I found slightly disturbing as a child; two heavy volumes of the *Engineering Educator*; several smaller books with names such as *Steam Engine Theory and Practice* and bookplates that record their award to H. Jack, Fife Mining School, Cowdenbeath, for coming first in the paper on heat engines or graphic statistics, sessions 1922 to 1924.

What this shelf shows is how my father spent his working life: as a mechanic earning the money that, among other things, bought the books that furnished his curious mind.

Somewhere to Call Their Own

February 1991

About 1,500 feet up in the Chota Nagpur hills, in eastern India, there lies a sprawling monument to racial fears and racial fancies, and to an idea of nationhood that shimmered temptingly in the years between the two world wars and then vanished leaving this as its only trace.

It has an odd name: McCluskiegunge. Several place names in India share this conjunction of West and East; McLeodgunge, Frasergunge, Daltongunge, Tollygunge. Usually they are named after some British district collector or military officer who, in the days of empire, benefited his patch of Indian countryside by building a road or a canal, or by simply being perceived as a decent man deserving a memorial (the word 'gunge', or '*ganj*' in Hindi, means a storehouse or market). McCluskie, however, was not a British official nor any kind of white man doing good. He had Indian as well as Irish blood, and this remote place in the hills was built as a settlement for his kind of people. 'Anglo-Indians' is the official name, though for a couple of centuries they felt the spittle of other descriptions: half-breeds, half-castes, mixed-bloods, cheechees, Chutney Marys, those with a touch of the tarbrush.

Had history worked out differently, McCluskiegunge might have become the capital of their small Indian state and McCluskie honoured as the Herzl of Anglo-India. That was the idea. Like the Jews, McCluskie's followers saw themselves as a wandering people, reviled and abused. Like the Zionists, they wanted a homeland and a redoubt; as the publicity for the project described it, the site promised 'a natural fortification offered by a chain of hills'. But that grand, perhaps even mad, ambition was never realised. Today McCluskiegunge is a scattering of bungalows strung together by a dusty road and divided by a railway line. Steam locomotives haul a slow passenger train up from the junction at Barkakana twice a day. At night, the sound of drumming echoes across the scrub from the tribal villages nearby. There are many poisonous snakes. Electricity is uncertain. Cautious residents, before they snuff out their candles, spread a little carbolic acid on the floor at the side of their beds as a defence against kraits and cobras.

I first went to McCluskiegunge a dozen years ago, drawn as much by the name as the fact that my wife's aunt and uncle had bought a bungalow there, where, during the Calcutta holidays, our uncle would take his rifle and hunt wild pig while our aunt worried about the snakes and made marmalade. Under clear night skies we drank rum and water and listened to my mother-in-law and her sister singing the Bengali songs they had sung from childhood. McCluskiegunge was their idea of a rural idyll, snatched from the acrid turmoil of metropolitan Calcutta, and I too came to be captivated by it, less because it was a wilderness (the reason it appealed to the Calcutta hunters) than because in the middle of the wilderness there were small pieces of Europe, of Britain, which had somehow got marooned.

Whichever way you came, by train or by road, everything suggested a passage out of Westernised, modern India. Calcutta was fewer than 300 miles to the east, but the overnight railway journey took fourteen hours and a lot of shunting. Long before Barkakana Junction was reached the reassuring, fertile fields of the Bengal plain had slipped away; the morning view from the carriage window showed raw hills where children chased goats among the rocks. The forty-mile drive from Ranchi, the nearest town, was no easier; the metalled road eventually gave way to a rutted track. Taxi drivers who had picked you up at the airfield would curse and want to turn back.

And yet at the end of these journeys lay not the unknown but the known. Two churches, the remains of a fountain, well-kept gardens, houses labelled Retreat, the Hermitage, Hill Cottage and (of course) Dunroamin.

Inside these houses, elderly Anglo-Indians kept to their old ways. They made rose cookies, plum cake, guava jelly, spiced beef. They had clocks that chimed mournfully on the hour, and pictures of

Constable's England and jokey mottoes on the wall: 'I am the boss in this house – and I have my wife's permission to say so!' Several of the men had retired from the railways. Mr Jim King's proudest possession was a photograph of the locomotive which had hauled King George V to the Delhi durbar, driven by his father. Mr Noel Ramsbotham, another old driver, liked to revive a more painful memory. He had been hit by the Bangalore Mail in 1932. Oddly, he had been stretched out asleep on the main line at the time. 'She saw me and whistled up,' Mr Ramsbotham would say over his evening drink, 'but by then it was too late.' And if you asked these men how they were, they would reply, 'Oh, pulling along, pulling along,' as though they themselves were engines, like those created by the Reverend Awdry.

The women wore frocks and (in the cool season) cardigans and socks. They were kind and lively. 'Have some more plum cake,' said Mrs Rosario. 'Try my guava jelly,' said Mrs Thipthorpe, who in McCluskiegunge was known as Mrs Tip-Top, perhaps because of her home-cooking or perhaps because the name was easier to say. Many of their children had emigrated. Photographs were passed around: Conrad in Romford, Tyrone in Ontario, brown men in white countries trying to adjust to the ignorance of the indigenous population, who thought they were simply immigrant Indians – strange people with strange customs – when in fact they had reached their literal fatherland and could drink and swear (and down plum cake) as well as the next man.

Few people in McCluskiegunge saw their racial origins as problematic or any irony in describing Britain as Home. They seemed easy in themselves. The one exception was Miss Dorothee Bonner, who lived in a bungalow near the level-crossing and had retired from the executive ranks of the Imperial Tobacco Company in Calcutta rather than from some hick railway town. Miss Bonner was grand and fierce, with a face that resembled Somerset Maugham's and a penchant for trousers and secateurs. Her house had the most melodious chiming clocks, her garden some of the finest roses. She presided over the McCluskiegunge burial board – and burying people, her fellow board members agreed, was one of the great concerns of McCluskiegunge. Alone among her fellow Anglo-Indian settlers, she had visited Europe and there, in London and Paris before the War, she had discovered something about herself.

She would think of her roses and say defiantly: 'I am a hybrid, and here among my fellow hybrids is the only place I can feel at home.'

I went back again and again. McCluskiegunge was quaint and nostalgic; some residents even remembered the time when it had been known as Chota (meaning 'little') London. The place's very obscurity gave it a charm. McCluskiegunge appears in no histories of British India and gets only a line in *Murray's Handbook to the Indian Subcontinent*. Outside the settlers and their relations, nobody in India seemed ever to have heard of it. Soon I was suffering symptoms of the traveller's disease, that absurd feeling of ownership which anyone who thinks he has 'discovered' somewhere so easily falls prey to. Then came disenchantment. The more I discovered about McCluskiegunge's history, the less quaint it became. In its origins, if not its present inhabitants, lay the pathetic desperation of a people struggling – and failing – to assert their self-worth.

People of mixed race had changing fortunes in imperial India, fortunes which hung almost totally on the attitudes of the ruling whites. Miscegenation was a fact of life for the early European settlers. Men needed women and the only available women were Indian. Their children were tolerated – the girls even prized as brides to be carried off to England. Then, in the late eighteenth century, an event in a French colony on the other side of the world had repercussions within India which replaced tolerance with fear. The mulatto revolt in Haiti toppled its rulers. The British in India grew alarmed that their own mixed-race population might get the same idea; they were threatening to outnumber the whites, and European genes (so it was thought) might infect them with European notions of political liberty. The government began to treat them as a race apart, to exclude them from jobs, to shun them.

That policy changed, however, in the second half of the nineteenth century. The mutiny in Haiti switched the focus of distrust to Indians at a time when the new technologies of steam and telegraphy needed great numbers of trustworthy workers who could speak and write English and who, as vital cogs in the imperial machinery, would remain unquestioningly obedient to the British flag. It was too expensive to recruit this entire new class of technicians from Britain – though many were recruited, to form the lowest expatriate class in India, 'the domiciled European' – and so Anglo-Indians became a familiar part of the new colonial landscape; sola topis, sagging telegraph wires and rushing trains.

Out of their subordinate role came a culture which defined them as much by class as by race. Every railway town had its Anglo-Indian settlement, and every settlement had its musicians, card games and dances. A lot of tobacco was smoked and grog drunk. It became the conventional picture of Anglo-Indian life: fun-loving and feckless, with a style and language that betrayed its English origins in Indian army cantonments and platelayers' huts, and (further back) in mean northern industrial towns and the impoverished Irish countryside.

But nobody much liked them. The British rewarded their loyalty with a contempt fostered by the new ideology of racial purity, in which the white (particularly Anglo-Saxon) race was peculiarly blessed; to them Anglo-Indians, despite their usefulness, represented no more than the shaming evidence of sexual transgression by the lower ranks, 'a temporary weakness in an unaccustomed climate.' Indians found their pretensions laughable, their bullying offensive, and, Indians being no less conscious of caste and class than the British, their habits and ancestry deeply impure. And so Anglo-Indians found themselves in one corner of a contemptuous triangle, despising and despised.

How could they attain self-respect? The traditional method would not be applauded by modern psychology. It was to deny, or at least to suppress, the maternal, Indian side of their ancestry. Throughout the nineteenth century they had lobbied Indian governments for some form of official name and status which would acknowledge their Britishness, and, in their eyes, progress had been made. 'Half-caste' and 'mixed-blood' were replaced by 'East Indian', which was in turn replaced by 'Indo-Briton' and then 'Eurasian' – an accurate name (many were of Portuguese as well as British ancestry) which Eurasians nonetheless hated and successfully converted into 'Anglo-Indian' around the time of the First World War. The last name had been their great goal for several decades; it was what the British in India called themselves and was therefore the logical conclusion in the process of self-delusion. (But of course, soon after the new kind of Anglo-Indian adopted it, the old kind of Anglo-Indian, judges and generals, dropped it like a hot potato.)

Many Anglo-Indians, the fairer ones, did successfully pass themselves off as 'domiciled Europeans'; census officers in British India reckoned that the number was as high as three out of ten. But it soon became obvious to the leaders of the Anglo-Indian community that this combination of genetic half-truths and semantics was no solution to the problem of identity for most Anglo-Indians. Within Anglo-Indian society it led to a hierarchy and snobbery of colour; even today there are few people who can talk so dispassionately and uninhibitedly about complexion – X has 'a little tint in her', Y is 'swarthy', Z is 'as black as the bottom of a pot'. And contrary to the popular idea that every Anglo-Indian male stood manfully astride a locomotive footplate, large sections of the community lived no better than the poorest Indian slum-dweller, illiterate, unemployed, ill-fed and diseased (in 1920, a survey of Anglo-Indian boys in central Calcutta found that less than half were free from worms).

By the 1920s even the Anglo-Indian elite began to feel insecure; for economic as well as political reasons many jobs which they had regarded as theirs by right were now being opened up to Indians. A sense of crisis developed. Thoughtful Anglo-Indians began to chastise their community's dependence on the British both for their employment and for their insecure self-esteem. A new solution was propounded: race-pride. Anglo-Indians should see themselves as a separate and independent race, proud of their mixed blood. Writers pointed out that racial purity was a chimera and produced lists of great men and women with miscegenation in their ancestry, including whole shoals of people in the Bible and several members of what they always chose to call 'Britain's leading families'.

But if Anglo-Indians were an independent race, might they not also be a nation? And if they were a nation might they not need a homeland? Step forward Mr T. E. McCluskie.

Not much is known about Timothy Ernest McCluskie, other than that he rarely visited McCluskiegunge and certainly never lived there. In his photograph he looks a dandy – bow tie, moustache, rimless spectacles – but the people I met in McCluskiegunge were post-war settlers and had never seen him. Eventually, nine years ago, I traced his eighty-year-old niece, Mrs Gladys Meredith, to her flat in Calcutta. There was a now-familiar motto on the wall: 'I am the boss in this house . . .'

What kind of man had her uncle been? 'Oh,' said Mrs Meredith, 'very jolly and jovial, though he wasn't much of a drinker. A convivial sort of fellow. And very fair-complexioned, Dutch-looking. There was hardly a tint in him.'

His father was an Irish railwayman, a platelayer on the Bengal–Nagpur line, who had adopted and then married a Brahmin outcast girl from Benares. The couple moved to Calcutta, where the platelayer died of grog and his wife, so Mrs Meredith remembered, grew into an old Indian lady who chewed cheroots. But their son did well, first in insurance and then as a small-time share and property dealer. He was generous. His niece recalled how he would hire a paddle steamer and take parties down the Hooghly to shoot tiger and crocodile. In his house in Calcutta there were preserved in a frame on the wall the contents of one crocodile's stomach: anklets, bangles, beads and human teeth. His wife, a Portuguese woman much older than himself, played the organ in Calcutta's Anglican cathedral.

In this way he became a luminary of Anglo-Indian society, a member of Bengal's Legislative Council, and a friend of the most powerful politician and lobbyist the Anglo-Indian community ever produced, Sir Henry Gidney.

Gidney was a military surgeon, another son of an Irish railwayman and another dandy. With spats and a monocle and an orchid in his buttonhole, he would take to the dance floors of Indian clubs and hotels and there present his audience with what his biographer described as 'a fascinating exhibition of the Argentinian tango'. Womanising made him notorious – there were jokes about his ever-changing series of companions, always described by Gidney as 'my nursing sister' – but, as Gidney was fond of pointing out, 'God never intended one's wedding bells to be one's funeral bells.'

Like McCluskie, he was also a big-game hunter, with a Calcutta flat bristling with tigers' heads. Together these two men, with their possibly over-romantic view of the open-air life, arrived at the idea that the best way to save their community was to convert engine drivers and ticket clerks into a hardy race of pioneer farmers.

Gidney's first scheme ended in disaster. In the early 1920s he proposed that the Indian government should subsidise a mass exodus of Anglo-Indians to the Andaman and Nicobar islands, in the tropics of the Bay of Bengal, which they would colonise as coconut growers under the protection – the natives were reported to be fierce – of a conscripted Anglo-Indian army and navy. Doubters pointed out that since the fourteenth century malaria had killed off almost every attempt at settlement; just to make the islands reasonably healthy by draining the swamps would cost several million pounds. But Gidney put his faith in the coconut crop. Lord Leverhulme, the Lancashire soap king (and always something of a sucker for uplifting schemes in unlikely places), had promised he would take every bucket of coconut oil the Andamans and Nicobars could produce; and that, Gidney estimated, would yield £4 million a year.

A committee was formed and in 1923 twelve Anglo-Indian ex-servicemen sailed from Calcutta as the colonisers' advance party. Three of them soon died on the islands, and the others returned after a year. For Gidney's critics it simply confirmed an old racial prejudice; crudely, that Anglo-Indians were a useless bunch of dreamers who lacked stamina and organisation.

Other, more realistic schemes of migration were proposed – to British Guiana, to British East Africa, to New Zealand (thought, alone in the white empire, to be free of racial prejudice). But Gidney persisted with his vision of a separate Indian homeland. In London in 1931, as the Anglo-Indian representative at the Round Table Conference called to discuss the political future of India, he urged that the community be given 200,000 acres; an area slightly larger than the Isle of Wight, and one acre, more or less, for every Anglo-Indian in the census.

The government rejected this demand, but McCluskie in the mean-time had found a site. After thirty months spent prospecting throughout India for land that offered what he called 'the Three Rs' – Road, River, Railway – he had persuaded a rajah in Chota Nagpur to lease him 10,000 acres near a station then called Lapra on the newly built loop line from Barkakana. Gidney ridiculed the idea – Lapra seemed to him remote and barren – and the two men fell out. McCluskie persevered on his own and formed a co-operative society, the Colonisation Society of India Limited, through which Anglo-Indians could buy plots at Lapra and set themselves up as smallholders. He wrote in the prospectus: 'I present a complete scheme to my people . . . where they may make a home and grow into a nation by unity and co-operation'.

Sitting at his desk in Calcutta, McCluskie presented Lapra as a kind of Eden. The climate was excellent ('with breezes reminiscent of

Darjeeling'), the land fertile. Almost anything could be grown or reared: fruit, tea, vegetables, cattle, sheep, pigs, goats and poultry. Nor was remoteness a problem: the loop line down which coal trains trundled from the Bihar coalfield would soon be converted into a new trunk route between Calcutta and Bombay. And the site offered scope for almost limitless expansion; another 200,000 acres were available for settlement, if and when the society wanted them. Anglo-Indians were told that this was 'the most historical move of the community, fighting for its very existence and solving its own salvation in its darkest hour'. Success would bring 'the respect and admiration of the world'. Apathy and failure would mean 'contempt and ridicule'.

The response was heartening. Anglo-Indians across the subcontinent bought shares. The society's monthly magazine, the *Colonisation Observer*, printed lists of shareholders, and there was hardly a railway town between Baluchistan and Burma without at least one inhabitant who had invested his savings. Soon the *Colonisation Observer* was publishing photographs of colonisers in the act of colonising. Men in sola topis and baggy shorts posed outside tents or half-finished bungalows, sometimes resting on their axes. Such scenes (the captions implied) gave the lie to the racial stereotype of enfeebled dependence on the white boss class. A verse from Longfellow was quoted:

> In the world's broad fields of battle,
>   In the bivouac of life,
> Be not dumb, like driven cattle!
>   Be a hero in the strife!

For the foundation ceremony on 3 November 1934, the settlers erected a triumphal arch of homegrown vegetables. A crowd of 300 watched as a memorial fountain was unveiled, and then sat down on benches to eat salmon mayonnaise. Speeches by Anglo-Indian notables made the usual exhortations. Anglo-Indians should give up smoking and drinking; clean-living, thrift, education – these were the watchwords. They should breed dogs and rear cattle. They should 'try to meet a large part of India's needs of ham, bacon, chilled turkey and pickles'. This was their big chance. As the Reverend P. E. Curtis wrote in a letter read to the assembly: 'The Jews rejected both their leader and his message and they are still a wandering, homeless nation, scattered, persecuted and reviled. Shall we not take a lesson out of their book of history? Shall we not make every endeavour to prevent such a fate befalling us by the rejection of our leader and his message?'

The crowd apparently took this to heart and by popular vote decided that from that day on Lapra would be known as McCluskiegunge, in honour of 'our noble founder – Old Mac'. Whether Old Mac was there to hear this tribute is unclear; the ambiguity of the *Colonisation Observer*'s report suggests that he was not, that he was relaxing in his Calcutta flat with a whisky and soda. He died there the following year.

McCluskiegunge as an ideal survived its founder's death. Sir Henry Gidney took over the role of the colony's father figure; the settlers even planned to tempt him to come and live among them by building him a house, Gidney Castle, in a section of the colony to be known as Gidneytown. Sir Henry wasn't tempted, though by 1936 almost 400 of his followers had bought land. A school, a bank and a clubhouse opened. A Roman Catholic and an Anglican church were built. A dentist, a doctor and a baker arrived. A cannery began to produce tinned fruit. To read the *Colonisation Observer* for those years is to see a heartbreaking portrait of people who thought they had given history the slip. People might say that Anglo-Indians would never take to pioneering conditions, wrote an editorial, 'but we know better'.

Not for long, however. Certain basic drawbacks of McCluskiegunge began to take their toll. The place lacked water, but paradoxically had plenty of black-water fever; the loop line never carried the promised Bombay expresses; farmers faced difficulties both in growing and marketing their crops. And then there came the familiar note of self-doubt and racial despair. History had not been shaken off, after all. There was something wrong, the *Colonisation Observer* decided, with 'the mentality of the settlers'.

What the magazine meant by 'mentality' was demonstrated by the complaints and dissension in its own letter columns. Racial antagonism broke out against so-called 'pseudo Anglo-Indians' – Goans and South Indian Christians – who had been allowed to buy land ('Let this evil be stamped out by insisting on proofs of European parentage on the father's side'). Anglo-Indians might be trying to think themselves into a new role as an Indian people or tribe, but evidently paternity (no matter how distant or humble) remained the sole criteria for membership. In the *Colonisation Observer*'s etiquette column, Mr Query asked if it was proper to eat a sandwich with one's fingers. And Professor Owl replied: 'Yes, if you can do so gracefully; if not, use a fork.' Those were the benefits of Europe, the small things that might set McCluskiegunge's pioneers apart from – and above – a population which could scoop entire meals with the skilful use of its right hand.

By 1940 the game was up. No more than a fifth of the society's share capital of 500,000 rupees had been subscribed; only 6,800 acres of land had been sold; there were only about a hundred settler families left. The great majority of India's Anglo-Indian workers had clung, perhaps wisely, to their jobs in railway yards and footplates and telegraph offices, and of the few who had answered McCluskie's call many were sucked back into Calcutta by wartime wages. The *Colonisation Observer* published its last issue in 1942 and by the end of the war the cannery and shops had closed. The Colonisation Society itself persisted and even tried to liberalise itself by removing, at Indian Independence, passages in its charter which were offensive to Indians. But it too collapsed, after a bitter Anglo-Indian wrangle, in 1955.

McCluskiegunge became a place to which people retired – Mr King, Mr Ramsbotham, Miss Potter, Mrs Tip-Top – and then died. When I first went there, in 1978, only a couple of dozen Anglo-Indian families survived. That year, for the first time, the Indian priest at the Anglican church had conducted the Christmas service entirely in Hindi, not a word of English spoken. That was reasonable; the congregation now contained far more Christian tribals than Anglo-Indians. But, of course, there were complaints to the bishop.

McCluskiegunge is a chastening place to think about race. A separate racial identity did not seem to have been the solution for Anglo-Indians, but then what was? Perhaps, as a group, there was none. After the British quit the Indian subcontinent, many of them emigrated and many of those who remained simply became, as individuals, one more kind of many kinds of Indian. And yet the feeling of superiority hardly died away. It remained a defence; to lose it was to lose Europe and get lost among the mass. You let your side down. This had happened to some people in McCluskiegunge. There was the perpetual drunk who lived in a tin hut behind the Roman Catholic chapel. And then there was Kitty Texeira.

I first heard about Kitty from Mrs Tip-Top. 'She's a good-looking girl is Kitty but terribly wild. She goes to the station and sells produce. It's sad. She got mixed up with some tribal fellows and now she walks about barefoot and all, and only speaks to her mother in Hindi.'

Mrs Tip-Top was right. When I saw Kitty at the station she did indeed look pretty and wild, with her loose hair and bare feet, like a browner version of one of Russell Flint's dancing gypsies. She hawked little oranges to passengers who passed money out through the bars on the carriage windows, and then, in the long gaps between trains, helped some tribal men to brew country liquor in a drum at the foot of the signal post. She and her mother lived in a bungalow called Woodlands high up on a tree-covered hill to the south of the station. There was no road to the house and the trees completely obscured it; even old McCluskiegunge hands tended to forget it was there.

On the final day of my last visit I decided to walk up this hill. I took the path east from the station, past the pink spoil-heaps of loco-motive cinders, and then followed it south up a sloping field of red earth until I reached an unkempt orchard of lime, guava and mango trees. This was Mrs Texeira's land and in the middle of it stood the ruin of her bungalow, Woodlands. There was only a little glass in the windows and the holes in the asbestos roof had been stuffed with rags. Kitty's mother, Marjory, took me into the parlour, where goats were nuzzling some old wicker chairs and the floor was strewn with leaves. A Winchester shotgun lay upright in one corner.

'Mine,' said Mrs Texeira. 'You need it in these parts.'

She was old, poor and under-nourished, as tattered as her bungalow. She wore a ragged blue cardigan and white crêpe stockings on her stick-like legs. At first she seemed half-mad with bitterness and despair. The tribals had put a spell on her daughter; the Bengalis who wanted to buy her land were cheats. It was providence that I had come, she said, because I could answer two questions. Was the river Euphrates really drying up? And when was Halley's Comet next expected? I said I didn't know (though apparently, thanks to dams, the Euphrates isn't the river it used to be).

'Revelations,' she said, 'it's in the Book of Revelations.' She was waiting for the end of the world.

We talked for an hour or two and Mrs Texeira sucked on her *biris*, her cheap Indian cigarettes, and grew calmer. She was pleased by my interest in her ornaments. There were still a few pictures and books. On the wall hung a tinted photograph of a couple in smart European clothes holding a baby – the woman with bobbed hair and a neat white blouse, the man in a blazer and white flannels. That was Mr and Mrs Texeira and the infant Kitty. On a shelf stood copies of *Little Women* and *What Katy Did*, crisp with age and white-ant holes.

Mrs Texeira saw me looking at them and quoted from *As You Like It*:

> And so, from hour to hour
> we ripe and ripe,
> And then from hour to hour
> we rot and rot,
> And thereby hangs a tale.

Mrs Texeira's tale was this. She was born Marjory Roberts in 1912 in a hill-station, Shillong, and baptised in the Welsh Presbyterian Chapel in the Assamese town of Gauhati. Her grandfather, a Welshman, had served in the East India Regiment. (She had preserved his discharge papers; he was the only link to that other civilisation which murmured from her walls.) During the war, she had worked as a nurse in a military hospital and there had met her husband, who as the son of one of McCluskie's pioneers had brought her to this lonely house on the hill. Here Kitty had been born and her husband had died – buried, so Mrs Texeira said, without much regret. She sucked on her *biri*. 'The marriage was a misalliance. My husband was a waster.'

But by now in her conversation she was almost cheerful. The undertow of her every sentence said: my birthplace is an accident, the world to which I properly belong lies elsewhere. She recited the names of cheeses – Camembert, Roquefort, Edam, Caerphilly. She spoke lovingly of kippers and lemon sole. And once, hearing I was from Scotland, burst into 'Ye Banks and Braes'.

We walked together through the trees and I shook her hand on the edge of the mango grove. 'It's been so nice to meet you,' she said, 'so nice to talk to my own kind for a change.'

Down at the station I saw Kitty again. 'My daughter,' Mrs Texeira had said with a shake of the head, 'is a perfect little tribal.' Now she was preparing a basket of oranges for the evening train and joking in Hindi with the brewers of country liquor. She seemed to have made her peace – perhaps not with India, which is too large and complicated an idea, but at least with that small part of it where she was born.

Dentists

November 2005

My mother had all her teeth removed at the age of twenty-three, my mother-in-law at thirty-five, my father before he was fifty. Long afterwards, when asked why – *why on earth! how come?* – they would say, 'Oh, I just thought it was better to get it all over with' or 'It saved a lot of trouble later on.'

I remember the night my father had his done. A basin of water was placed at his feet before the fire in the living room and he spat and spat, filling the basin with unfurling red trails, Lady Macbeth at work, making the clear water incarnadine. I thought at the time it was like the advertisement for Rowntree's Fruit Gums, which depicted a similar basin filled with a similar red sea – this one dotted with pineapples, lemons, oranges, blackcurrants and tipping into a roll of sweets, the liquid actually becoming the sweets as it streamed so wholesomely into the packet, as if the chief constituent of a Rowntree's gum was the freshest juice from the ripest fruit rather than sugar plus flavouring: the enemy of teeth. The word 'gums' may have helped suggest this image, now I come to think of it again. Anyway, it was the callous thought of a six-year-old who had no idea how vulnerable and undignified his father felt with all his teeth gone and a future of Steradent awaiting him: the bedside glass, the goodnight plop, the tiny bubbles clinging to the submarine grin.

'Gas,' he said. 'I had gas tonight. It makes you laugh.' Soon after, I had gas too and discovered there was nothing to laugh at. 'You have to put this in your mouth,' the dentist said. 'It's like a little doggy's bone.'

It was a metal device which jammed your mouth open when you were unconscious, after the mask was placed on your face and the dentist began his count to ten. The mention of 'little doggy' did very little to counter the terror of it. At another surgery, where the dentist had given up gas in favour of the cocaine syringe, I was told that my baby teeth being yanked out would make a sharp little crack 'like a toy gun makes when you shoot a toy rabbit'. Could the dentist really have said that? I believe he did. Doggies, bunnies: they were meant as relaxants, but even if the surgery had contained a death-camp orchestra playing 'The Teddy Bears' Picnic' my eyes and mind wouldn't have strayed from the steaming antiseptic box that contained the pliers.

With second teeth dawned the age of fillings. Here again the dentist tried to help. 'Look, it's like a Meccano crane,' he said, swivelling and lowering the silver drill towards a wide-open mouth, which wanted to speak and deny the likeness, Meccano being green and red. This dentist, Mr Macdonald, was perhaps then the grandest man I had ever met, with a Jaguar and a big Victorian house and a new phrase, 'Excuse my French', which he used after he said 'bloody' or 'damn' when there was some mix-up with his instruments. I went there after school and usually in winter, so that in my mind's eye I am always staring out of his big bay window into a Scottish dusk, watching fresh child victims being delivered up the garden path by their mothers in scarves and hats. When Mr Macdonald pushed back the drill with a finality that suggested he was not merely replacing one drill-bit with another, a faster for a slower whine, there came a sweet, slapping noise as he mixed the filling – a sound that said there would be no more pain today, which remains for me the best of sounds.

Archaeologists and forensic scientists rely a great deal on teeth, and sometimes I think of my life as being marked out by their slow elimination, just as Giorgio Pressburger uses them in his lovely novel *Teeth and Spies*, with its chapters headed by dental notation, UR5, LR6, etc. I had buck teeth as a child. They were my playground nickname and a misery to me, and then, thanks to Mr Macdonald, I got an appointment at the Edinburgh Dental Hospital, where I met an orthodontic consultant in a bow tie (another first) who gave me a pink plate to wear at night, which I did for many years. At bedtime I would put mine in as my parents took theirs out; a day- and night-shift dental system, you might say, though I think we didn't share the same containers.

Teeth came to means treats. Every visit to the dental hospital meant a visit to the Royal Scottish Museum, just across the road, where a great whale skeleton hung from the roof and you could press buttons to set models of coal mines and locomotives in motion. When I had to go to another hospital to have an impacted molar extracted, there was the familiar lie ('We're taking you to the theatre – cowboys and Indians films') and then, when I packed my pyjamas and left my bed, another treat in the shape of a visit to an unknown town (Bathgate) where my mother indulged a visit to the railway station.

Then for several decades teeth meant nothing, their presence taken for granted, the occasional pain rectified by cheap but apparently able dentists in Glasgow, Hackney and New Delhi. 'I think this one will have to come out', but who cared really given that there seemed so many?

Now I go to a dentist in Hampstead, whom I see as the important curator of the teeth that remain. I lie on my back and look up at his painted ceiling, a blue sky with fluffy clouds and a cherub peering from behind the cornice, the equivalent of the bunny-and-dog talk of old. Music plays, most of it sounding like 'The Girl from Ipanema', as my dentist tells me about implants and root-canal work and the need to establish a 'chewing platform'. He is an excellent dentist, though not cheap, but I would say he was good even if he were otherwise, because I see him a lot, he may read this, and which of us doesn't remember the scene with Laurence Olivier in *Marathon Man*?

Recently we were talking of his Balkan ancestry and the many bad Balkan episodes in the Second World War. 'Scratch many of us and you might find an SS man underneath,' he said, before asking me to open a little wider and ordering me to relax.

Girls and Dolphins

December 2005

As a Christmas present in 1955, my father gave me a handsome book called *The Birds of Britain* which had colour paintings of each species pasted on the recto pages and cost forty-two shillings, a lot of money at the time. I knew a little bit about birds, could tell (thanks to my father) a chaffinch from a robin and recognise the cries of the peewit and the curlew, and sometimes joined raiding parties for eggs. The book promised to teach me so much more, but did I want to know? I wasn't really all that interested in birds. I recognised that my father wanted to interest me in something that interested him and that he saw, wrongly, nascent in me. That night I took *The Birds of Britain* to bed and cried over it, blubbing to my mother that it was such a lovely and expensive book but I couldn't live up to it. I think I wasn't crying over my own disappointment but my father's, because even then I could see that he meant well. A boy who could thrill to the sight of a skylark or a sparrowhawk might be a better kind of boy, a better companion to his father, than one lost in a world of mechanical objects: trains, ships, fighter planes, guns.

It is very hard to direct children in their likes and interests and one might as well give up. To try to fan a spark of interest into a flame of enthusiasm is often a mistake. Their passions are self-directed and seem to the parental eye to come out of nowhere. I don't mean the obvious consumables – iPods, Playstations, the music of Green Day or the Arctic Monkeys – but the cults that can't be easily explained by marketing money or peer pressure. For example, why do girls like dolphins?

My daughter, aged thirteen, has loved dolphins for several years. Her bedroom wall is covered with pictures of dolphins. She has books about dolphins and models of dolphins. Together with 77,000 other people, most or many of them girls, she belongs to the Whale and Dolphin Conservation Society and pays £3 a month to 'adopt a dolphin'. Has she ever seen a dolphin in the flesh? No, they are difficult to see. Does she intend to see one? Yes, certainly. Many hours have been spent on ferries and small boats in the Hebrides peering across the waves for the sight of a dorsal fin, to be followed (she hopes) by the leaping body of a mammal and its smily mouth. So far, nothing other than seals and harbour porpoises, though she did see a minke whale near Coll and was unlucky to miss a pod of killer whales (misleadingly named – they belong to the dolphin family) that had been spotted earlier by our skipper off the west coast of Lewis. Like amateur harpoonists, we spent an hour circling in a grey and swollen sea, the rain coming on, our eyes mistaking curling waves for fins.

As an enthusiasm, this may be smaller than the girlish one for ponies, but considering the accessibility of the pony over the dolphin, and the fact that you can stroke a pony and ride on one (a feat not performed with the dolphin outside Greek legend and Hollywood), it is still remarkably large. There's profit in it. At the Homebase stores, you can buy dolphin quilt covers, dolphin shower curtains, dolphin wallpaper, dolphin lavatory seats. In summer, many boats cruise the coasts of the West Country, Wales and Scotland filled with young dolphin-spotters. The Moray Firth is said to be especially dolphin-rich, the location of the adopted dolphins that are identified by their fin markings and given numbers and sometimes names ('Nevis', 'Lightning'). The Moray Firth, to my mind a chilly place, is of course where my daughter wants to spend next summer.

If you ask a dolphin-girl about the peculiar attraction of creatures which take so much trouble to see, and, if seen, then only for a few seconds, she will list their intelligence, the humorous shape of their mouths, their liking for each other's company, their acts of kindness to human beings that include rescue from sharks and shipwrecks. All of this is ancient lore, best told in the story of Arion, the finest lyre player of his day (*c.*600 BC), who was returning to Greece from a musical tour of Italy when he was forced overboard by his ship's treacherous and thieving crew. A dolphin, attracted by Arion's singularly high-pitched singing, befriended him and carried him to shore complete with lyre, thereby demonstrating (according to Carlos Parada, a writer on Greek mythology) that 'to this clever animal alone nature has granted what many philosophers seek, namely friendship to no advantage; for the dolphin has no need at all of men, and yet it is their genial friend'.

Children's films such as *Flipper* and *Free Willy* carry a more cloying version of the same message, and it was surprising to me that no dolphins made their way into *Finding Nemo*, which did a lot for sales of tropical fish and nothing at all for Homebase's lavatory seats. But why their attraction to girls in particular? I speculate: because at a certain age, or perhaps at all ages, they have a keener sense of friendship, and friendship to no advantage; and also because the beauty and mystery of living things interests them more.

I don't know about the last thought. Son and daughter both have it – it's one of the most striking and heartening differences between the children of my generation and theirs. Nature seemed to me unremarkable compared to the delight of *man-made* objects, the gendered phrase: the different turning circles of a Spitfire and a Hawker Hunter or the sight of the Aberdeen Express. Mother Nature, gender again, was only a setting; it would always be there. Thanks to television documentaries and teaching in schools, children now treasure it more, aware of its fragility and of our role as custodians. In that way, my own would be better companions for their grandfather.

Chavs

January 2006

Once again the government has declared war on yobs. The word 'yob' is Victorian back-slang: boy, lout, hooligan. According to the Shorter Oxford its first recorded use came in 1859, though I don't think I heard it until the 1970s, perhaps because in the first post-war decades there were so few people to be identified as such. The word 'chav' has more mysterious origins. It may have a gypsy ancestry – 'chavi' is the Romany word for child – and therefore be a slang description of gypsies. Or it may come from Chatham, where it's said it first described young Chathamites. Or its roots may be some mixture of both.

'Chav' seems to me a less pejorative word than 'yob', but pupils at my children's school think it's an acronym for 'Council House and Violent'. When I heard this piece of playground semantics I didn't know how to react. I could, on the one hand, deliver my son a lecture on social prejudice and snobbery and the uplifting role of public housing in British history, including its part in his parents' and grandparents' lives as well as those of some of his friends. On the other, I could let it go as a piece of schoolboy banter. I decided that was wiser. My daughter, after all, had been given as a Christmas present something called *The Little Book of Chavs* (100,000 copies sold) and I'd raised no objection to its cod anthropology. 'Chavs are identifiable by their attitude (anti anything to do with authority, art, culture or the good of society) and clothes . . . Jodie Marsh and Jordan are chav icons . . . Reality shows, like *Big Brother*, are favourite chav TV programmes . . . the *Sun*, *Daily Star* and *Sport* (or the *Daily Mail* for the more cultured person) are about the only things chavs even consider reading.' We are all Nancy Mitfords now, when we are not being Richard Hoggarts.

How did it start, this superficial deconstruction of society? I suppose with the idea that consumption is the most significant badge of human identity. Advertising demographics had something to do with it. Thirty years ago Peter York co-authored the *Sloane Rangers Handbook*, which may be the first in the field, and York is an advertising man. To mock upwards – at classes above you – was publicly allowable then, as it had always been. To mock downwards, at least in the post-war era, only began to happen in the 1980s. Harry Enfield, impeccably middle-class and southern, created a funny Geordie character who smoked 'forty tabs a day'. Around the same time London football fans waved ten-pound notes at supporters of northern teams and chanted 'You're all unemployed.' You might argue that these developments were symptoms of the crumbling of an old monolith, the working class, and the exit of a form of politeness or even political correctness. You might also argue that amusing condescension to its sometimes dangerous remnants, the yobs and chavs, is a way of masking fear.

My first council estate, the one I was born into, had very little fear in it. If an emotion could be attached to the houses it might have been optimism. The streets had the names of flowers: Iris, Begonia, Orchid. We lived on the corner of Lily and Lupin after my parents switched from Iris; their first house with a bathroom. As a small boy I was hardly equipped to recognise social difference – all adults seemed pretty much the same – but a family at the top of the street stood out because they were scruffier than the rest, with children who had dripping noses and wore clogs (this was Lancashire in 1950) and no socks. This led to pity rather than fear: 'Them poor Ramsdens.' What fear there was sprang from Pansy Road, where the houses were bigger and meant for large families: a sign of fecklessness and domestic misrule: 'You want to watch out for those Pansy Roaders.' I walked past it quickly on the way home from school.

I left the estate when I was seven and went back to walk around it more than fifty years later. Many of the front-garden fences had vanished, the gardens untended and trampled, the front doors scratched. A man said the place was full of drugs. Theft was a problem. Few people were to be seen on the streets. The corner shops had closed – and of course the mills too. None of this should have come as a shock, and yet it was.

Pansy Road looked neither worse nor better than the rest – odd to remember that a few boisterous lads were once imagined as the worst the world had to offer. I left rejoicing that I didn't live there.

Tony Blair mentioned this kind of doleful transformation in his recent speech outlining the government's plans for 'the eradication of anti-social behaviour', a speech that was better than he was generally given credit for. He was careful not to sentimentalise the 1950s – 'Try telling ethnic minorities that there was more respect fifty years ago' – while pushing the hardly challengeable idea that 'the self-reinforcing bonds of traditional community life do not exist in the same way' and that it was time to consider changes in the law which would 'restore the liberty of the law-abiding citizen'. Whether such changes will have any effect is a different question; increasingly, politicians seem small and frightened people, whistling in the dark. But it was absurd of David Cameron to chide Blair for his 'pessimistic view of human nature', which is one of the cornerstones of Conservative philosophy and a hard view to deny if you have in your hand *The Little Book of Chavs*.

Some sweet little corners of optimism remain. Catching my number 19 bus home last week I found that I'd only a ten-pound note and the driver had no change. He let me on, and I tried him again before I got off. Still no change. Instead he handed me a printed slip which said it entitled me to complete my present journey without having paid a fare 'on the strict understanding that you will pay the fare due immediately to the address shown below'. I liked 'the strict understanding' – a concrete example of the old social contract. All across London, people (yobs, chavs and otherwise) charge on to the new multi-doored 'bendy buses' and never dream of paying a fare. I estimate that on the numbers 73 and 38 three-quarters of passengers travel free. Nonetheless, I shall send off £1.50 to Transport for London, perhaps by postal order, in memory of how things once were and (one can never tell) might be again.

A Seaborne Disease

April 1998

The people of Sri Lanka (or Ceylon as it was then known) first saw the power of steam in ships, and then the railways came. Much later, in 1981, I met a madman on the platform of Colombo railway station, the narrow-gauge side. The Tamil war on the island was just beginning. I was working for a Sunday newspaper in London at the time and had filed my copy for the week. Now, on a Sunday afternoon, I could relax. I decided to take a look at the little branch line, rumoured to be still worked by steam locomotives, which runs up from the capital to the town of Ratnapura and the tea and rubber estates in the foothills. That was how I met Mr Goonawardene.

No trains were expected. The station was deserted. He must have been watching me for some time from his position behind the pillar. He may even have seen in my behaviour a kindred spirit; the way, for example, I walked up and down the platform peering over the edge for telltale signs of locomotive cinders on the tracks – what could that be but derangement? His approach was startlingly direct.

'Sir, sir, allow me to introduce myself. My name is Goonawardene and I am a racialist.' He was a thin man in grubby white clothes and black lacing shoes which lacked shoelaces. He wanted to tell me his theory of the world, how it had developed and where it had gone wrong.

The guilty party, he said, was Western science. Out of science had come industry and medicine. The industrial countries of the West had enormous appetites for raw materials – cotton, tea, sugar, rubber, oil

– and to feed these appetites they had behaved like capricious gods, plucking people from one country and dumping them in another without a thought for tomorrow. Think of it! Africans dispatched by sea to the Caribbean to cut sugar; Indians exported by sea to Africa to build railways; and here, in Sri Lanka, Tamils shipped by ferry from India to pick tea. Then Western medicine had come along with its bag of tricks and permitted all these black and brown people to multiply; 'to breed like microbes', was how Mr Goonawardene put it.

He shaped a globe with his hands and waggled his fingers to show it pulsating. I imagined a round Dutch cheese alive with grubs. 'A mess, a most terrible mess. Blacks, whites, browns, yellows, all mixed up. They must be sent back to where they came from and then we shall have some peace.' His fingers stopped moving. The globe was now calm and orderly. 'That is why I call myself a racialist.'

I was anxious to get away. 'Well,' I said, 'no trains to Ratnapura today. I should be getting back to the hotel.'

But it was not so easy. 'No, no, train is coming soon. A little train, lots of smoke. You'll like it.' He dusted a station bench with his sleeve. 'Sit, please, sir, sit.'

We sat. Mr Goonawardene leaned forward, as though he had noticed me for the first time as a person as well as an audience. 'Which is your country?'

'Britain.'

He broke into a broad smile. 'Ah, then you are the guilty-party-in-chief. Step forward into the dock. I shall be the prosecutor. Now tell me, Mr Britisher, who perfected the steam engine?'

'James Watt.'

'Correct. A Scotchman, born I believe in the seaport of Greenock. A great man. It may be that he and Isaac Newton are the only two British scientists of what we may call world class, at least until the atomic age. Now give me the place and date of the first railway in the world.'

'Stockton and Darlington. Was it in 1825?'

'Very correct. George Stephenson was the engineer. Imagine! A boy who worked at a coal mine, who could neither read nor write by the age of eighteen, and yet he built the world's first really successful steam locomotives. But I can see you know everything; your knowledge is A1.'

We sat together like a schoolmaster and his prize pupil. Then

Mr Goonawardene winked and became playful. Could I tell him who had perfected the internal-combustion engine? I fumbled; not Henry Ford?

'No, no. Herr Rudolph Diesel, 1897. And Diesel was a native of which country?'

I guessed Germany and Mr Goonawardene said that was right, though in fact Herr Diesel had been born in Paris. The inventor died in mysterious circumstances, vanishing from the deck of a cross-Channel steamer in the year before the outbreak of the First World War. Mr Goonawardene suspected suicide. 'Like many great men he may have suffered mania and depression. I am also suffering from the same condition and I have been tempted by the same fate. But do you see what I am trying to tell you?' His arms went out to make a see-saw. 'Britishers invent the steam engine. Britain goes up. Germans invent the petrol engine. Germans and their cousins the Americans go up. Britain comes down.' These days, he said, only backwards places such as Colombo ever saw a steam locomotive and even here they were rare.

The afternoon wore on. It was a grey day in the tropics. A curtain of rain swept in from the Indian Ocean and hammered on the station roof. Mr Goonawardene began to shiver.

'When is the train coming, Mr Goonawardene?'

'Soon, soon.'

A lie; but he couldn't let me go, our quiz was too delightful a conversational form. What tune had the band played when the *Titanic* went down? Who was the most powerful man in Stalinist Russia? ('Stalin?' Tsk, tsk! 'Beria, the head of the secret police?' Tsk, tsk again. No, it was Maxim Litvinov, the Soviet ambassador in London and Washington, though I can't now remember why.) And then he named three prominent Britons: a journalist, a peer and a politician. Did I know these people? I said I knew of them. Then would I write to them on his behalf?

'I want them to set up a commission of inquiry, to come to Colombo and establish my sanity.' For the past twenty years he had lived in the Angoda lunatic asylum – it was, he said, 'a fine three-storey building of the British period' – but he had never believed, because he knew so much, that he could really be insane. 'And you must admit,' he said finally, 'that I am knowing a pretty damn lot, isn't it?'

No train ever came, at least on the narrow-gauge side. My companion went home to his asylum and I returned to my room overlooking the ocean at the Galle Face Hotel. There were ships on the horizon, their shapes occasionally blurred by the rain which came and went in squalls and dark patches which moved across the sea. They were square shapes. I imagined a flat hull loaded with containers and not the raked funnels and curving sterns of my childhood. That night, remembering Mr Goonawardene and the ships, I wrote to my father, who was dying.

It was not a good letter. Nobody had told my father he hadn't long to live, though perhaps in his conscious moments he understood this well enough. My letter was part of a cheerful pretence. I knew that more than fifty years before he had sailed into Colombo as a junior engineer on a cargo steamer, the SS *Nuddea*, and so I described Colombo: how a lighthouse still stood in the main street, how the tea now went by containers, how some people still remembered the British India Steam Navigation Company, the line which had owned the *Nuddea*, though the puritanical black-and-white funnels of its ships no longer popped up above the dock's high walls. In my father's time it had been one of the biggest shipping companies in the world. I made a few jokes – cheerfulness, that was the thing – and hoped that he was feeling better.

He died a couple of months later. For most of his life he had worked as a steam mechanic, a fitter, one of the men who were on the down-swinging end of Mr Goonawardene's see-saw. One of Watt's children; I had never heard him mention Herr Diesel, though the German had perfected his engine five years before my father was born. The saddest change in him, my mother said, was the way that, long before the end, he had completely lost interest in the world. He had read a few sentences of my letter from Colombo and then lain it down on the bedspread and said nothing. 'And you know what your father was like,' my mother said, 'he was always so interested in things.' I remembered a saying of his, spoken from the heart of a man who had grown up among the gossip of a small Scottish town: 'Stupid folk talk about other folk. Intelligent folk talk about things.'

Five years later I came back to Sri Lanka. The Tamil war was now in full swing. Tamil guerrillas had beaten back the Sri Lankan army in the north of the island. Troops were regularly ambushed or blown up by landmines, and the Sinhalese in the south were frightened and angry. Bombs went off in Colombo, while in the countryside entire villages were rounded up and massacred, Sinhalese by the Tamils and Tamils by the Sinhalese. Tourists and businessmen no longer came. Colombo's hotels were empty. At the Galle Face they said I could have any room – even the Royal Scandinavian Suite – for less than half the listed price.

Mr Goonawardene's diagnosis looked in the case of his own country to have been right. Ethnic differences within the same nation had exploded into savagery (though science and the West could hardly be blamed; Sri Lanka's Tamil separatists were not those Tamils imported from India by the British to pick tea; they had arrived long before European colonisation.) But where was Mr Goonawardene? Now, on another Sunday with another newspaper story safely filed, I went down to the railway station again. Nobody in the stationmaster's office had seen him. What kind of man was I looking for?

'Thin and old,' I said, 'and slightly mad, but he knows a lot. He said he came here often in the afternoons – the platforms on the narrow-gauge side.'

'We have seen no such person.'

Sitting alone in the wide open spaces of the Royal Scandinavian Suite and listening to the sea, I began to think I'd made him up. The next day, I asked at the British Council library. The women behind the counter said she thought she knew who I meant. He had died a year back. 'He came here every morning to read the *Encyclopaedia Britannica* and the London newspapers. He wrote a lot in his notebook. He was interested in everything, all kinds of facts.'

That was all she remembered: Mr Goonawardene as a heap of facts who was locked up every night in the Angoda asylum. He had left no other trace of personality. An old version of Europe – the Europe of Watt and the British India Steam Navigation Company, the Europe of curiosity and enquiry – had sailed to Sri Lanka and planted seeds in him. And the seeds had sprouted to cover his personality like bindweed. His was a seaborne disease.

Addicted

February 2006

Fourteen years before Peter Pan first trod the boards, his author published a novel. *My Lady Nicotine* isn't much of a novel – its origins as a series of essays for the *St James's Gazette* are only too clear – but it may be the only work of literature to take giving up smoking as its central theme. J. M. Barrie wrote it in his late twenties, when his career was taking off largely thanks to the intervention of the *Gazette*'s editor, Frederick Greenwood, who steered his writing towards the folksy Scotchness that would make his name; and later break it, especially in Scotland. Barrie had been trying to make his living as a man of letters for several years (a book about early English satirical verse was one of his failed projects) when he hit on the idea of turning some of his beloved mother's early Victorian memories of Kirriemuir into a piece and posting it south. There had been many rejections of other pieces, but Greenwood wrote, 'I liked that Scotch thing. Any more of those?'

My Lady Nicotine was published six years later, in 1890. It isn't particularly Scotch – no more Scotch than Peter Pan. Barrie by now was living in London and no longer an anonymous magazine contributor trudging Grub Street. He went for drinks to the Garrick. He had four books behind him. He was rich enough to take a summer houseboat on the Thames and in Scotland rent a holiday farmhouse large enough to take the whole Barrie tribe (his parents, his many siblings and nieces and nephews) while at the same time leaving enough space and quiet for the author to work on his 'big novel', which turned out to be called *The Little Minister*.

And also rich enough to smoke: good briar pipes, fine cigars, the best brands of cigarette. According to Barrie's biographer Janet Dunbar, the author would later remark 'in his whimsical way' that he'd never smoked anything when *My Lady Nicotine* was written, but this is contradicted by pictorial evidence – an early portrait of him at his writing desk with a pipe clenched in his mouth, 'blazing away' like Mr Quilp – as well as by the text of the novel itself. Of course, we must beware of the idea that fictionalists must have themselves experienced something to write convincingly about it. Richard Ford and Lionel Shriver write well about parenthood while not being parents. But if Barrie wasn't a tobacco addict then I've never bought a packet of Marlboro Lights.

My Lady Nicotine is the first-person account of a man, 'a bachelor drifting towards what I now see to be tragic middle age', who is told by his wife-to-be that he can have smoking or her, but not both. The fact that he's given up smoking is made clear from the start and the narrative is retrospective: how he began to smoke, the pleasures and companionship of smoking, the addiction of smoking, the struggle to stop smoking. The last scene has him sucking secretively on an empty briar late at night after his wife has gone to bed, listening enviously through the wall to the sound of a neighbour scraping out his pipe for the last refill of the day. Substitute cigarettes or cocaine for the sweet-scented 'Arcadia Mixture' and you have the makings of a contemporary novel, a key text for Addicts Anonymous, though also almost certainly a similar artistic failure. A book with chapters headed 'Smoking and Matrimony Compared', 'My Tobacco-Pouch', 'How Heroes Smoke' is nothing if not single-minded in its concerns, as if Simon Gray's *The Smoking Diaries* were to be vandalised and reconstituted to nothing but arguments for and against Silk Cut.

It has some nicely ironical passages, however, which still bring self-recognition to anyone who has ever smoked – seriously smoked. There was the financial cost computed at £33 4s 6d a year: 'With that you can buy new Oriental rugs for the drawing room, as well as a spring bonnet and a nice dress . . . Once a man marries his eyes are opened to many things that he was quite unaware of previously, among them being the delight of adding a new article of furniture to the drawing room every month and having a bedroom in pink and gold, the door to which is always kept locked.'

There was the cost to health: 'There were nights when I awoke with a pain at my heart that made me hold my breath. I did not dare move . . . I never mentioned these experience to a human being.' There were lies: 'Though a medical man was among my companions, I cunningly deceived him on the rare occasions when he questioned me about the amount of tobacco I was smoking weekly.' There were the reformed smoker's post-food jitters: 'Occasionally I feel a little depressed after dinner still, without being able to say why, and if my wife has left me I wander about the room restlessly, like one who misses something.' At least one sentence could come straight from the confessions of Allen Carr: 'No blind beggar was ever more abjectly led by his dog, or more loth to cut the string.'

The book's fictional element was marriage, which wasn't a prospect to Barrie when he published it. He met Mary Ansell, an actress, the next year but didn't marry her until 1894. A completely different way to read the book, in fact, is to see it as a long exercise in wishful thinking. A hypothesis in his own mind: to get married might *even* be worth giving up nicotine. He was a self-consciously small man – never more than five feet two – who was aware that women showed insufficient interest in him. He worshipped his mother, who worshipped his dead brother – a great tangle of asexual longing and morbidity that found expression in *Peter Pan*. In Barrie's case, it was not the wife who kept the bedroom door locked. She found a lover and divorced him.

Barrie's subsequent career as a smoker isn't recorded in his biographies, but he had a very bad chest and when he was in his early sixties began to like, and eventually to crave, the relief of heroin. It was one of the last things he asked for before he died in 1937, aged seventy-seven, which is not a bad age for an addict.

Cured

February 2006

I wrote recently that J. M. Barrie's *My Lady Nicotine* may be the only work of literature to take giving up smoking as its central theme. Before the day was out my friend Diana Athill came to the house to tell me there was another: Italo Svevo's *Confessions of Zeno*. A reader mentioned the same book in a letter last week.

I'm sorry for my ignorance. I'd never read the book, and now I've managed to read only some of it. So far the introductory notes on the author are by far the most interesting thing. Svevo was born Ettore Aron Schmitz into a family of German-Jewish descent in Trieste, then the chief port of the Austro-Hungarian empire, in 1861. His family had Italianised itself, and over the question of his city's nationality he became an Italian patriot; his adopted name means 'Italus the Swabian'. James Joyce taught him English at the Trieste Berlitz School and encouraged his writing. He is said to have written a poor kind of Italian – 'pidgin Italian' say the introductory notes – in books that were heavily influenced by the then relatively new practice of psycho-analysis (Freud lived in the same empire just a train ride through the mountains). *Confessions* was first published in English in 1930, two years after the author died in a car crash, and could be crudely summarised as a fifty-year-old ironist's retrospective view of the inci-dental nature of his life and the part that the attractions of the forbidden have played in it. Smoking has only a minor role, though the first chapter begins:

When I spoke to my doctor about my weakness for smoking, he told me to begin my analysis by tracing the growth of that habit from the beginning. 'Write away!' he said, 'and you will see how soon you begin to get a clear picture of yourself.'

Will you? As someone who has recently given up (touch wood), I shall try the doctor's advice.

It may be that from quite an early age I associated cigarettes with sex. I remember my mother talking to a travelling salesman, his suit-case of brushes and Brasso opened on the doorstep, and his offering my mother a cigarette and my mother refusing, saying she no longer smoked. News to me that she ever had, offering the possibility of a different, younger woman, an unmother, a woman of a kind that a brush salesman might flirt with. Years later, in my early teens, the sight of a dog-end with lipstick on it would sometimes fill me with an unfocused desire. Impossible to know quite why, other than its evidence of louche behaviour (that is, in Fife). What is certainly true is that I caught the habit from girlfriends, first with their Peter Stuyvesant ('Oh, how I long for a nutty-flavoured PS!', one girl wrote to me from her holiday with her parents on the Antrim coast) and then with their little Players Number Six.

For a few years I was no more than an experimental smoker. In a little film by Jean Luc-Godard, *Tous les Garcons s'appellent Patrick*, a young man goes to a booth in Paris and asks for a packet of Sweet Afton. 'Eh?' says the man behind the counter. '*C'est une cigarette Irelandaise,*' says the young man. That was me – a tobacco tourist. After I saw the film I went out and bought a packet, to discover they were made in Dundalk and had lines from Burns on the packet, 'Flow gently, sweet Afton, among thy green braes!'

Around the age of twenty-one I started to buy cigarettes regularly, usually ten Gold Leaf, before I started my nightshift on the subeditors' desk of a Glasgow paper. Nearly every man – there were no women – on the desk smoked either pipes, cheroots, cigars or cigarettes, and sometimes a combination: a pipe put down and a fag taken up. At first only the difficulty of headline writing needed a cigarette: how to express a council dispute in three lines of type of no more than eight charac-ters to each line, with the middle line shorter or longer than those above and below to give it a pleasing symmetry? That called for a Gold

Leaf, and then other things did too. A better first paragraph, a good caption, a Guinness in the supper break. The dreadful escalation had begun, the progress from tens to twenties, from Gold Leaf to Piccadilly to Benson & Hedges to Silk Cut to Marlboro Lights. Eventually almost any moment of difficulty – and writing is one long series of such difficulties – needed a cigarette. It helped you to think. In my case, it went on helping for nearly four decades.

Do I get a clear picture of myself from this brief history? If so, it's a very ordinary one. An adolescent boy sees cigarettes as quite literally sexy (think of the come-and-get-me tilt of cigarettes in the pictures of Jack Vettriano, a Fife man still in thrall to the idea); then he sees them as companionship; finally, in this Victorian slide show prepared by the recently repented, he just needs them as a chemical supplement, shouts at his children when deprived of them, etc.

Svevo's narrator remembers that the first cigarettes he ever smoked had the double-headed eagle of the Hapsburg empire stamped on the box. My first cigarettes were mint-flavoured Consulate, 'Cool as a Mountain Stream' in their green and white packets, the nicotine equivalent of an alcopop. I bought ten one Saturday afternoon in winter and smoked a couple far from home on a shore strewn with sea coal near Methil. The feeling and scene are still vivid. Black beach, abandoned houses, an empty dock that reflected the coal hoists around it, minty smoke sucked into the lungs, a slight dizziness. Many, many thousands smoked since, but these are one or two that I actually remember.

And now I look across at the ashtray on my desk, wondering how soon ashtrays will join pipe racks and spittoons as pieces of antique bric-a-brac – and marvelling that it remains empty.

Serampur

January 1990

I.

In Serampur I had an awful dream. I dreamed of my mother and brother. They stood on the slopes of a public park. Behind them lay a Victorian bandstand – octagonal with a curved roof like an onion – and behind that a line of trees. The landscape was in shades of green. The rich green of grass that has thrived on a summer's rain, the pale green of copper mould on the bandstand roof, the dark green foliage of oaks and elms. And all of this green under a sky of grey clouds which held the last of the evening's light. It looked like the end of an August day in Scotland, around nine o'clock, just before the street lamps string the towns with rosaries of bright orange and old people begin to mourn the passing of another summer, telling one another: 'Aye, the nights are fairly drawin' in.'

But this, the visual element, was only a dream within a dream. The larger dream had no pictures. It was simply a kind of soundtrack which said: 'These people and this scene are dead.' And so it was a cunning dream, a dream that told you that you were only dreaming, that the scene was not a real scene, and that the reality was that you would wake and never again see and hear the people in it.

I woke up in tears. I had lost my childhood, the people I loved, the kind of country I came from – there would be nobody else who knew me as these people had done, memories could no longer be exchanged, the sense of isolation from the past would be permanent and absolute. Only slowly did my surroundings penetrate and diminish this self-pity. First, the fan racing and creaking from its pivot on the ceiling, and then the chants of the Krishna worshippers who had set up camp a few hundred yards away on the banks of the Hooghly. Life began to fall into place. I looked at the luminous hands of my watch. It was two in the morning, a warm April night in Bengal. My mother and brother were alive, though my mother was old. By subtracting the time difference it seemed possible that they were settled in front of their gas fires and televisions in Fife and Edinburgh and watching the evening news. I crawled out from under the mosquito net and felt the coal smuts and tiny cinders on the floor scratch under my feet on the way to the bathroom, where I bathed in scoops of cold water from the bucket and, remembering my tears, thought ruefully: That was a dream of the middle-aged and homesick.

For the rest of the night there were no more memorable dreams. When I woke again at seven the Krishnaites were still chanting – they worked in relays – but now their shouts mingled with the sounds of Christianity from the chapel opposite my bathroom window. There a sparse congregation drawn from the Christian students and teachers of Serampur College were singing a hymn, a low murmur of piety easily pierced by the cymbals of Krishna and, for a moment or two, just as easily drowned by the steam hooter of the Serampur jute mill over the wall, which sounded to call the morning shift to work. Twenty minutes later the singing stopped and there was a knock on my door: my next-door neighbours the missionaries, having sung in the chapel, were summoning me to share their breakfast.

Mr and Mrs Knorr had said that this would be the best arrangement, otherwise I would have to share rice and dal in the students' canteen. 'You should eat with us. It's no trouble. We've hired a cook.' The Knorrs were Baptists, energetic and practical Canadians with personalities so apparently unshaded by ambiguity or introspection or melancholy that they stood out in Serampur like a daub of primary colour on a fading sepia engraving. There was nothing false in them; to me, they were kind and direct. But Mr Das, their Bengali cook, seemed by contrast to represent a different race separated not just by continent and colour but by an infinite wistfulness and obliqueness, as though he had stood in the wrong queue when the rations marked 'Energy' and 'Happiness' had been given out. Now he served the porridge with the silence and gravity, though not the precision, of an undertaker. Mrs Knorr arched her eyebrows. 'Poor Das,' she would say, 'he has simply no idea.' And then she bent her head as her husband said grace.

The Knorrs were not new to India – they had worked for decades in what they still spoke of as 'the mission fields' of the south – but they were new to Bengal. They did not intend to stay long. Knorr said it was 'a kind of vacation'; he was here to consult the college archives for a book he was writing on early Baptist missions. They compared the district unfavourably with their old home in the uplands of southern India, a place of vigour and competence where the women wore flowers in their hair and the smell of fresh coffee drifted across station platforms to meet the morning train. The little they had seen of Bengal perplexed them. They saw lassitude and decay, a state government that was at least nomin-ally Marxist and therefore perhaps nominally atheist, a lazy river in a flat landscape, small and squalid towns, tall mill chimneys made of brick, and a cook who made heavy weather of the porridge. On the journey from Calcutta they had passed station buildings and factory walls painted with hammers and sickles, portraits of Marx and Engels, and slogans urging the continuation of the class struggle. But Mrs Knorr discounted these as symptoms of energy. She said: 'I don't know why, but the people here have no go.'

We ate. Knorr said the college library was closed again that day so we would have another day off: there would be no opportunities for research, either mine or his. Therefore the day guaranteed nothing but frequent meals. The Knorrs were hearty eaters. At breakfast, Das came out of his kitchen with bananas, tea and toast as well as porridge. At lunch there might be rice, vegetables, dal, curried chicken, followed by fruit and a rich Bengali sweet of boiled sugar and milk. For afternoon tea, always promptly observed at half past four, the table was laid again with biscuits ('Britannia' brand), fruit, dishes of salty Indian mixtures made from lentil flour and dotted with bright green peas, and – perhaps the cook's greatest success – loops of sweet and sticky jelabis plucked crisp from the frying pan. Finally, for dinner, Das had been persuaded to switch to the old British mode which had reached him, perhaps more as a rumour than a recipe, via some previous employer. Soup would be followed by plates of chips, tomatoes and omelettes, rounded off with more fruit. Before each meal we bowed our heads as Knorr thanked Christ for what we were about to receive – almost, I began to think, more as a warning to the bowels than a blessing.

In the interval between eating that morning, I sluiced from the cold-water bucket again and walked along the river bank. I was grateful to the Knorrs. For the past three weeks I had been travelling alone upcountry in Bihar on a diet of hard-boiled eggs and oranges, and now the profound weight of so much food and religious certainty had a dulling, convalescent effect, burying the embers of my dream like spadefuls of sand on a fire.

Early morning is always the best time in an Indian summer. The sun is still friendly. On the road beside the river I passed old men in their dhotis and sandals taking their daily exercise, while in the river itself families bathed from the muddy shore; the men struck out boldly into the river and held their noses and bobbed under, while the women stayed close to the bank and soaped themselves discreetly under wet saris. Each splash sparkled in the sun. Crows cawed and the horns of cycle-rickshaws honked like flocks of geese down the bumpy road from the bazaar. The jute mill chimney put out more smoke and a low hum emerged from the weaving-sheds. From this distance it was almost a noble sound – industry as Victorian idealists liked to think of it, something akin to the busy-ness of bees – but inside the sheds, I knew, the hum became a hellish clatter of shuttles and looms, so loud that communication was confined to a crude sign language between loom-hands and their foremen.

By midday it was too hot to walk and by afternoon the fierce light had bleached the landscape. Trees that in the morning looked green now looked grey, the brown and blue of the river had turned to a sheet of silver. The crows and rickshaws fell silent, the lizards stuck motionless on my bedroom walls. Even the Krishnaites sounded defeated, their chants ragged and tired. I lay under the fan and read, and slept and sluiced again. 'Hot enough anyway,' said Mrs Knorr over the teatime jelabis, though by that time the sun had slid down the sky and Serampur was coming back to life. When I went out again there were groups of students smoking cigarettes in the shadows of the road that ran along the river and the rickshaw pullers were beginning to light the oil lamps that were suspended from the axles of their tricycles.

I walked to the end of one of the little jetties that carried narrow-gauge railway lines from the jute warehouses, where barges were loaded with finished jute and towed downstream to Calcutta docks. Once it had been a considerable traffic, dotting the river with barges and steam-tugs trailing banners of smoke, upstream and downstream for dozens of miles. Now the river traffic was much less considerable – most jute swayed down the Grand Trunk Road in large, elaborately decorated lorries – but the shine on the rails and the grease on the crane indicated that sometimes a fleet of barges would still arrive and coolies would still push wagons to the end of the jetty and attach bales to an iron hook and watch the bales swing into the hold.

The river had changed from silver to dark glass. Downstream on either side chimneys pricked the evening sky from mills which bore Scottish names: Dalhousie, Waverley, Angus, Kelvin, Caledonia. Nearer, a hundred yards or so upstream from the jetty on the same bank, stood a grand block of flats – impossibly grand for a place like Serampur; 'mansion flats' they would be called in London or Calcutta – with bay windows and balconies and crude classical pediments on the roof and the gateposts. That morning I had met an elderly Bengali out on his stroll and asked about this building: who had lived there? 'Scotch,' he said. The jute-mill manager, perhaps? No, he said, the manager had a separate villa. Assistant managers, foremen, engineers, that kind of person had lived there. 'Scotchmen and their families, all of them. But they went away a long time back.' The flats were still occupied – I could see pale electric light shining through the shuttering on the third floor – but they did not look well-kept. Damp from the monsoon had streaked the yellow lime-wash on the walls, the plaster of the facade was crumbling, the gardens had run riot.

The evening hooters began to sound, first from the Serampur mill and then from the other mills up, down and across the river. There was nothing alarming or rousing in the noise, nothing that suggested fires or air raids, or even that a day's work had been completed and a night's work was about to begin. It was a slow, reedy expulsion of steam and it resembled nothing more than a collective sigh, as though old men were turning in their sleep.

It completed a scene of the purest melancholy. I remembered my dream then, as I stood on the jetty and watched the flickering fire from the Krishna camp and the black silhouettes of the figures who walked and danced around it; the evening had renewed their vigour. That night I wrote in my diary of the dancers and the missionaries, Hindu and Christian: 'I suppose both are meant to supply a balm, if not an answer, to the universal human terror which seemed (was) so real to me last night. But in my family's case it failed and in my case it'll fail too. This morning I felt I'd grieve over this childhood memory of love and kinship until it died with me. And I suppose I shall – intermittently, of course, otherwise life would be both unbearable and insupportable. But I've too strong a sense of transience and what was, and almost none of what is to be.'

Did I really feel this commonplace so forcefully? I suppose I must have done; I wrote it down. The diaries of solitary travellers are often littered with banalities and depressions which seem unreal and over-heated after the writer has come home to the distractions of the social present. And then there is the old Scottish problem, of minds held in thrall to their childhoods and the sentimentalisation of the past (think of Scott, Stevenson, Buchan, Barrie, all of them gifted with imaginations which in some sense were immunised from adult life; children's writers). Perhaps my dream owed something to each of these, the loneliness plus what might be called the cultural disposition. But Serampur, and more than Serampur – Calcutta, Bengal, Bihar, Bangladesh; all these places were reflected in it too. Sometimes as I travelled that winter and spring it seemed that these might be the last places on earth which preserved the old industrial civilisation of Britain, people as well as scenes, manners as well as objects, frozen in the Victorian economy of the lower Ganges. Sometimes it even seemed, particularly in a place such as Serampur at dusk, that I had come home; or if not home, then to some tropical version of the time and country that my Scottish parents and grand-parents knew, as if I might turn a corner of a Serampur lane and meet them dressed in dhotis and saris. That was absurd. But among the mill chimneys and the steamboats and the hissing locomotives this waking dream persisted, like a tribal memory.

2.

I came to Serampur from the north by the Danapur Fast Passenger, the 328 Down. Arriving in an obscure and unfamiliar Indian town can be a daunting experience, particularly if the town lies on the northern plain and your train arrives at night, and you have no friends of friends to meet you, nor letters of introduction, nor any clue about where you might stay. Usually, there are rapid swings in mood. Panic first, then grati-tude (a bed), and then, in the morning light, bewilderment. To a European eye the town seems unknowable. It is very flat. No street has the faintest incline, there are no bridges, no landmarks apart from the station and the cinema, the lanes are dense and complex. Soon another thought strikes you. The town is not only unknowable, it is not worth knowing. In old imperial gazetters, consulted in Delhi or Calcutta, it has looked interesting, even romantic: 'The district is identified with the Vyaghraprastha or "place of tigers" of the *Mahabharata*. Several ruins have been identified as hunting lodges built by the late Moghul emperors.' But the sheer mess of the town quickly kills that literary romance. The streets look to have no history; they contain nothing of beauty – no aesthetic sense seems ever to have touched them; apart from the station and the cinema, the buildings might have loitered here for 300 years, or sprung up yesterday; there is a lot of smell and noise, open drains and Bombay film music. You fail to find the ruins of the Moghul hunting lodges.

Serampur, however, was different. The river gave it an easy topography. The town ran north to south along the Hooghly's western bank – that was its eastern boundary – while inland, cutting through the middle of the town, the Grand Trunk Road and the railway followed the same north–south axis. And so it was easy to visualise as a vertical kind of town, bounded and divided by three vertical lines of transport which passed through on their way elsewhere; south to Calcutta, which was only fifteen miles away, and north to upper India, to the plain of the Ganges and eventually (by bending west with that river) to Delhi.

These days most of Serampur's bustle came from the road and the railway, but it owed its history almost entirely to the river. The place was an ancient centre of Hindu pilgrimage. The worshippers of Jagannath, the Lord of the Universe, had been coming here for hundreds, or possibly thousands, of years to struggle chanting through the river mud and launch their clay gods into the Hooghly. In India only Puri had made more of Jagannath than Serampur – Puri with its great moving platforms, or juggernauts, which carried gigantic images down the main street – and yet Serampur took its name from the hero Ram or Rama; the signs on the station and the entry in the timetable said Srirampur, the place of Lord Ram, as if the Indian railways were trying to obliterate two centuries of corrupt Anglicisation. Ram was the seventh incarnation of the god Vishnu, the preserver, while Jagannath was another name for Krishna, Vishnu's eighth incarnation. Perhaps at some point in the distant past Jagannath had supplanted Ram as the local deity, or perhaps the difference between two successive incarnations of the same god had never mattered. Nobody I met in Serampur could say, but then mainly I met Christians.

That was the role of the river as a sacred thing, a child of the Ganges after the mother river slowed and broke apart to find several exits to the sea. It was a purely Indian role and it must have developed, unrecorded, over centuries. But the next important stage in Serampur's development came from Europe and it left behind dates and documents. At the beginning of the seventeenth century European traders began to push their way upstream from the Bay of Bengal, their ships alternately tacking against the current and floating with the tide, to penetrate closer to the heart of a rich textile industry – silk and cotton woven into taffeta and muslin – and the provincial capitals of the Moghul empire. The trading companies of several European nations did deals with the provincial governors and established trading depots, called factories, eighty miles and more upriver from the sea. The Portuguese came first but were soon displaced by the English, French and Dutch. By the second half of the century there were clusters of white men inside stockades under different flags at half a dozen points up and down the Hooghly, at each of them exchanging silver bullion for silk and cotton cloth which was finer and cheaper than anything Europe could produce.

At Serampur the flag was Danish. The Danish East India Company founded a settlement there in or about 1676 and called it Fredericksnagore after the Danish king. Denmark's intrusion into Bengal may now seem an oddity, rather like, say, a British-made camera trying to compete with Japanese Nikons and Canons in the late twentieth century, but late in the seventeenth century Denmark had made a serious attempt to squeeze itself into the sudden European boom in trade with India. Like many of its rivals, the Danish East India Company enjoyed royal patronage but unlike several of the ill-fated companies which followed it and joined the rush too late – the Holy Roman Emperor's Ostend Company, for example, or Frederick the Great of Prussia's Bengalische Handelsgesellschaft – the Danish company persisted in denting what soon became an Anglo-French monopoly. Trade flourished. Accounts from the eighteenth century describe hundreds of ships riding at anchor in the reach opposite Serampur, ships which had often sailed from the Baltic via the other small Danish settlements at Balasore and Tranquebar on the Indian coasts of Orissa and Coromandel. And then, in 1845, faced with a new imperial spirit, the Danes sold all three of their Indian colonies to the British East India Company for £120,000, leaving in their wake at Serampura a church called St Olaf's and several oil paintings of the Danish monarchy.

But that was not all. A smaller oddness lay inside the larger oddity of the persisting Danish presence on the Hooghly. In 1800 Serampur became the home to a small band of English Baptist missionaries led by a self-taught preacher and former shoemaker, William Carey. As Englishmen they might have been expected to settle downstream in Calcutta, which had become the capital of British India. But the government of the East India Company did not encourage missionaries, English or otherwise, because they saw in missionary activity a kind of yeast that might have unpredictable, destabilising effects among the native population. There were two fears. The simple one was that the fearless arrogance of Christian preachers, with their talk of ignorance and sloth and hellish warnings for the unreformed heathen, might cause understandable and perhaps violent hostility among Hindus and Muslims. The other, more complex, stemmed from other parts of the Christian, and particularly the Nonconformist Christian, message which preached the equality of the Christian brotherhood. The missionaries could fail and cause one kind of insurrection, or they might be too successful, make many converts and plant the seeds of another kind. Either way the British governors of Bengal saw them as a potential danger to British rule, contravening the philosophy that the British were in India to trade and to raise revenue but, so far as the first two were compatible with this last, not to disturb the society of the people they governed.

Carey had already been in Bengal for seven years, living upcountry and describing himself for the sake of government records as an indigo planter, when four other missionaries sailed from England in 1799. They carried with them a letter of recommendation from the Danish consul in London to the governor in Serampur; a useful precaution because they were shortly prohibited, on pain of arrest, from entering British-controlled Bengal. And so with Carey as their leader they set up their headquarters in the Danish colony, as refugees from their fellow Englishmen and fellow Christians. To Lord Wellesley, then the British Governor General, Serampur was a 'peculiarly obnoxious' town in which 'adventurers of every nation, jacobins of every description . . . all our public defaulters and debtors' sought sanctuary from the penalties of British law in Calcutta. But by the time Carey died there, in 1834, it had become one of the major glories of British Christianity, a place name proclaimed from country pulpits and public platforms in the new industrial towns by English Nonconformists and Scottish Presbyterians; to evoke the rewards of abiding faith and hard work and to inspire the congregation with the idea – difficult, but then few of God's tasks were easy – that Britain's new spiritual objective was to Christianise the East.

When the British took over Serampur, Carey's legacy spoke well of his achievement: aside from places of worship, the mission had established a college and library, a school, botanical gardens, a hospital, a printing press and newspapers in English and Bengali. The college was the grandest of the buildings, with a tall Ionic portico and a double staircase of iron and brass imported from Birmingham, and it survives both as a noble piece of architecture and as an institution (a special clause in Britain's treaty of purchase with Denmark preserved the statues and privileges the college had been granted by the Danish king, including the principle that 'no caste, colour or country shall bar any man from admission'). But as the century progressed and the memory of Carey faded, so the rest of his legacy dwindled. The newspapers closed, the printing press was moved to Calcutta, and then for several weeks in the year 1865 riverboats arrived loaded with the bricks and machinery which eventually buried the mission's botanic gardens under the Scottish jute mill. The town, meanwhile, had become popular with rich families in Calcutta as a resort noted for its 'salubrity' and its river views. Bengali merchants from the city built large and rambling villas, and commuted to them by river – a couple of hours traditional row in a *budgerow*, or river barge, if the oarsmen were fresh and the current was right; much less in one of the new paddle-tugs which were beginning to thrash up the Hooghly even before Carey had died.

Since then, of course, the town had changed; electric lights, electric trains, the pallor from televisions flickering across interior walls. But its history was still obvious, the rudiments of the various transformations yielded by the river were still in place. Temples and bathing ghats lined the bank, and then behind them in a row from south to north, stood the college, the jute mill, the Scotsmen's houses, and the old (and now crumbling) suburb of the rich Calcuttans: the river as religion and sanitation, the river as commerce and industry and colonisation, and finally the river in a new European (or very old Indian) sense – as something non–utilitarian, a luxury, a view, a rest from the dust and ink of the Calcutta counting-houses.

I missed this river view on my first trip in Serampur, by rickshaw from the station to the college, because once through the bazaar we took a short cut to the back of the college through the jute workers' colony which lay behind the jute mill, through cramped lanes where little huts selling tea were perched across black drains and dogs foraged in the rubbish. But the journey felt cheerful enough. The Danapur Fast Passenger ran several hours late, as people said it always did, but I had reached Serampur in time for lunch. The college expected me, so there was no call for panic on that score. These were moments of expect-ation. With luck I would spend the afternoon in the library; with further luck the library would contain papers relating to the activities of the mission in 1820; and with a completely improbable amount of luck these papers would contain references to William Carey's steam engine.

According to information buried inside Victorian biographies of Carey, long out of print, the missionary had imported the first steam engine ever seen in India, perhaps even the first in Asia. It was yet another forgotten oddness inside the neglected story of the Danes and Bengal and Carey; a Russian doll of historical oddities.

3.

It soon became obvious that there was trouble at the college. The prin-cipal was absent, the teachers had gone on strike, students congregated outside locked classroom doors. They said I should see Mrs Allegory, the college secretary, and in the thirty minutes it took me to find her I thought of her as such, as a figure of speech, an abstraction. But I had misheard the name. It was Aligodi and she was flesh and at that moment, judging by the crowd of college servants around her office, she repre-sented the only focus of organisation in the college.

I was to stay in Carey's old residence, the house which, according to its plaque, the missionary, philanthropist and oriental scholar had lived in for the last eleven years of his life. Mrs Aligodi took me there and showed me how to work the locks. It was a big block of a house, its lines softened by moulded Greek pediments above the lintels and a balustrade around a flat roof. We went up stone stairs to the first floor. My apartment had many large rooms and high ceilings supported by iron beams. On one side, facing east, the windows looked across the lawn to the river. But there was almost no furniture apart from a bed, some cupboards and a table. On the table lay a chrome dinner plate and a water glass, both upturned against the dust.

'The principal's,' said Mrs Aligodi.

I was to live in the principal's home then; but where was the principal?

'Calcutta,' said Mrs Aligodi. 'His residence is there. When he chooses to come, he comes by train and then goes back in the evening time.'

There was something in Mrs Aligodi's tone – a touch of reproof? – which suggested that the principal's presence was not as frequent as it should be, as though he might even now be lying under a fan in his Calcutta flat and feeling the heat, and thinking of the journey to Serampur, first crowded tram and then crowded train, and deciding against it. And I was right to detect this implication, because when I met other members of the college staff and mentioned the principal their tone was always the same. It transpired that he was a young man, recently appointed, and unpopular; perhaps, I thought, it was his unpopularity which had driven him back to Calcutta, leaving as a token of his claim on the flat – and flats so spacious and well-built were like gold to poorly paid academics – the upturned glass and dinner plate. But there was more to it than that. The college charter, so carefully protected when the Danish sold out to the British, was partly to blame. It had specified that the professors of the college must profess Christianity and though the charter had since been amended – because the college was now part of the state education system of West Bengal – the fact remained that Christian beliefs were still required of the principal. That cut the choice of suitable candidates quite drastically; Christians are only a fragment of the population of eastern India. Eventually the governors had settled on the young man, who was certainly a Christian but a Christian of low caste. This had caused resentment among his staff, Hindu and Christian, from higher castes, though whether this was caused by the principal's caste as such, or by characteristics which his staff now blamed on his caste, or merely by these characteristics themselves, it was difficult to say. As my days passed inside his flat I began to see a sadness in the bare table and the upturned utensils.

Christianity, of course, rejects the idea of caste. Islam, Sikhism and Buddhism also reject it. Over hundreds of years, millions of Hindus at or near the bottom of the caste pile have converted to these faiths at least partly because of this rejection. But caste and religious belief, social position and the individual spirit, these are different things and to change one does not necessarily, or in India even usually, alter the other; just as class differences in England would not be resolved by issuing the poor with Old Etonian ties. If you collect sewage for a living and become a Christian you do not stop collecting sewage, all that happens is that you become a Christian sewage-collector. That was an Indian truism, even though India now was a much more fluid society. But what I had never considered until later that day was the grief and pain that conversion could cause to the converted, or that it might become a cause for regret like a secret wish from a partner locked for years in a failing marriage, a wish that it had never happened.

Lunch had been arranged with the rector of the divinity department and now he came to collect me. He was in his thirties, tall, fair in the Indian sense, and grave, though underneath the gravity there was a bitter sense of humour. He was not a Bengali, he said; his name was Ravi Tewari and his family came from Agra in Uttar Pradesh. Tewari was a Brahmin name.

We were to eat in his flat which was in a block inside the college grounds, a newish and unmemorable block, post-Independence, which formed one side of a quadrangle fronted on the other three sides by faded but still handsome buildings from the Victorian British period: pilasters, terraces and shutters painted green. As we walked I asked about the strike: were the teachers very discontented?

Ravi said I had been misinformed. It was not the teachers but the administrative staff who had struck, but tomorrow their strike would be over. It had lasted only two days and they were simply obeying some dictat from union headquarters in Calcutta.

So tomorrow the library would be open?

'I'm afraid that will not be the case,' said Ravi. 'You see tomorrow the teachers will go on strike, or rather they will go on holiday.'

News had been received that day that a former principal, a Scotsman who had retired twenty-five years before, had died in Edinburgh. Some members of the academic staff had met the principal and persuaded him to declare a holiday in memory of this man's life and work in Serampur.

So the dead Scotsman had been a popular man, a big figure in the history of the college?

'No, not at all. In fact, apart from my father I don't think anyone else here can even remember him.'

Strikes, spontaneous holidays: it seemed to me that the students' work would suffer, that the teaching staff would have a harder job. Didn't they find it frustrating?

Ravi laughed. 'Why should it frustrate them? They like it. The holiday is their idea after all. And only the poor students suffer.' For a second I misunderstood that, not taking the word 'poor' in a comparative and literal sense. But Ravi explained: 'The poorer students do not have families who can afford private tuition. Richer families will pay for their children to make up for their lost lessons. Some teachers at the college will teach these lessons privately and make money, so naturally they are not against strikes and holidays. You might even say the more the merrier.'

By this time we had taken off our sandals and were walking barefoot on the shaded concrete – refreshingly cool – which led into the Tewaris' flat. Father and son lived alone. They were both Christian theologians, son following father in the same college, living and teaching as his father had done. Their food was plain and good: rice, dal, vegetables, curd made by old Mr Tewari himself, and – though nobody touched these – some cubes of processed cheese in silver paper and ghee, clarified butter, in a little plastic pot. At the end of the meal the old man served *sandesh*, a superior Bengali sweet a little like crisp fudge, and grapes. These were treats; today was his seventy-eighth birthday, though he looked ten years and more younger. He was fair like his son but leaner and somehow more refined, with his slender figure draped in loose white clothes, kurta and pyjamas, and his sparse white hair combed sideways across his scalp. He was alert – an alertness which picked up my diffidence towards his grapes and correctly identified the reason. 'You shouldn't worry,' he said. 'I have washed them in a solution of potassium permanganate. You can eat them without fear for your stomach. I also wouldn't touch them if they had just been put under a tap. The bazaars are very filthy.' He said he had learned this hygiene when he had stayed for six months in Gandhi's ashram, at Wardha in central India. That would be in 1934, when he was a young man, but he had never forgotten it.

I wondered what else he had learned from Gandhi. 'Oh quite a lot,' said the elder Tewari. He pressed me to stay for tea while his son went off to look into the arrangements for the Bachelor of Divinity final examinations. And then when we were alone, he said: 'I shall tell you about Gandhi certainly, but first you should know a little of my life.'

4.

Over the fifteen years I had spent as a journalist coming and going from the Indian subcontinent and travelling inside it, I had been struck by how simply and directly some people, especially old people, could describe the central experience of their lives. This did not seem to be because they led simple and direct lives – many of them were modern, complicated and obtuse – nor even because they were religious and saw their lives shrunken by this larger context, though many were and did. Quite often you would be startled by this directness. Usually it was men – a man you had known for a few hours might say: 'For those ten years in Bombay I was very unhappy.' But women were not immune: 'I am sad. My husband does not love me.' (In my old newspaper office in London a woman had once confessed that to an acquaintance and her openness was considered so striking that for years afterwards her colleagues thought of that whenever they saw her: 'My husband does not love me.') Perhaps in India this frankness came from self-absorption, or self-dramatisation, or the thrill of confession to strangers, but whatever the cause I sometimes felt inadequate in the face of it. Sometimes I was asked to explain my own life, and that was always hard, not because it was richer or more complex but because it was sheened with irony – many protective coats – and most easily defined itself in terms of work and what interested me outside myself. These days, on a train, I found I could lose myself – the exact phrase – for hours in the tabled minutiae of Newman's *Indian Bradshaw*, working through journeys I would never take to places I had never seen. Other passengers would become curious and amused, and though the Tewaris did not have quite that reaction to my curiosity about Carey's steam engine – they saw that it might be interesting, for a European – I felt now as I faced old Mr Tewari in his flat that he and I were like the buildings which faced each other on the opposite sides of the quadrangle, that he was unadorned concrete while I had pilasters and classical plaster-work which disguised brittle brick.

And so, in the Indian way, he outlined the essentials of his life. He was born in 1911 in Uttar Pradesh of a prosperous and well-respected Brahmin family and had attended an English-medium school in Agra, the town of the Taj Mahal. There one day in the early 1920s he had met a Christian brother from an English mission who had told him the story of St Francis of Assisi: of how long ago in Italy a wealthy merchant's son had led a gay and abandoned life until, halted by a dream, he repudiated his wealth and gave away his clothes and became a hermit, committed to poverty, chastity and obedience. The story impressed him. It had a Hindu feel – renunciation, the solitary life among the animals of the forest – though in Hinduism this retreat from the world is usually postponed to the period after middle age, the final stage in a man's life. Through the Christian brother Tewari met other mission priests and then suddenly one night, he said, 'I found myself in the presence of Christ.' This was his conversion. He had married by then, to a young Brahmin girl chosen by his parents, and was studying for his Bachelor of Arts at college in Agra. The apostasy outraged and bewildered his father, but when Tewari left Agra and travelled almost a thousand miles east to read divinity at Serampur, his father continued to maintain him.

Serampur was a disappointment. 'It was too wordly, too filled with certificate-hunters. I hadn't imagined that the Christian life would be like that.' So he became a sadhu, a questing holy man, and left Serampur to wander across India, a journey that still in his mind combined penance, discovery and adventure. 'I shouldn't, of course, have become a sadhu. That was selfish of me. I had a wife at home and I should have been with her.' But the journey had led him to Gandhi.

How had this happened? The answer was a coincidence, one of the kind that seemed to occur regularly in Indian life stories as they once did in Victorian novels. One day, several weeks after he began his journey, he reached a village in what were then the Central Provinces. A rainstorm came. The village lanes turned into swirling mud. An Englishwoman – an unexpected sight in an Indian village – called out to him and offered him shelter in her bungalow. He smiled at the memory of the kindness and strangeness of the meeting. 'The woman was Miss Mary Barr and she was a disciple of Gandhi. So there in that house in the rainstorm I confessed my doubts to her.' Was he fitted to be a Christian? Was it the true religion? Would he be strong enough to resist the pull of his family and community? 'Miss Mary Barr said that, though Gandhi was a Hindu, he was the only man she knew who followed the true Christian path.' So, after the rainstorm had ended and he had rested, he began to make his way towards the ashram at Wardha. 'By the time I arrived Gandhi had already opened a file on me.'

By the word file, Tewari implied a sheaf of official documents tied with red string, the tool of the Indian bureaucracy since the days of the East India Company. Gandhi was by that time India's leading politician, a world figure and the centre of a small bureaucracy himself, with secretaries and assistants to deal with a large correspondence. But Tewari used the word as a joke. Gandhi had received only two letters about him. Miss Barr had written: 'Here is a young Christian who needs guidance.' His father had written: 'Please restore my son to his family and his ancient faith.'

Gandhi offered Tewari a choice of jobs, which were both by rigid tradition the work of the lowest Untouchable castes. He could 'cut' (that is, skin) dead animals or he could clean latrines. Tewari chose latrine-cleaning, though that soon became the second of his daily tasks. Every morning, after he rose at four, he would knead dough for the ashram's supply of bread; the formula – 'four parts flour to one part water' – had stayed with him for more than half a century, together with the efficacy of potassium permanganate. (Also, he remembered the plainness of the food, though it was not as plain as that served in another Gandhian ashram he had visited – run by the Gandhian Vinobe Bhave – where the rice and vegetables were boiled without seasoning of any kind. Bhave had taken pity on him and allowed him his own pot of lime pickle – 'otherwise I would not have been able to eat at all' – and it was the memory of that indulgence which had produced the processed cheese and the ghee at the lunch table; they were for me, in case I found his food too plain.)

I thought then that Tewari's story had taken a wrong turning: suddenly Gandhi had become a domestic scientist rather than a spiritual advisor, with Tewari still gripped fifty years later by the marvellous consistency of the scientific method and perhaps the only practical knowledge he had ever learned – four parts flour to one part water, knead, and the result (every time, said Tewari, marvelling) was dough. But it was not a wrong turning, not a sidetrack. That was what he had learned from Gandhi; there had been little spiritual counselling. When he had asked one of Gandhi's oldest and closest friends, the Englishman C. F. Andrews, which church he should join, Andrews had replied: 'None.' Gandhi himself had simply said that Tewari should consider his father's wishes, and then asked him to befriend another disciple in the ashram, a girl from Birmingham, and walk with her in the evenings. It seemed to have been proposed as a temptation. 'You can be sure,' said Gandhi, 'that anything you do or don't do with this girl will reach me.'

'He could be very stern,' said Tewari. 'And I was frightened and did not misbehave with the girl from Birmingham.' Several weeks passed, kneading and latrine-cleaning, walking with the girl from Birmingham, until one day Tewari decided he had had enough and told Gandhi he was leaving. 'And Gandhi put his hand over his heart and said: "You have hurt me here."'

That was the end of the Gandhi story. Tewari went off to fetch tea and Britannia biscuits, and when he came back he outlined the rest of his life. He had taken a Master of Arts degree from Kanpur and then returned to Serampur to teach. He was a New Testament scholar, specialising in the gospel of St John. He knew some classical Greek (but wished he knew more) and Sanskrit, as well as English, Hindi and Bengali.

I asked about his wife. Tewari shook his head. 'Eventually she also converted, but she would always say: "I am a Christian by religion but a Brahmin by caste."' There had been many quarrels. She refused to eat with inferior castes, she insisted on the ritual purification of the kitchen by plastering it with sacred Ganges mud. 'When she died – long ago now, in 1952 – I had her buried in the ground and not cremated on the ghats at the river. That upset her family and cut me off from them. I was already an outcast from my own.'

He lived with a great weight of regret for the past, aggravated by distress for the present. These days scholarship seemed to count for little. Scholarship was his Brahminical inheritance, the study of texts, the interpretation of puzzles. The college had even removed Sanskrit from the syllabus – Sanskrit, the ancient language of the Hindu scriptures, the language of his forefathers, the pundits – and though his son had restored it to the syllabus, the fact was that most divinity students were now tribals, from Assam and the hills of Bihar, or low castes from south India, and did not care at all for Sanskrit. They identified it as the language of caste oppression. They hated it, and this hatred for a language which expressed the canon of Indian philosophy – whatever else, said Tewari, Sanskrit was interesting – had taken him by surprise and made him miserable.

But of course it was only part of a new morality. In the evening, said Tewari, you could see young men and women 'consorting' in front of the college on the road that ran by the river. That was new, and disturbing. He had protested to a colleague: 'The town's prostitutes might at least spare the dignity of Serampur College.' The colleague had laughed. They weren't prostitutes. 'Tewariji,' he had said, using the friendly honorific, 'these are your own sons and daughters,' meaning that it was the college's own students who were talking and touching in the dark. And now Tewari himself laughed at his mistake, his failure to comprehend how India had changed. Something of his brighter mood returned. Earlier, when he had remembered Gandhi's small, unheeded piece of advice – consider the wishes of your father – his voice had slowed and darkened.

5.

That evening, before my first supper with the missionary Knorrs, I went out for a long walk with Ravi. He wanted to know what his father had talked about and what I had made of him. I said he had described his life and that, for me at least, it had been an interesting afternoon.

'Did he talk about his conversion?' Ravi asked.

'A bit, not much. I don't know how to say this, perhaps I shouldn't say it, but it seemed to me that he might almost regret it.'

Ravi seemed to have been waiting for this opportunity. It released a flood of words. 'You are very correct. He does regret it. But he won't talk to his family about it, only to people outside. You know a friend of mine once put it to him: "If you could be twenty-four or twenty-five again, would you still become a Christian?" And my father said no, the pain he had caused others and the loneliness he had caused himself, these were too high a price. My father would never have told me this, of course, but my friend was blunt and got an answer. Only in this way do I know how much he suffers.

'And now I want to tell you something shocking. His children, my brothers and I, we're glad that my mother died when she did. We agree among ourselves: it was a good thing for her to die. She was a Brahmin lady forced to lead a completely unnatural life. She was very unhappy.'

Ravi was right: it did shock me. His mother had died young, a woman in her thirties. But I left the subject alone and wondered about his father's loneliness. He was so sprightly and engaging, and he lived among his Christian peers.

Ravi said: 'He is a scholar and he is in some ways still a Brahmin. This is no place for him. He cannot feel among equals. Therefore he has very few friends.'

We walked north beside the river and, near the Scotsmen's houses, caught up by accident with the father, who was also taking his evening stroll. I said hello and I thought we might stop and fall in with the old man, but Ravi walked on. 'Oh, I was hoping to avoid you,' was all the father said to the son.

'He's very stubborn,' said Ravi and gave instances. Despite pleas from his children, he refused to even consider the idea of writing about his childhood, even as a private keepsake for his grandchildren. And when, in the old days, his students had pressed him to deliver his own opinion on a theological dispute – 'Sir, what do you think?' – he would always decline. Ravi said it was the Brahmin way. 'They have this Pauline idea that everyone should work out their own salvation. They believe knowledge is to be acquired and hoarded and never shared.' In India, he said, these ideas were still pervasive and he himself was not immune; he taught no more knowledge than was 'generally available' and kept the rest to himself.

Now we were walking in the old suburb of the Calcutta traders, which Ravi said was called Chatra, the Sanskrit word for 'umbrella'. We had already passed quite substantial villas which Ravi identified as the old home of the Danish governor and the former summer retreat of the Bishop of Calcutta, but now some of the houses were the size of palaces. Formerly they were homes of *zamindars*, the great landlords of Bengal, said Ravi, though they had since been divided and subdivided. Again, the Greek revival in Britain was the obvious architectural influence, though decay and piecemeal improvisation were slowly removing the evidence. Broken plasterwork revealed bricks slipping out of dusty mortar, small shrubs had taken root among the television aerials on the roofs, advertisements for fans and motor oil had been nailed to the facades. Goats were tethered to the pillars and hens pecked among them. Ornate verandas, places once meant for recreation, hookahs and evening games of cards, were festooned with bedspreads and quilts put out to air. Electric wires and cables emerged haphazardly from the walls and zigzagged overhead down the street. The rooms inside looked poor – bare light bulbs, commercial calendars tacked to the wall – but their occupants were probably the Bengali middle class: public servants, shopkeepers, lawyers with too few clients. 'No inclination for proper maintenance,' said Ravi.

The light was fading. The place felt remote – the remoteness of disintegrating European architecture many thousands of miles from Europe and centuries from the period that created it, the remoteness of Bengal from the new currents of Indian life which swept through Bombay and Delhi and much of the country to the west and south, currents only the eddies of which had so far touched the old capital, Calcutta. I used the word to Ravi.

Yes, he said, remote. It was sometimes how he felt. He was forty and hadn't married, an unbidden life of chastity. He said that suitable brides were scarce; there weren't enough Brahmin Christians from Uttar Pradesh, particularly in his particular subcaste. But if he went outside this community? 'You mean Bengali Christian Brahmins? Those Mukherjees, Chatterjees and Bannerjees? They stick to their own caste even more than the Brahmins who remain Brahmins.'

'But you have your work.'

'Yes, I have my work. I teach comparative religion to students who have not the slightest interest in the topic. I tell them about Jainism, Sikhism, Islam, Buddhism, but they are not all interested. They are evangelical Christians. They have the The Truth, you see.' His father had become a Christian, but he had been born one. The first was an intellectual decision, the second fate, an accident. He said that for his doctoral thesis he had compared the work of Paul Tillich, the modern Christian philosopher, and Shankaracharya, the ancient Hindu sage. He had reached a conclusion: 'Hinduism has everything that Christianity contains except Christ.'

'And do you think that matters?'

Ravi didn't reply. He had begun to look watchful. We had turned into the narrow alleys that led back to the town. They had a Mediterranean look, with painted houses and doors which led straight on to the street, filling it with domestic noise and the smell of fish sizzling in hot mustard oil. Ravi said he hadn't dared to walk in this part of Serampur for months, was only walking in it now because in my company he felt safe. That seemed ridiculous, but Ravi said no, his life had been threatened. It was the story of another quarrel among Serampur's Christians. A member of the theology department – a Baptist – had been carrying on simultaneous affairs with another colleague's wife and her daughter, and failing to turn up for his classes.

I said that seemed a risky business in a small Indian town.

'Correct,' said Ravi, 'but you see as a Baptist he had no fear.' Baptists believed in 'the priesthood of all believers', their church was 'a fellowship' – here Ravi smiled as he had done when he mentioned his students possessing The Truth – and they did not defer to a hierarchy of bishops and archbishops. Nonetheless Ravi, as head of the theology department, had sacked him and the lecturer had taken his case to the district court, which found in his favour. That did not surprise Ravi. District courts were politicised and the lecturer had friends in the state's ruling Marxist party. The college had appealed and a judgment was now awaited from the High Court in Calcutta. In the meantime a friend of the sacked man had approached Ravi and said: 'Give him back his job or you'll be dead within a month.' This friend ran a 'country liquor' store in the part of the town we were now walking through – 'country' as opposed to 'foreign' liquor, cheap, clear spirits distilled from grain – and was well known as a *goonda*, a local thug. That was why Ravi was scared, but in the company of a foreigner, a white man, he did not think he would be attacked.

We had walked for two hours. We had become companions (though later, when I met Ravi and his father again, that companionship was never acknowledged and never reclaimed). And now that we had reached the evening jostle of the railways station and the bazaar, he was more cheerful. He took me to the station booking hall and pointed out the plaque to William Carey and Carey's famous maxim – ATTEMPT GREAT THINGS FOR GOD, EXPECT GREAT THINGS FROM GOD – which the Eastern Railway had painted in a semi-circle beneath an arch. Ravi said the railways had got the maxim back to front, in Carey's original the expecting came before the attempting, but he was pleased to see it there, as a token of how India could honour foreigners and foreign faiths.

After the bazaar, we entered a compound; a square enclosure with a gate in one wall, like a fort. Inside there were stalls heaped with wooden toys, bottled pickles, stone utensils for the Hindu sacrament, and upright columns of glistening plastic bangles, all of them lit by the white glare of hissing gas lamps. The stalls formed a rectangular arcade. At the head of it, against the wall furthest from the gate, stood an old shrine to the god Siva. The mood of the crowd here changed from the bazaar. It was both more reverent and more relaxed. Ravi himself seemed infected by it. 'A *mela*,' he said, 'a Hindu holy fair. Very popular.' I bought some grapes as a gift for Ravi's father, and he chided me ('You should not have given the money with your left hand'), and chided me again when I gave money to a beggar ('You should have looked into his eyes, to tell if he was sincere').

That was how the Christians had come unstuck in India, he said. They had paid no attention to etiquette, to the rules of Hindu society. They had clumped into houses in their buckled leather shoes, attacked pieces of meat with knives and forks, sweated, not washed, enough, talked too much and too confidently, baptised anyone who asked to be baptised. (From Ravi's description I imagined them like red-faced gluttons eating roast beef in eighteenth-century cartoons; and some of them, long ago, were like that.) The result had been that intellectual, exclusive, Brahmin India disdained them; they had succeeded mainly among the lowest castes and tribes, and that limited success had only made their work harder among the higher castes.

In India at large the issue was no longer important, if it had ever been. But to Ravi it mattered, as an irreconcilable quarrel between belief and behaviour. I tried to console him. I said that in Britain this quarrel had died away, that the large utopian beliefs were vanishing, that perhaps it was important for people (though I don't know if I really believed this) to have such arguments beating about inside them. I generalised. In Britain, I said, what mattered were the particulars of the here and now, the purchase of things, the pax consumia that held the West together in a way that politics and religion had never done. Ritual, the belief in old ways of behaviour, could never be part of this because economic growth demanded constant social change. My father's way of living could never infect mine in the way that old Mr Tewari's had done Ravi's – perhaps that was why we were so interested in the past, because we felt safe from it, we could switch it on or off in our lives like a light in a vault. Perhaps, I said, it was this view of history as an entertainment and distraction – a consumable item, 'heritage' was the word in Britain – that enabled my interest in William Carey's steam engine. And perhaps it was not entirely healthy; perhaps it contained and concealed a different kind of pain, a sense of baffling loss.

But Ravi was not consoled. He was attracted by history and the preservation of memory – that was why he had asked his father to write down his life. It was, he said, yet another difference between him and the way most Indians felt. 'We care nothing for history, only for eternity,' he said, shortly before we left each other at the college gate. 'We are a *horrible* people.'

6.

Eternity. It was not just an Indian enthusiasm. It was the enthusiasm, in fact, that had sent William Carey, the Northamptonshire shoemaker, to

India. In India, he wrote, before he had reached the place, there lived 'millions of perishing heathens, tormented in this life by idolatry, superstition and ignorance, and exposed to eternal miseries in the world to come'. They were pleading, he wrote, though he had yet to meet a single one: 'Yea, all their miseries plead as soon as they are known, with every heart that loves God, and with all the churches of the living God.' Carey had the remedy. He would answer the plea. He would preach the Gospels, heathens would accept Christ as their saviour, their morals and industry would be transformed, the eternal misery of the next life would be replaced by 'endless perfection', hell would be exchanged for heaven. He intended to achieve all this, not by proselytising at the periphery of Indian society, among outcasts and half-castes, but by striking at the 'very seat of Brahminism' on the Hooghly in Bengal. If enough men followed him, the entire subcontinent would be saved for Christendom.

I had brought a couple of biographies of Carey with me, picked up from the fullest and most neglected shelves ('Theology') of second-hand bookstores in London. I had intended to read them – thoroughly, for once – on my journey through Bihar, so that when I reached Serampur I would have some kind of understanding of its history. But I had given up. They were like the Baptist Sunday School prizes ('for regular attendance') that my father had kept in our bookcase at home, Victorian fables about lives of good works in which Christ was never faraway and often lent a hand. Carey was 'God's lamplighter in the East', as great an Englishman as Shakespeare, Milton and Newton, and had not died but 'passed within the veil'. Both books had been published less than a century before – one of them much less, in 1923 – but it seemed almost impossible to believe that they and I shared the same country and the same century. Many of their allusions to British religious history were obscure; Arminianism, Socianism, a debate which had once divided Scotland called 'the Marrow of Divinity'. Their language was ecstatic and divine. They were so simple, so sure; their simplicity and certainty were ridiculous. And yet my father and my grandmother had once read books like these and admired the lives contained in them, they had been part of normal ways of thinking and feeling in Nonconformist, Presbyterian, Imperial Britain. The allusions would have been understood.

Now, in the house that Carey had lived and died in, glancing through the windows at the view of the river which had scarcely changed since his day, I tried reading them again. Previously I'd been too careless, too easily diverted by Newman's *Indian Bradshaw*. The divinity was still a barrier, the allusions seemed no less obscure, but they no longer disguised the power of Carey's story. He had been a remarkable man.

7.

William Carey was born on 17 August 1761, in the village of Paulerspury, about eleven miles south of Northampton on the southern fringe of the English Midlands. He came, unusually for the place and time, from a family who could read and write. His grandfather was the village's first schoolmaster; when he retired the job had passed to his son, William Carey's father, who until then had earned his living as a weaver. The boy grew up among stories from the outside world. An uncle had returned from Canada and William helped him in his work as a gardener, listening as he weeded to adventures set in Britain's North American colonies (here his biographers referred to Millais's picture *The Boyhood of Raleigh*). But he was an inquisitive rather than a romantic child; observable fact interested him more than make-believe. He studied the material easily available to him in an eighteenth-century English village: flowers, plants, insects, birds. And he read. He wrote later: 'I chose to read books of science, history, voyages, etc., more than any others. Novels and plays always disgusted me, and I avoided them as much as I did books of religion, and perhaps from the same motive.' Villagers gave him a nick-name: Columbus.

Britain in the time of Carey's boyhood was a country approaching the edge of its greatest transformation. Military victories against the French in India and North America had laid the foundations of an empire. The profits from trade, most notoriously the slave and sugar trade, were piling up to finance the world's first industrial revolution. Already, in a few parts of the country, heaps of raw earth rose above the hedgerows to mark the path of new canals. In other parts, the blur of smoke from a crude steam-pumping engine signalled the draining of water from a coal pit or a tin mine. But these were rare events in the landscape. The country still depended for its power and movement on animal muscle, relieved occasionally by the windmill and the waterwheel. Its tools were the packhorse, the handloom and the walking shoe.

Carey wasn't robust enough for work in the fields – he was a small youth, with a form of scurvy which erupted when his skin was exposed to the sun – so he got into the shoe trade. A local shoemaker took Carey as an apprentice when he was sixteen and he worked with nails and leather over a last for the next twelve years. At twenty he married his employer's sister-in-law, Dolly Placket, who was five years older and so illiterate that she was unable to write her name in the parish register. The couple's first child died of fever. By twenty-two Carey was as bald as an egg (his biographers blamed 'ague, caused by a neighbouring marsh') and took to wearing a cheap wig ('stiff, ill-fitting and odious') on his long walks across Northamptonshire to collect broken shoes and return repaired ones. Eventually he threw the wig overboard – an overdue fit of disgust – on the voyage to Bengal, but that was ten years away. Nothing, at this stage, suggested that Carey would ever break out of the cramped, insanitary boundaries of rural England.

What changed Carey and made his escape possible – though the biographies didn't refer to it as an escape – was his susceptibility to new information about the nature of the world and new ideas about how it might be remade. The information and ideas came from a wide assortment of sources – Europe in the late eighteenth century was a lively place. They came from Captain Cook's newly published narratives of his South Sea voyages, from Rousseau's belief in the common and equal rights of all men, from the pamphlets of the anti-slavery lobby. The ideas were secular, but religion was the fire inside Carey which melted them down and coalesced them into the belief that men could be improved, and that Christianity was the proper instrument to improve them. The Church of England which had christened Carey, where many generations of Careys had worshipped, stood against these ideas. It represented social and doctrinal conservatism and the establishment; to get into the universities, to become a naval or military officer or an employee of the state, you still needed to belong to it. To Carey its ministry was 'lifeless and carnal'. Through the influence of a fellow apprentice he began to attend meetings organised by non-Anglican, evangelical groups, the new Nonconformist churches, which had sprung up in the wake of John Wesley's crusades across England. Among the most radical of them, with their dramatic symbolism of an adult rebirth in Christ, were the Baptists. At twenty-three Carey was baptised in the River Nene in Northampton and began to work for his new church as a travelling part-time preacher. Five years later, in 1789, the year of the French Revolution, he gave up cobbling for good and moved to the charge of a Baptist congregation in the town of Leicester.

The French Revolution excited him. It was 'a glorious door opened . . . for the Gospel, by the spread of civil and religious liberty'. He became a republican in politics and a radical in religion. He refused to drink the loyal toast, he burned his playing cards, he banned West Indian sugar from the table ('on account of the iniquitous manner in which it is obtained'). His biographers tended to pass this off as youthful excess, but it was a personal revolution of a very modern kind, by a man who had hung a map of the known world on his cottage wall, who could see the international repercussions of his actions and beliefs. In 1792 he published a pamphlet: *An Enquiry into the Obligations of Christians to use Means for the Conversion of the Heathens, in which the Religious State of the Different Nations of the World, the Success of Former Undertakings, and the Practicability of Further Undertakings are Considered by William Carey.* As much as religion, it reflected his enthusiasm for exploration and geographical statistics, and it contained a calculation which distressed him: of the world's 731 million people, only two-ninths were Christian. The remedy, Carey wrote, lay in overcoming fears and prejudices about the remoteness of barbarians, their willingness to kill strangers, their inedible food and incomprehensible tongues. Maps could be made and friendships established, languages could be learned and European diets adjusted.

At a meeting in Kettering later the same year Carey and his fellow ministers founded the Baptist Society for Propagating the Gospel Among the Heathen, to be funded by subscription and church collections. All that was needed now was a suitable group of heathens to convert. There was already a scattering of Moravian and Wesleyan preachers in the West Indies and west coast of Africa, which seemed to rule those places out on the grounds – rather un-Christian but quite common among missionaries; David Livingstone was a later example of it – that there was little glory in coming second. Carey himself favoured Tahiti. Captain Cook's logbooks had made a lasting impression. Nobody seems to have given any thought to India at all, if only because the East India Company's opposition to missionaries was well known, until a ship's surgeon called John Thomas turned up in Northampton and roused a meeting attended by Carey to a peak of compassionate weeping. Thomas had made two voyages to Bengal on East Indiamen and for a time preached there, upcountry and well away from Calcutta. He told his audience that the people there were wretched – 'My heart aches for them body and soul' – and at the end of his speech Carey stood up, shook hands with him and volunteered to go. Whereupon, said the biographies, 'Thomas fell upon his neck and wept'.

This was symptomatic. Thomas was unbalanced, impulsive and feckless. He borrowed money wherever he went – London, Calcutta, the trading outposts where he had preached – and rarely got around to repaying it. Later, like Carey's wife, Dolly, he went plain mad. He was the last man, in fact, that Carey should have trusted to lead him further than the outskirts of Leicester let alone the creeks and backwaters of Bengal. Carey, however, could not be dissuaded by the pleas of his family or his congregation. His father thought the journey was 'the folly of madness'. Dolly, who was eight months pregnant, stubbornly refused to go. More obstructively, the East India Company's office in London rejected their applications for licences to settle in Bengal, which meant that their passage on British ships would be difficult to obtain. In the end the captain of Thomas's previous ship agreed to take them, but it was a false start. Thomas and his family and Carey and his eldest son, eight-year-old Felix, set sail from the Thames and a few days later found themselves anchored in the Solent, were they were to wait six weeks for a convoy to assemble. Here one of Thomas's London debts caught up with him and the missionary party and their baggage were put ashore on the Isle of Wight. Carey and Thomas returned, frantic but apparently unchastened, to the Midlands to talk the Baptist Mission Society into supplying more money for a second attempt by a Danish ship which was due to sail from Dover in a few days' time. Dolly Carey had by this time given birth to a son, Jabez, but Carey could still not persuade her to leave with him. Thomas tried with more success: she would come if she could bring her sister, Kitty. The next day an enlarged and flustered party of Careys set off for the south by coach; it was the last English journey William and Dolly Carey would ever make.

The voyage round the Cape of Good Hope to the Hooghly took five months. Carey, who had already taught himself Hebrew, Latin and Greek, now spent the time learning rudimentary Bengali from Thomas and worrying about the Godlessness of the other Europeans on board. They reached Bengal in November 1793. A terrible famine had swept the country twenty years before. About 10 million people, a third of the population, had died of starvation. The loss in terms of fields and field labour had still not been recovered. 'I see one of the finest countries in the world, full of industrious inhabitants,' wrote Carey, 'yet three-fifths of it are an uncultivated jungle, abandoned to wild beasts and serpents.'

Carey and Thomas were soon nearly destitute themselves. They had arrived with a little money from the Baptist mission, but they badly needed to earn more. Thomas looked for work as a surgeon; Carey thought he might become a smallholder. Calcutta, with its large European population, was their obvious home. But in Calcutta they felt too close to official disfavour and the cost of living was much too high. To Carey, the town was 'a great snare', into which Thomas (who, unlike Carey, had already experienced the desperate loneliness of life upcountry) was only too eager too fall. 'The grandeur, the customs and the prejudices of the Europeans are exceeding dangerous,' Carey wrote, catching the essential tone of British expatriate life, then and now. 'They are very kind and hospitable, but even to visit them, if a man keeps no table of his own, would more than ten times exceed the allowance of a mission; and all their discourse is about the vices of the natives.' So they wandered north by river to deliver sermons in native towns which were rarely frequented by Englishmen, guided by a Brahmin whom Thomas imagined he had evangelised (this wasn't so; the Brahmin, Ram Ram Basu, had attached himself to the party for the usual pecuniary reasons). In Nuddea they preached to other pundits – Nuddea was 'the Oxford of Bengal', the centre of Brahminical learning – but the only effect was novelty. No conversions, no prospect of work, but plenty of bad water. Dolly and the children fell sick with dysentery. They returned to Calcutta abjectly, on the brink of pauperdom. Dolly had never reckoned that the penalty of marrying a Northamptonshire cobbler would be this simultaneous sweating, shaking, retching and shitting in a small boat on a subtropical river. She was never quite sane again.

And now, not for the last time in Carey's life, there came a paradoxical salvation. The people who saved Carey were the people whom Carey, with innocent presumption, had come to save. A Hindu banker, Nelu Dutt, allowed the family to live rent-free in his country home outside Calcutta on the banks of the Hooghly. Carey could not live there for ever, but it allowed Thomas time to borrow money (from another Hindu banker) so that they could hire fresh boats and servants and set off again, south and east this time, to the area of creeks, marsh and jungle in the Ganges delta known as the Sunderbuns. Here Carey hoped to take advantage of a British scheme to clear the jungle by parcelling out plots of it to natives, who would then make money by felling and selling the timber until the day when fields had been created and they could work the land as rice farmers, contributing to the general prosperity and government revenues. Nothing about his family's health or Carey's physique suggests they were fitted for a life of back-breaking labour in a country infested with tigers, crocodiles and cobras and ridden with cholera and malaria. But their luck held. After a four-day journey they stopped at a place called Debhata, where the East India Company owned a salt warehouse which was supervised by an Englishman, Charles Short. Again Short was not a Christian; he was, to Carey's almost incredulous displeasure, a deist. But he was a very welcoming, lonely deist. He put up the women and children in his bungalow, travelled with Carey to his plot and helped him build a house from bamboo, and proposed marriage to his sister-in-law, Kitty. The proposal was accepted. Life looked up. Carey had now one fewer mouth to feed, the beginnings of a farm and the prospect of an income.

Had Carey remained in the Sunderbuns he might have become a more romantic (and more obscure) figure, a small-time Livingstone or Schweitzer, who sat over his diaries in candlelight to record the slaughter of maneaters and the hubbub of native panic. But he stayed among the tigers and the marshes for only a few months before he moved north by river again, further north in India than he had been before, almost to the foothills of the Himalayas. His biographers explained the move as a call from God, acting yet again through his unlikely agent, Thomas. (The lines 'God acts in a mysterious way / His wonders to perform' were written by William Cowper; the poet had been a neighbour in Northamptonshire and Carey travelled to India with a book of his verse.) That was the divine way to see it; some men who knew Thomas slightly, indigo planters in northern Bengal, now offered Carey and him well-paid jobs as managers at their factories in Dinajpur. But behind the offer lay a strange history of cause and effect – the divine mind acting at global levels of mysteriousness – which had recently made indigo the first piece of British industrial endeavour on the subcontinent.

Indigo is a tropical and subtropical plant. As Europe exploited the tropics, it had slowly replaced woad as the source of blue dye. Now, thanks to the same political ideas that had transformed Carey, the usual sources of supply had dried up. The American War of Independence had interrupted the indigo trade from Carolina. In French Haiti the slave rebellion led by Toussaint L'Ouverture had cut off Europe's single largest source completely. And yet the call for blue dye had never been greater. The wars against revolutionary France increased the need for blue cloth, because blue was the colour of most naval and military uniforms. So, just as egalitarian ideas were diminishing supply, the same ideas, or the nations which opposed them, were increasing demand. The East India Company saw its opportunity. It needed a crop which could help pay for the cargoes of finished textiles which were sailing down the Hooghly. It organised and subsidised indigo plantations near the fast snow-fed rivers of northern Bengal, sown with seed brought from western India. With the plantations came the factories. Large iron and copper boilers began to be towed upstream on rough barges, at the end of ropes made taut by coolies straining and chanting as they plodded up the riverbank.

The processing of indigo needed great care and, above all, careful timing. The seeds needed to be sown just before the spring rains and the plant harvested at the moment of perfect ripeness, after the monsoon but just before the rains returned in the autumn. Then the crop had to be carried quickly – any delay might cause decay, and decay was fatal – to the factories where, in vats flushed with changes of clear river water, it was submerged, beaten and fermented until a fine blue sediment lay on the bottom. The water at the top of the vats was then drawn off and the remainder boiled and strained until the sediment was like soft soap, which was then pressed and dried and cut into half-pound cakes. The process took a great deal of time and manual labour; the drying stage alone lasted two months and it was coolies, equipped with only the most basic technology, who lifted the water from the river and beat the mixture in the vats with bamboo paddles. It also needed space; indigo grown on land measuring 2,000 square feet would shrink in the end to only one of thousands of half-pound cakes. And finally – so it was thought – it needed European supervision, because manufacture in bulk meant that each stage of indigo's passage from plant to dye needed to be sampled and tested and passed fit, otherwise defects in the final product would be discovered too late and whole batches would have to be destroyed or sold too cheap. Each indigo factory had several out-factories, and each of these several out-factories was managed by a solitary Briton.

And so, at an out-factory called Mudnabati, Carey exchanged one kind of loneliness for another. In some ways his new life was an advance. As an indigo planter he got a licence to settle in Bengal from the East

India Company; he drew a salary of £250 a year with a share in the profits; and Mudnabati was not, like the Sunderbuns, a wilderness. But there was a price to pay. Carey was now part of an agricultural industry that remained a reproach to British rule in India for the next 130 years, until Gandhi's time (it was the cause of his first big Indian campaign), when the products of German chemistry finally wiped out indigo as a cash crop. At the root of indigo's wretched reputation was the three-way relationship between the British factory managers who bought the crop, the Indian peasants who grew the crop, and the Indian *zamindars* who owned the land where the crop was grown. At the start of each growing season the managers would give the peasants cash advances to buy seed, and then when the harvest came in they would deduct these loans from the price they paid. But the price fluctuated with the demands of the European market; many peasants got into debt, while many others preferred to stick to tradition and grow rice, which was a more useful crop both to themselves and their Indian landlords. Bitter quarrels arose between managers, peasants and landlords. Peasants who could not be persuaded to grow indigo were often compelled to grow it by beatings and threats. In many places the factory manager, fearful in his isolation, became the despotic apex of an oppressive system.

This worried Carey because it interfered with his primary duty as a Christian missionary. The whole concern of 'the poor labouring people', he wrote, was 'to get a little rice to satisfy their wants, or to cheat their oppressive merchants and *zameendars*'. Consequently they had 'scarcely a word in use about religion . . . no word for love, for repent, and a thousand other things'. Nonetheless Carey never tired of preaching to them in a form of sophisticated Bengali which few peasants and coolies understood. He hired boats and travelled to remoter districts, and walked in these districts from village to village urging curious crowds to abandon their old faiths and avoid an eternity in Hell. He began to learn Sanskrit and to translate the Bible into Bengali. He opened schools ('to promote curiosity and inquisitiveness among the rising generation; qualities which are seldom found among the natives of Bengal') and from a dispensary treated malarial fever with 'Jesuit's bark' – cinchona – imported from South America. The last was a popular success; the bark had a practical, demonstrable effect, and Carey thought the mission should be 'furnished yearly with at least half a hundredweight'. But his evangelism was an utter failure. By 1800, seven years after he set foot in India, years of recurrent dysentery and fever for himself and his family, he had not made a single Indian convert. In the meantime another of his children had died and his wife had gone completely insane, alternately crackling with reproach and wailing with depression. Carey unburdened himself to his nearest European neighbour, Thomas, who managed another factory eighteen miles away, and Thomas replied: 'You must endeavour to consider it a disease. The eyes and ears of many are upon you . . . if you show resentment, they have ears, and others have tongues set on fire. Were I in your case, I should be violent; but blessed be God, who suits our burdens to our backs. Sometimes I pray earnestly for you, and I always feel for you. Think of Job. Think of Jesus.'

Little of this, however, intruded into Carey's correspondence with the Baptist Mission Society in England. His letters concentrated on descriptions of the country and its inhabitants and the great Christian fruit that they might bear. Send more missionaries! Onwards and upwards to Bhutan, Tibet, China! The society published the letters in annual volumes, with inspirational effect. Other missionary societies were formed in London, Edinburgh and Glasgow, while the Midlands Baptists themselves decided to send reinforcements to Carey and settle them in a new mission station at Serampur. Four men sailed with their families to the Hooghly, but two of them died not long after they had landed. The survivors, William Ward and Joshua Marshman, formed with Carey what the biographies called 'the Trio'. Like Carey, Ward and Marshman were self-improving, non-metropolitan men. Ward was a Derbyshire printer turned journalist whose last work in England was editing the *Hull Advertiser*. Marshman had started out as a bookseller's apprentice in Wiltshire before progressing to weaving and country schoolmastering. They brought printing and publishing skills and the enthusiasm of the self-taught for new facts; Marshman, as Ward noted, didn't chew books but swallowed them whole and had a memory 'very tenacious of dates, or circumstances in History, &c &c'. Their company in Serampur released Carey from the isolation and oppression of indigo. During the monsoon rains of 1799, before he left Mudnabati, he had begun to worry about himself. He had written: 'I . . . appear to myself to have lost much of my capacity for making observations, improvements, etc., or of retaining what I attend to closely . . . I try to observe, to imprint what I see and hear on my memory, and to feel my heart properly affected with the circumstance; and yet my soul is impoverished, and I have something of a lethargic disease cleaving to my body.' Of course, he was being far too hard on himself. He had been stuck in a remote house for six years with a mad wife, in a climate which for half the year swaddled human energy like a wet, warm towel. It was the self-criticism of a man who expected wonderful achievement – 'Expect great things from God' – which was eventually fulfilled in Serampur. There he stuffed his life with words, deeds, facts, improvements; almost – or so it seemed to me as I read his life – as though intellectual curiosity for the here and now sustained him more than his faith in the eternal.

He became a professional linguist. The British Governor General of Bengal, Lord Wellesley, had realised the need to breed a new kind of imperial civil servant. He established a college at Fort William in Calcutta; the first centre of Western art and science in the East, 'a light amid the darkness of Asia'. There the servants of the East India Company were to be reformed from heedless young men, guffawing over their cards and claret, into sober and industrious administrators with some know-ledge of the people they ruled. In 1801 Carey was appointed the college's first professor of Sanskrit and Bengali, and for the next thirty years divided his weeks pretty equally between Serampur and Calcutta, sailing down to the city on Mondays and returning upstream on Fridays. His sheer intellectual energy during these years is daunting; there was hardly an hour in which Carey did not either learn something new or pass on the results of his learning. In the course of a day he might read or speak in nine different languages. On a stifling June day in 1806, for example, he rose at quarter to six in the morning and prayed and read from the Hebrew Bible until seven, when he attended prayers with his servants in Bengali. Between morning tea and breakfast he read some Persian under the guidance of a *munshi* (a native teacher of languages) and studied a part of the Bible in Hindustani. After breakfast he worked with a pundit on his translation of the *Ramayana*, the Hindu epic, from Sanskrit to English. At ten he set out for the college at Fort William, where he taught Sanskrit, Bengali and Marathi until one or two in the afternoon. Then, at home again, he checked the proofs of his Bengali translation of the Book of Jeremiah until a late lunch. After lunch, with another pundit, he translated some of the Gospel of St Matthew into Sanskrit. At six in the evening he sat down with a third pundit to learn Tilingua (Telegu; the language spoken to the south of Bengal). At seven he composed his evening sermon in English. At half past seven he preached the same sermon. At nine, when his congregation had dispersed, he wrote to the mission society in England and then rounded off the day by reading from the Greek Testament and praying. 'I have never more time in a day than this,' he wrote to the mission society with an air of playful apology, 'though the exercises vary.'

At Serampur his scholarship was put into print. Earlier, when he was still in Mudnabati, Carey had ordered a printing press from Calcutta for £40. It was transported to Serampur and there in 1801 Thomas Ward and Carey's son Felix set the type for Carey's New Testament in Bengali; a copy was presented to George III at Windsor. In the years that followed Serampur became the foremost printing and publishing centre in India, outdoing even the government presses in Calcutta. By 1837, when Marshman died, the mission had translated the Bible into forty-five Asiatic languages, including Chinese, Malay and Thai. Carey alone, said his biographers, translated the entire Bible into Bengali, Oriya, Marathi, Hindi, Assamese and Sanskrit, and parts of it into twenty-nine other languages. Much of this was the work of Hindu pundits working under Carey's supervision, but Carey always took responsibility for the finished product. 'I never suffer a single word, or a single mode of construction to pass without examining it,' he wrote. 'I read every proof sheet twice or thrice myself, and correct every letter with my own hand.'

New languages required new type fonts in non-Roman scripts. The mission hired a blacksmith who had helped an earlier Englishman cut the first Bengali type, and set him to work on the thousand combinations of characters in Devanagari, the formal alphabet of Sanskrit. Twelve Bengali pattern-cutters were lured from the cotton trade to cut Chinese ideograms in wood. By 1812, the mission had begun to manufacture its own paper and ink. It employed a professional type-cutter from England – his job was to shrink the previous type sizes so that the Bible could be published in one volume rather than five – and dozens of natives as typefounders, compositors, pressmen, binders and copyists. In that year a big fire at the press destroyed almost its entire stock of paper, manuscripts and books, including a polyglot dictionary of all the languages derived from Sanskrit, a work in progress which Carey never restarted. Carey was sanguine: 'The Lord has smitten us, he had a right to do so, and we deserve his correction.' But in Nonconformist Britain the fire was reported as a great tragedy which threatened the entire objective of a Christian subcontinent, and collection boxes far removed from Carey's

Baptist heartland rang to the sound of copper and silver. During the course of a single Sunday in the Clydeside town of Greenock, so his biographies said, every place of worship had raised money for the restoration of the Serampur press. It was in full production again within six months.

As well as Bibles, Serampur produced grammars, dictionaries, schoolbooks, tracts, and took on commercial contracts for the colonial governments of Britain and Denmark. Carey's own Bengali–English dictionary and grammar became the standard work and laid down the sinews of modern Bengali prose (and this claim was more than hagiography; distinguished Bengali historians themselves said that Carey had raised Bengali 'from its debased condition as an unsettled dialect' to a language 'capable . . . of becoming the refined and comprehensive vehicle of a great literature'). Slowly the boundaries between the religious and the secular began to wear down, and ideas began to leak into Bengali society which could no longer be described as purely, or even mainly, biblical. When Carey's son Felix published a translation of the *Pilgrim's Progress*, that could be defended as an evangelical book. But could the same defence be mounted when Felix published a Bengali edition of Goldsmith's *Vicar of Wakefield* and gave his Bengali readers their first taste of a new European literary form, the novel?

The truth was that, because Carey identified Christianity with Western material progress, he had become a propagandist for much more than Christianity. His purpose was one thing; his effect another. In 1818 the mission press launched English and Bengali editions of a monthly magazine called *Dig-Darshan* (*The Signpost*), probably the first periodical ever published in an Indian language. It was meant to provide 'entertaining as well as instructive reading' for young Indians and its first issue contained articles on new industrial advances in Britain, botany, zoology, and Carey's boyhood hero, Christopher Columbus. In fact, Carey hadn't given this particular project his wholehearted support because he suspected that the government in Calcutta might disapprove; it still wanted India untainted and unthreatening – the English journals published from Calcutta were regulated and censored. But the anticipated displeasure never emerged and *Dig-Darshan* was quickly followed by a Bengali weekly for adults, *Samachar Darpan* (*The News Mirror*), which was then unique in all Asia as the first Western-style newspaper to be published in an oriental language. Once again the object was to 'disseminate useful knowledge'; the paper's statement of intent prom-ised 'brief notices concerning the most remarkable events and discoveries in Europe, and . . . articles, amusing and instructive, calculated to whet the edge of curiosity in the subscribers, and to ensure the continuance of their support'. It worked. The intelligentsia of Bengal subscribed in large numbers, and together with a third periodical in English, *The Friend of India*, the paper played a fundamental role in shaping the outlook of a small but vital section of nineteenth-century India. But by Carey's own criteria it saved very few Indians from the eternity of Hell. For Carey, curiosity (and the application of curiosity, science) was the ally of faith; that was how he had found his own. Science, there-fore, would help undermine false faiths such as Hinduism because it would demonstrate the superior power of Christ. What he couldn't see was that it could (and soon would) be equally inimical to his own beliefs, that once curiosity was let out of the bag it didn't pick and choose among the cats it killed. But that in Carey's time would have required a rare far-sightedness. The cracks between science and religion had still to widen into a gulf. Scientists and inventors in Britain were still overwhelmingly Christian, in particular they were English Nonconformists and Scottish Presbyterians, just as many ministers of religion were amateur scientists. To take one example, one of Carey's strongest supporters in Britain, the Reverend Thomas Chalmers, lectured his Glasgow congregation on astronomy and political economy before he went on to found the Scottish Free Church. Darwin and Huxley were still to come. The Christian cosmogony – its theory of world history, the Creation, Original Sin, the Flood – was still intact.

Carey's own favourite sciences, botany and zoology, had begun as hobbies in the countryside of his childhood. The fertile plains of Bengal offered them immense scope. There was so much here for the European mind to discover, document and classify, such an apparent jumble of plant and animal life for a man of Carey's even, enquiring temper to sort out and understand. His letters grew full of exacting demands. From Serampur he wrote to his son William, who was now himself a missionary in Carey's old home in north Bengal: 'Can you not get me a male and female khokora – I mean the great bird like a kite, which makes so great a noise, and often carries off a duck or kid? I believe it is an eagle, and want to examine it. Send me also all the sorts of ducks and waterfowls you can get, and, in short, every sort of bird you can obtain which is not common here. Send their Bengali names. Collect me all the sorts of insects, and serpents, and lizards you can get which are not common here. Put all the insects together into a bottle of rum except butterflies, which you may dry between two papers, and the serpents and lizards the same. I will send you a small quantity of rum for that purpose. Send all the country names. Let me have the birds alive . . . Spare no pains to get me seeds and roots, and get brother Robinson to procure what he can from Bhootan [Bhutan] and other parts.'

But this research was only one part of Carey's scientific project. The foreign natural landscape was like foreign religious belief; first you discovered and defined it, then you changed and improved it. The land must be improved, Carey wrote, because from it was 'suspended the comfort and happiness of the larger part of . . . numerous millions'. The model was the Northamptonshire countryside Carey had left behind, which itself had been recently transformed in the drive to make British agriculture more productive and profitable, by the amalgamation of smallholdings, by better drainage, by innovations in crops and machinery. And so in Carey's mind 'improvement' meant European agricultural tools, European plants and crops, European farming methods. He filled his letters home with a different kind of demand, but no less exacting. He would transplant England in India, and teach Indians how to benefit. There were requests for plough wheels, sickles and scythes, acorns and all kinds of nuts, copies of botanical books and magazines. He would consider it 'a great acquisition', he wrote to his supporters, if they could send the seeds of sour apples, pears, nectarines, plums, apricots, cherries, gooseberries, currants and strawberries, all 'put loose in a box of dry sand and sent so as to arrive in September'. At Barrackpur, across the river from the Serampur mission, he started an experimental farm where peasant farmers were taught the gospel of manure and good drainage. In Calcutta he founded the Agricultural Society of India through which he hoped to reward 'industry and virtue in the room of idleness and vice'. Gold medals were given to the farmers who could grow the best coffee, cotton and European fruits, whose trees provided the most luscious mangosteens (freshly transplanted in Bengal from the Pacific), whose churns could supply the sharpest cheese. On a grander scale, he wanted to plant Bengal with forests of Burmese teak and settle the arable lands with British landowners, whose energy and science would set a good example to their Indian neighbours.

At ground level, among individual fields and farmers, some of these schemes bore good results. In Serampur, for example, Carey's head gardener became famous for the quality of his English cabbage. But as a plan for the future of British India it remained a lonely and romantic vision. Outside irrigation canals and cash crops, the British administration never significantly altered the toiling heart of rural India, and India never became a British colony in the sense that Carey had hoped, as a country of white settlers like North America or Brazil. Instead he had smaller memorials. Several of the Indian plants he had classified were named after him. He edited and published the first standard work of Indian botany – the *Flora Indica* – which had been compiled by his friend William Roxburgh, the superintendent of the East India Company's botanical gardens downriver from Calcutta. And during what he described as 'intervals of relaxation' he stocked his own botanical gardens in Serampur with plants from across the world, which Carey had exchanged for Indian specimens. Some of them thrived. Thirty years after his death, his gardens were still famous for their South American collection. In small ways that were perhaps more enchanting than useful – an English daisy here, an Amazonian berry there – he had permanently changed the Indian landscape.

The Serampur gardens were Carey's great delight. He would wander through their plant beds, stopping, stooping, poking, instructing. And when, during his old age, he was too frail to walk, he would conduct his horticultural supervision from a mobile platform like a trolley, which his servants towed up and down the garden paths. The Almighty continued to give him some bad breaks. In 1823 monsoon floods swept away most of his botanical collection, which Carey arduously replanted only to see a great part of it uprooted by a cyclone eight years later. (Carey wept at the sight.) In the meantime he had become embroiled in a protracted row with mission headquarters in England. Many of his original supporters had died and the severer men who replaced them resented the independence of the Serampur mission, regarding it as a wayward outpost that needed to be steered away from commerce and botany and back towards its original Christian purpose. The dispute lasted a dozen years. At its heart was a straightforward argument about money and property – who owned Serampur, the mission society or the missionaries? – but the charges against the Serampur men as they appeared in England often revolved around words such as 'comfort' and 'luxury'. To their English critics it seemed that by this stage Carey and his colleagues had simply sat back to enjoy an expatriate life: coolies and carriages. Where was the self-sacrifice?

There may also have been, unvoiced, the feeling that the Serampur Trio were tradesmen who had used evangelism to jump above their proper social station; 'a nest of consecrated cobblers' in the words of the Reverend Sydney Smith, the Anglican essayist whose wit and armchair prejudices had been fattened at Winchester school and New College, Oxford. The fact that a self-taught former shoemaker could share a supper table with a Governor General was annoying to some and pleasing to others: you could blame the melting effects of the Indian sun on the English hierarchy or praise the intervention of the Lord. But what were his supporters to make of the fact that the former shoemaker had married into the aristocracy (admittedly only the Danish aristocracy), or that he had made the marriage only six months after he had buried poor, mad Dolly?

The biographies called her 'The Lady Rumohr'. Carey married her in Serampur in 1808, when he was forty-six and she a year or two older, and she was a surprising story in herself. She was born Charlotte Emilia de Rumohr in the Danish duchy of Schleswig, the only child of the Chevalier de Rumohr and the Countess of Alfeldt. She was a frail child. When she was fifteen her family's home caught fire and she injured her spine during her escape. She became a permanent invalid. She was hardly able to walk. She could not climb stairs. There were long hours in every day spent on day-beds, reading. Her family sought cures and in the end came down to the healing properties of sunshine. They sent her to Italy and the south of France, and then, when Mediterranean heat had no effect, arranged her passage to India – surely a desperate last resort – with a friend in the Danish East India Company. Tranquebar in the south was her original destination, but the ship put in first at Serampur, where she met a relation who was the governor and, perhaps for that reason, decided to remain. Bengal, among the British, was a byword for sickness and a short life; the fresh soil of its graveyards often stuck to their boots; it ended careers in raging fevers and calls for surgeons whose only treatment (European and useless) comprised a sharp knife, a punctured artery and a bleeding-cup. The Lady Rumohr may have been the first and last visitor to have imagined the place as a sanatorium.

She arrived in Serampur about the same time as Carey and a house was built for her on the river bank next to his mission. She was an educated woman: the contrast with Dolly could not have been greater. She understood several European languages besides Danish; she read books; she could converse delicately about abstractions. On the voyage out she had read Pascal in French. But she was a sceptic and not a believer and she could not speak English. Carey remedied both soon after they met. In June 1801, the year after she arrived, she became the first European woman to be baptised in India. In the years that followed, years when Dolly still lived, Carey continued to tutor his new friend in the Scriptures and English and Bengali, and during those years it is easy to imagine Carey spending more time in her home than his own; closing the door on his deranged wife, walking a few hundred yards down the Hooghly, sitting with a serene woman to whose physical frailty he could address 'the consolations of religion'. Who would blame him? The biographies made brief allusions to gossip and opposition among his fellow missionaries – a round robin was signed deploring the couple's engagement – but their authors were quick to stress that Carey always behaved towards his first wife with 'true Christian gentlemanliness' despite her being 'a peasant woman with a reproachful tongue' who had never learned to share his aspirations and ideals, above whom 'grace and culture had immeasurably raised him'. They did not mention the fact that it was her husband's adventures, part selfless and part selfish, that had begun to unhinge her in the first place.

With the Lady Rumohr, Carey found a soulmate. Both had discovered love at a late age in an unlikely place, when, if they had ever pined for love between the sexes rather than between the sexes and God, it must have looked certain to have passed them by. They were happy. When the Lady Rumohr travelled north up the Ganges, now searching for health in temperate breezes rather than heat, she sent her husband tender letters: 'Though my journey is very pleasant, and . . . the freshness of the air and the variety of objects enliven my spirits, yet I cannot help longing for you.' It reminded one of the biographies, the more modern, of Robert Browning and Elizabeth Barrett. Often she was confined to bed for months at a time, and even when she was well her life was mainly spent indoors. She shunned the sun which had brought her to Bengal and emerged in the fresh air only at dawn and at dusk, when she would be carried to a small carriage drawn by a single coolie, who would pull her in the contraption up and down the road along the river for an hour or so. This went on for a dozen years. It seems to have prolonged her life and her study of the life to come. In this way she was, Carey wrote, as though tending a marrow, 'gradually ripened for glory'.

She died, fully ripe, in 1821 at the age of sixty-one. Two years later Carey married again, this time an Englishwoman more than fifteen years younger and like himself married twice before. His biographers didn't make much of her. They slid her parenthetically into the narrative, hoping, it seemed to me, that the reader might not notice. She was called Grace Hughes; Carey had baptised her; they had lived in great happiness; she had been a devoted helper in his final years.

Carey was now at the climax of his career. Great works were all around him. The buildings and gardens of the Serampur mission had grown to cover five acres and now acted as the headquarters to a series of sub-missions which spread across the East. Three of Carey's four sons had followed their father's calling; Felix went to Burma, Jabez to the Moluccas. Indians themselves were being trained as missionaries in the college built for that purpose, described as one of the finest pieces of European architecture in Asia. Young teachers, fresh from Britain, tramped up and down its grand staircase of Birmingham iron, and from one of its classrooms pungent smells and smoke emerged. A Scotsman, the Reverend John Mack, had sailed from Britain in 1821, accompanied by chests filled with retorts, test tubes and pipettes, to tutor what was probably the first Western science class in India.

Carey shared his last Serampur house with Mack, which for the young graduate of Edinburgh University was a considerable honour. Carey had become a distinguished figure: a fellow of the Linnaean Society, a member of the Royal Horticultural Society, the Geological Society, the Asiatic Society of Bengal. He was the object of veneration and curiosity. Fellow scholars and divines often made the journey from Calcutta to pay their respects. The Burmese ambassador came with a retinue of cheroot-smoking women and servants who shaded him with golden umbrellas. Lady Bentinck, wife of the Governor General, was regularly rowed across the river from her country retreat in Barrackpur. Others, less exalted officials and travellers, turned up in Serampur merely to see what he was like. What they found was a small, stooped man leaning on a stick, strands of white hair curling over his collar, whose manners and accent had never shaken off rural Northamptonshire; the kind of man who might easily have a brother who worked as a nightwatchman in the London docks (which was the case). He wore black in the cool season and white in the hot. His clothes came from another age; stockings and nankeen breeches, a waistcoat, a battered old hat.

Because he was old and famous, people now took the trouble to write him up in their diaries, to record his personality for posterity. To visitors he was 'equable and cheerful'. Those who knew him better thought he united the apparently contrary qualities of meekness and firmness. He had, one witness remembered, 'a quaint kind of obstinacy or rather dourness, a "bovine way" such as one sees only among the peasantry of England . . . a want of delicacy and reserve'. And Carey's own assessment of himself seemed to bear this out. When visitors praised his genius, he demurred. He wrote to his nephew Eustace: 'I can plod. That is my only genius. I can perservere in any definite pursuit. To this I owe everything.'

What Carey called plodding, others saw as science. Andrew Leslie, another young Scotsman at the mission, wrote that Carey was 'so scientific' that he had banned from conversation the common English names of plants and flowers. 'If, therefore, I should at anytime blunder out the word Geranium, he would say *Pelargonium*, and perhaps accuse me of ignorance, or blame me for vulgarity.' Carey, Leslie noted, 'carries method into everything he does; classification is his grand hobby, and wherever anything can be classified, there you find Dr Carey . . . Visit his dwelling and you find he has fitted up and classified shelves full of minerals, stones, shells, etc., and cages full of birds.'

In this house, surrounded by the objects of the natural world, Carey grew old and sometimes lonely. Many of his earlier companions had died, two sons had died, he had stood at the graveside of two wives. Religious belief and scientific dispassion were only his most obvious characteristics; wrapped up among them, and now increasingly visible, was sentiment. He missed people and places. There was no point in returning to England, he said, because he knew almost nobody there. He cried easily. He told his friends that when he died he should be forgotten. Both biographies told a story. During Carey's final illness, the Scottish missionary Alexander Duff had travelled up from Calcutta to sit by his bed and pray. On his way out, he heard Carey's feeble voice calling him back. 'Mr Duff,' he said, 'you have been speaking about Dr Carey, Dr Carey. When I am gone say nothing about Dr Carey – speak about Dr Carey's Saviour.' And Duff went away 'rebuked and awed'.

Europe and its excitements seemed closer now. News no longer wandered round the Cape of Good Hope on the five-month journey by sailing ship. In Carey's last years the British government opened a new mail route to India – by steamer across the Mediterranean to Alexandria, by riverboat to Cairo, by camel from Cairo to the Red Sea, by another steamer across the Indian Ocean to Bombay and Calcutta. Despite the obvious hazards of this journey – mechanical breakdown, coal shortages, dust storms, mailbags lost or stolen during their numerous transfers – despatches reached Serampur from London in almost half the time. And, as if to demonstrate Carey's conviction that material and moral progress went hand in hand, one of the first pieces of news brought by the new steam route caused him enormous gratification. In September 1833, reports reached Serampur that the British government intended to free the slaves on sugar plantations in the British West Indies. Carey had prayed for their emancipation for almost fifty years. He thanked God with tears in his eyes and proposed that for the next month a special thanksgiving should be offered at every mission meeting.

He went on working well into the next year, reading and correcting proofs from the mission press, but his energy was failing. He was seventy-two; he had lived in India for forty years; heat and recurrent fevers had stripped him of fat and muscle. 'I am,' he wrote, 'exceedingly emaciated . . . my clothes hang about me like bags.' Exhaustion could not be indefinitely postponed and when it came it was complete. A man who had interested himself in almost everything was suddenly interested in nothing. His biographers said he was too tired even to manifest symptoms of 'spiritual ecstasy' at the prospect of death.

He died in Serampur at sunrise on 9 June 1834. The hot season had reached its peak; the next day, the day of his funeral, the monsoon clouds burst and sent torrents of mud into his newly dug grave. But first his body lay in state, and for several hours a queue of his servants, disciples and fellow missionaries, British and Indian, filed into the sickroom to have a last look. In the crush and the heat one student noticed signs of continuing life: a line of red ants had climbed up the wall, entered the bed, and begun to attack the corpse. It was a piece of zoological observation that Carey himself might have been pleased to make.

8.

That was Carey's life as I read it in Serampur in the rooms where Carey had lived and died, emptied long ago of their cases of fossils and stuffed birds and all the paraphernalia of documentation and classification which had marked Carey out as a man of science. He and his wives were buried a mile or so away in the old Christian graveyard on the other side of the Grand Trunk Road. One morning I walked there. It was a water-logged, neglected stretch of ground where, among the broken columns and sinking headstones of the lesser dead, three mausoleums like small Greek temples stood over the graves of Carey, Ward, Marshman and their families. Carey's memorial tablet had two lines from the English hymn-writer Isaac Watts: 'A wretched, poor, and helpless worm / On Thy kind arms I fall.' Carey had chosen them before he died; the metaphor, appropriately if perhaps unconsciously, had been plucked from the naturalist's world.

When I got back to the college that day I discovered that the library had opened. Mr Chatterjee, the librarian, had come. The strike and the holidays were over. I could begin my research into the Serampur mission's steam engine.

Chatterjee looked ill, unshaven and uncared-for, as though he had just got out of bed. A traditional Bengali dhoti hung loose and unstarched about his legs; one eye sported a black eyepatch; a grubby bandage concealed several fingers on his right hand. It seemed he always looked like this, that his dishevelment came out of an ascetic respect for learning. In Serampur, Chatterjee was the custodian of Carey's memory. The library contained many of the missionary's earliest biblical translations, in manu-script and type, written and printed on paper coated with arsenic to stop it being eaten by ants and termites. Most visitors came to Serampur to look at these books; Chatterjee would take them from their case and crack their bindings open and explain that it was the arsenic which had turned the paper brown. But he also knew about the steam engine. He pronounced the first word in the Bengali way, with an aspirated S, which made it onomatopoeic. Esssh-teem engine. You could imagine the piston stroke and the hiss of steam escaping from the cylinder.

He unlocked a cupboard and brought out a square sheet of brass with engraved lettering in a mixture of Roman, Gothic and copperplate script, so that each line carried a different emphasis like an advertisement. 'Twelve Horse Steam Engine,' it said, 'manufactured by Thwaites, Hick and Rothwell, engineers, Bolton.' It was the builder's plate. But it was not quite all that remained.

'The first esssh-teem engine in India,' said Chatterjee, and then produced a model engine, brass mounted on wood, which could be worked by compressed air. Chatterjee said it had been brought to the mission by William Ward, when he returned from furlough in England in 1820, as a replica of the big twelve-horsepower engine which was on its way.

But why did the missionaries want a steam engine? The story went like this. The Serampur printing presses demanded increasing quantities of paper. Despite the fact that the overwhelming majority of his potential converts were illiterate, Carey never abandoned the Protestant conviction that it was the printed word of the Bible rather than the spoken interpretation of the priesthood which contained the power to change men's hearts. The Bible needed paper, stacks upon stacks of it. Indian paper was too rough, imported English paper too expensive. The missionaries began to make their own, but found they could not make enough. Pulping the raw ingredients by hand was slow and laborious. They introduced machinery, powered by a treadmill which was worked by relays of forty coolies. But the treadmill was so obviously inhumane – one day one of the coolies collapsed and died through sheer fatigue – that the missionaries cast around for another solution. Eventually it came via William Jones, a Welsh mechanic who had begun to work a seam of coal one hundred miles north-west across the Bengal plain at a place called Raniganj. Jones, like Carey, was a self-taught polymath, known to his Bengali neighbours as 'Guru Jones'. Apart from his coal mine, which was probably the first in India, he had started up a factory in Calcutta which made canvas and he dabbled in architecture and papermaking. At his suggestion, the Serampur missionaries turned to the new technology which had only just begun to reshape Britain into the world's first industrial nation, and an order was placed with the Thwaites company in Bolton, which made engines for the Lancashire cotton mills.

The effect of the Serampur engine was sensational. On 27 March 1820, a large and curious crowd gathered to witness what was known among Indians as 'the fire machine' on its first day of operation. The engineman who had sailed out from Britain to work it – mystifying new skills such as his could certainly not be found in India – grew hot and bothered and spent a great deal of his time ordering the crowd to stand back. The crush included Europeans. For many of them, especially those who had served a long time in Bengal, the steam engine was no less novel; the Lady Rumohr, for example, must surely have been brought in her carriage to view the spectacle. But the accounts which survive dwell on the Indian reaction, perhaps because in that awed response, brown eyes watching the relentless thrust of the piston in a machine which had a life of its own, Europe could see the effects of its new power. Four years later the *Calcutta Gazette* could report with some satisfaction that the engine was still 'drawing large crowds of the natives of every walk'; people who were travelling up and down the Hooghly by boat would anchor there, go ashore and 'spend long hours to witness its working'.

Carey may have shared in the racial pride: his biographers did not say. What was certainly true of him, however, was that he did not see steam technology and the science that lay behind it as a racial monopoly. By the middle of the 1820s several rooms in the college had been filled with the 'philosophical apparatus' which John Mack used to teach physics and chemistry. There were by that time many many more instruments than those Mack had brought with him. Carey had appealed to his supporters at home for funds for the new laboratory, and four gentlemen in Edinburgh and London had responded by sending out a great heap of objects, including – Chatterjee still had the list from 1821 – an electrical machine, a portable camera obscura and an 'elegant working model of [James] Watt's steam engine'. The library still contained books from that time, many of them too fragile to open. Chatterjee showed me another list: Newton's *Principia Mathematica*, Joseph Black on chemistry, Charles Babbage's enquiry into the economy of machine manufacture. How much impact the laboratory and the books made on the college's Indian students is difficult to say – Carey himself sometimes complained of their apathy – but at least one Indian craftsman saw that the Serampur steam engine itself was not a mystery, that its workings could be understood and reproduced. According to the minutes of the Agro-Horticultural Society for 9 January 1828, it was resolved at Carey's suggestion that 'permission be given to Goluk Chandra, a blacksmith of Titigur, to exhibit a steam engine made by himself without the aid of any European artist'. The machine and its maker were summoned down the Hooghly to Calcutta for the society's next meeting, where the engine was steamed among heaps of vegetables exhibited by 109 native gardeners. The judges pronounced it 'useful for irrigating lands' and awarded Chandra a prize of fifty rupees.

And that is all that history seems to know about Chandra. He had done a remarkable thing; he was probably the first man of non-European race to build an example of the machine which allowed Europe to dominate the rest of the world for the next hundred years. If there had been more Chandras, more enterprising country blacksmiths, more indigenous steam engines, then that European supremacy might never have developed to its full extent, or at least it might have been moderated sooner. But because Britain knew that, it kept a grip on the technology it had perfected; put simply, pioneering blacksmiths in Bengal would mean less work for steam mechanics in Glasgow and Manchester. Increasingly, Britain saw India as a market rather than a manufactory; by the time Carey died the outflowing tide of cotton cloth woven on the handlooms of Bengal had been replaced by an inflowing tide of cheaper cloth spun and woven in the steam mills of Lancashire. The native cotton industry was wiped out. It was the same story with the Serampur paper mill.

The steam engine there was a great success. For Carey's biographers, and probably for Carey himself, it was a source of considerable pride that here was a 'purely missionary engine' which puffed and rattled on the Lord's work, its owners trusting that India could be evangelised at the new speed of steam. In the old days, paper had been produced from buckets of pulp and spread like thick soup on frames, one frame to a page, and left to dry in the sun. Now the pulp was fed from vats across steam-heated cylinders in a continuous sheet, so that, as Carey wrote, 'it is dried and fit for use in about two minutes from its having been in a liquid state'. In 1845, another two steam engines were erected and set to work and the mill became the largest in Asia, producing paper for all kinds of secular uses beyond the demands of Genesis to Revelations. It was, in fact, too successful. Its paper began to compete with imported British paper, not just in India but throughout Asia. British producers complained. The Indian government imposed restrictions on further supplies of machinery and switched its own contracts for stationery supplies to British factories, despite the higher cost of the paper they produced. By the 1860s the Serampur papermaking enterprise had been crushed.

I asked Chatterjee about the fate of the steam engines. They had been sold, he said, to new paper mills elsewhere on the river which flourished after the government changed its policy later in the nineteenth century. And then? Chatterjee's one visible eye regarded me with exasperation. 'I think they have been scrapped for sure long ago.' Things, he said, did not last for ever.

But the question in Serampur was: did ideas?

9.

The clue lay with my neighbours, the missionaries. During our last lunch together I asked them a question I had hesitated to ask before because it seemed too childish and too antique, the kind of query that might follow a small hand held high in a Sunday school, with gas lamps and fog in the streets outside. What did missionaries think happened to people who did not believe in Christ? Would they go to Hell?

Mrs Knorr said ah, but that was a difficult question, and looked at her husband, who hesitated. All three of us now looked as grave as Das, the cook. Eventually Knorr said that it depended on the missionary – they had different points of view – but 'liberal evangelists' like himself took the agnostic position: 'We don't know. My job as I see it is to proclaim the Gospel so that people can hear it. After that it's a mystery. It's up to the Lord.'

But did he believe in Hell?

'Yes, in the sense of individuals being God-forsaken, lost, in despair, suicidal, without hope.'

But that was surely Hell on earth. What about non-Christians who were in none of these states? What about Hell in the life to come, Hell as fire, brimstone and eternal damnation?

'I suspect that's an allegory or a metaphor, but again I don't know. I could be wrong. It's another mystery. Only the Lord knows.'

I thought of Carey as a young man in Northamptonshire two hundred years before; his earnest reckoning of the seven-ninths of the world's population that needed to be saved, his frantic urge to get among them. Hell to him had been real. It had not been a mysterious state of other-ness which could slip through a conversation like quicksilver. It seemed unlikely that he would have sailed to India to save millions of people from a metaphor. Of course, an eternity of suffering was only one part of Carey's Christian message – the negative part, the stick as opposed to the carrot – but he had certainly deployed it. And it hadn't worked. That was the central sadness in Carey's story – sad, that is, from Carey's point of view – which his biographers for obvious reasons neglected to explore. The facts were available in the Serampur library. In the twenty years up to 1821, the total number of people in India baptised by British Baptists came to 1,407. The figure included conversions made by missionaries who were not attached to Serampur (which itself had twenty-five missionaries under its supervision by 1817), and about half of the converts were European and Eurasian rather than Indian. As for the Indians, many of them soon lapsed or were later excluded from the Christian community because of their 'doubtful character'. Nor, year by year, did the figures reveal a slow but steady growth; in 1810 there were 106 baptisms, in 1820 only fifty-one. In 1824, more than thirty years after he landed in India, Carey lamented in a letter to his son Jabez that its people appeared 'as insensible as ever' to the joys of Christianity.

Serampur had offered a false promise. Soon after Carey arrived there, after his several years of utter evangelical failure, he made his first Indian convert, a thirty-six-year-old carpenter from the French colony of Chandernagore a few miles up the Hooghly. This man, Krishna Pal, had already renounced traditional Hindu society by joining the Hindu equivalent of English Nonconformism – a movement known as the Kharta-bhojas, which moved around the country worshipping God directly by singing and clapping, and denied the authority of the Brahmin priesthood. (It was their spiritual descendants, the Krishnaites, who now danced around the fire near the Serampur jute mill.) In that way, Pal had already moved closer to Carey's brand of Christianity. The clincher came after an accident, when Pal slid on the muddy side of a Hindu bathing tank and dislocated his arm. John Thomas, the evangelical ship's surgeon, had met him and pushed his arm back into place. 'The next morning,' Pal wrote later, 'Mr Carey came to see me, and after enquiring how I was, told me to come to his house, that he would give me some medicine, by which, through the blessing of God, the pain in my arm would be removed. I went and obtained the medicine, and through the mercy of God my arm was cured.' For Carey, 28 December 1800 was 'a day of great joy'. His diary recorded that he had 'the happiness to desecrate the Gunga [the Ganges] by baptising the first Hindoo, viz. Krishna, and my son Felix'. One of his biographers painted a vivid picture: the baptismal party had waded into the river singing one of Carey's new Bengali hymns, but the uplifting sound had been mingled with 'the ravings of Thomas in the schoolhouse on the one side, and of Mrs Carey on the other'.

This breakthrough was followed by some minor triumphs. Pal's family and friends were brought within the fold, and in 1802 Carey baptised his first Brahmin. The converts were feted and treated as equally as European sensibility would permit; at marriage feasts Carey and his brother missionaries would take along their own table, plates and cutlery and sit down to eat like a supper party, while Christian natives knelt on the ground and dipped their fingers into the same food served from banana leaves. Thomas, meanwhile, sat in his schoolhouse and devised his own prognosis in the form of a strange arithmetical equation in which the number of Indian Christians was multiplied in seventeen-year cycles, each cycle at a different multiple, like a stuttering mania, until mathematical inevitability ensured that every one of the subcontinent's 200 million people was Christian. Thomas's figures took no account of the hundreds of thousands of Christians in southern India; Roman Catholics converted by the Portuguese in Goa, and the descendants of a colony of the Syrian church which had migrated to the Malabar coast as early as the fourth century. But then to Thomas, as to Carey, such people were hardly recognisable as members of the same faith. They were merely slaves to Mediterranean ritual, Mariolators and Papists, untouched by the Reformation and the later Enlightenment.

Carey's church had no hierarchy, no vestments, no idols, and little ritual other than the ceremony of immersion. That was its beauty and that was its problem. It relied on the invisible magic of ideas, on the persuasion of words and reason to prepare the heathen soul for its leap across the boundaries of faith. Reason and faith: Carey believed passionately in a muddle of both and saw one as the servant of the other. And that was also not a help, because his opponents, the Hindu pundits, had their own supple and robust faith and an interpretation of the world which was just as reasonable or unreasonable as that offered by the Bible. Reason squabbled with reason like two old drunks, and (to a reasonable man) there were many comic moments. Carey's colleague William Ward recorded in his journal the details of one argument, in which Carey tried to persuade a group of Hindus that Brahmins – true Brahmins – did not exist. How so? Because Noah was not a Brahmin. All real Brahmins had perished in the Flood together with everyone else, apart from Noah's wife, also not a Brahmin. One of the group replied that God may well have planted a fresh race of post-diluvian Brahmins, but, as Ward solemnly observed, 'he was unable to establish the point'.

Later Carey gave up his attacks on the faults of Indian religion and switched, with more success, to the positive story of Christ and his ability to save the greatest of sinners. But even here there were formidable difficulties. When Carey had complained from his indigo plantation that the local population had no equivalent word for 'repent', he was only touching the tip of a large intellectual iceberg, the great confusion between words and ideas. For Carey, words were supremely important. He worked so hard at translating the Bible because his evangelical model was the Reformation in Europe, when the new invention of printing and the first translations of the scriptures into modern languages had for the first time given the Bible a readership far beyond the priesthood. Carey hoped to emulate this success in India. He failed to appreciate that the Protestant Bible owed its earlier success in Europe to the fact that Christian ideas had been part of everyday life there for centuries; that the Bible, as it were, was falling on fallow ground. But in India, the words were preceding the ideas. If indigo coolies did not understand repentance as an idea there was hardly much point in struggling to find a word in their language which would convey the same meaning. (To put it another way: Bengal has six seasons and a different word for each. How would one fit the words to the four ideas of the seasons of Europe?) Moreover, some of the ideas that could be easily understood were repellent: the killing of fatted calves was not, in the Hindu view, a cause for celebration. Carey, however, pushed ever on with his relays of pundits and their different languages, translating word for word, verse for verse, chapter for chapter, book for book. There were so many millions to be saved, who needed to hear the words of salvation.

Later scholarship on the shelves of the Serampur library suggested he had done too much too quickly. Few of his translations survived to become the standard version. They contained too many flaws and absurdities. In the Pushto translation of St Matthew, the verse 'Judge not, that ye be not judged' became 'Do not practise equity, lest equity be practised against you.' Perhaps some Pathan tribesmen drew a finger along their sword blades and nodded sagely at this un-Christian advice, but Bengalis had a more puzzling experience in Corinthians, where 'a little leaven leaveneth the whole lump' became 'a little crocodile crocodilleth the whole lump'. In 1802, William Ward reported that several new converts had been seen attempting to raise a friend from the dead, claiming that if the man would not come alive again 'then the whole Gospel was false'. But should Ward have been so surprised? Christianity promised resurrection. All that the converts had got wrong was their timing.

These were some of the ideological obstacles to Carey's mission. Above them loomed a greater barrier, the sheer social and economic impracticality of becoming a Christian. In other parts of the world voluntary conversion might offer practical advantages – it tended to identify the converts with the colonial power – but the British government in India did not think better of Indians who abandoned their own faith; it was no guarantee of preferment. In material terms, Indian converts lost rather than gained. They became social outcasts; they were sacked from their jobs; people derided them in the street. Carey found solutions. He gave them work at the mission in the printing plant and the paper mill and, if work was not available, he might provide board and lodgings and a small dole. But the solutions became incentives. Soon the missionaries were charged with creating a new class of 'rice Christians' from the poorest and most ignorant classes in Bengal. Both Indians and Britons made the accusation; it prompted Sydney Smith's attack on the 'nest of consecrated cobblers'. The reply was simple enough – did Carey's critics have any better ideas? Replying to Smith's attack, Robert Southey, the Poet Laureate, wrote that 'the first step towards winning the natives to our religion is to demonstrate that we have one'. The Church of England, said Southey, simply didn't have the zeal, its 'age of fermentation' had died long before. It was the 'low-born, low-bred mechanics' of the Serampur mission who had done more to evangelise the heathen 'than has been accomplished, or even attempted, by all the princes and potentates of the world – and all the universities and [government] establishments into the bargain'.

Across Nonconformist Britain, where the steam engine and the Protestant Church formed their utopian alliance, Southey's view prevailed. It was the spirit of Carey's biographies, and by the end of the nineteenth century it was possible, in terms of numbers, to demonstrate that Carey had started an evangelical tide. The missionaries who followed him had won thousands of converts in the hills of Bengal and Assam among animist tribes which were beyond the pale of Hinduism. But what had happened on the banks of the Hooghly, at Carey's home, the 'very seat of Brahminism'?

In the library I looked up Serampur in the twenty-six volumes of the *Imperial Indian Gazetteer*, published in 1908 and a monument to the infinite European capacity for facts; Carey would have been proud of it, nothing before or since has touched its authority and scope. Serampur took up a page. The population in the previous census of 1901 had been 44,451, divided by religion into Hindus (eighty per cent) and Muslims (nineteen per cent). Of the remainder, 405 were Christian. That was less than one per cent. But the gazetteer also showed that the town had doubled its population in the last thirty years of the century, 'the progress being due to the important mills which Serampur contains'. The mills made jute and cotton. They had drawn workers from hundreds of miles away, taken them out of the dusty countryside and packed them into railway carriages with their families and cooking pots. Many of them came from upper Bengal – the plains of Bihar – and spoke a different language, Hindi rather than Bengali. Many were Muslim. They had exchanged fields for the factory floor, rural huts for brick tenements, and the pattern of their lives was now set by the factory hooter rather than the sun. Alcohol became a problem.

What had changed the town, and even the way the town spoke and behaved, was not Carey's religion but the puffing machinery he thought would disseminate it; not the idea but the idea's tool.

10.

But at least Carey's message had changed Mr Tewari, though whether it had given the old Brahmin happiness nobody could say. Now that my work in the library was over and it was time to pack and leave, I went to find him to say goodbye. I met his son Ravi in the quadrangle outside their flat. He said his father was asleep, his usual afternoon nap. It would be best to leave him be.

'So tell me,' Ravi said, 'what did you find in Serampur?'

He spoke wryly, as though he thought his own answer would be 'not much'. I told him about the model and the brass plate from Lancashire. Ravi nodded half-heartedly and pointed with his eyes to the mission's rear wall.

'And have you been round the back, to Birmingham?'

That was another wryness, and also – because Ravi had never been to England, never in fact left India – a historical allusion. By 'Birmingham', he meant the houses of the jute workers over the mission wall, the 'jute colony' which I had travelled through on my way from the station, where the tea stalls were perched above open drains and the dogs lay in the dust. I had, in fact, gone back there and discovered that the random squalor concealed an industrial symmetry. The lanes were arranged in straight lines of uniform two-storey houses, back to back like those of a Victorian industrial town in England, only here families didn't spread themselves up and down the luxury of two floors but were cramped inside two-room flats on each floor. It was in these tenements that field labourers had adjusted themselves to their new role as factory hands more than a century ago, their new work governed by machines which were in turn governed by the demands of the markets far away in Europe, hands and wheels quickening and slackening as textile prices rose and dipped on the marble floors of British mercantile exchanges. For the people who came from the fields it must have been a difficult adjustment – perhaps for a time a nightmare of regret – but that time had passed. Now the colony looked as though it had always been there. Men shaved and washed in the street or lay on charpoys picking their teeth and smoking cheap cigarettes. Generations of trade union posters with hammers and sickles encrusted the factory walls. Old habits, old struggles; it was home.

The lanes had a powerful combination of smells. Some were typically Indian: hot tea boiled with milk and sugar, mustard oil, sun-dried urine. Others reminded me of Britain in a different age: dishwater, coal smoke, coal dust. Ravi had thought of Birmingham, and that was right, but it was the Birmingham of long ago, plucked from descriptions in his schoolbooks.

Leaving Serampur, I passed through these lanes again on my way to the station. There was a commotion at the factory gate. A crowd chanting slogans – 'Victory to the trade union!' – was struggling with the factory guards, who wore military khaki and carried sticks. I stopped the rickshaw and got down. Somebody decided I had come to see the manager, and so I was taken upstairs by a peon, an office servant, and shown into a room filled with polished wood.

An assistant manager, Mr Mehta, came in. He wore a safari suit and looked, resigned. 'Labour troubles,' he said, 'a permanent condition.' Since the morning two other assistant managers at the factory had been *gheraoed*, a form of protest perfected in Bengal in the 1960s in which workers surround a member of the management and harangue him. A *gherao* can last for days, with the manager permitted food and water, but Mehta did not think this *gherao* would last that long. Even the workers knew that the jute business was in serious trouble. A strike might finish off the mill for good.

I asked about the mill. Mehta said it had been built by the great

Scottish company Mackinnon Mackenzie and sold to an Indian firm in 1955. It made cotton as well as jute and employed 5,700 hands on a three-shift system. I asked about its steam engines. Mehta looked surprised. 'No, steam engines now. We electrified the looms forty years ago.' But the chimney, the smoke? Mehta said that the furnaces and boilers were maintained because the mill still needed steam; it wasn't used as power but as an ingredient in the final processes of stretching, smoothing and pressing, the cloth. 'And also,' Mehta smiled, 'for our steam hooter.'

The shouting outside had moved into the yard. We went to the window and looked out. Down below, some workers were squabbling with the khaki guards. Mehta wasn't ruffled. He smiled again: 'A permanent condition.' Somehow, the work at the factory went on.

Up above, smoke tumbled out of the factory chimney. Somewhere inside the weaving sheds yards of jute and cotton were being stretched, smoothed and pressed. The smoke drifted south and down across Carey's college, through the Ionic portico and into Chatterjee's library, through the windows of Tewari's flat and Carey's old home. There, if someone woke up in the middle of night and went to the water bucket to sluice away his bad dream, he would feel under his bare feet the prick of tiny cinders that had settled on the floor.

Sepia

February 2006

In an office filled with younger people, often much younger people, mainly you get by by not mentioning Jimmy Edwards or the Glums, and certainly not Harold Wilson, who has fallen deep into the forgetting pit and might as well be Stafford Cripps. But sometimes you try to get a fix on how you might seem to younger people, an imaginative act underpinned by remembering how older people once seemed to you, or by counting the years between significant dates in your ancestors' lives and comparing them to those in your own. For example, the Boer War came at roughly the same point in my grandfather's life as Ted Heath's government arrived in mine. A fairly long Tube journey with nothing to read can pass happily in these calculations.

I think of Mr Gemmill who taught chemistry at my school. Mr Gemmill was a peppery man, a 'stickler' and maybe also something of a snob. Once, seeing a boy at my school lunch table eating his mince with a spoon, he called out, 'Boy, where are you from – Crossgates [an old mining village]?' 'No sir.' 'Townhill [an ex-mining village] then?' 'No, sir. Sir, I belong to Oakley [a new mining village], sir.' 'Ah, boy, I thought so. I suppose they don't even know what a knife and fork *are* in Oakley.'

He had a bad leg from the First World War. I suppose he was only a few years older then than I am now. What the Somme was to Mr Gemmill's memory in 1957 is what – in years not horror – learning to edit the *Glasgow Herald*'s fish-price reports (haddock, six shillings a creel at Peterhead) or hearing McCartney's 'Yesterday' for the first time is to mine. In 1957, the First World War seemed a long way away to a boy of twelve, even though I often went to see a grandfather who fought in it, but in Mr Gemmill's mind it must have been only as the *Herald*'s subediting room is in mine: the smell of the trenches as fresh to him as the whiff of the subediting gluepot is to me, a flickering Chaplin film seen on home leave as marvellous and close in his memory as the afternoon my girlfriend pulled the new Beatles LP from its sleeve and said, 'You should listen to this song, there's a chamber group playing on it, even a cello!'

I think of that afternoon as part of my continuous present − a long thread somewhere inside me − rather than a historical moment, and yet much more recent times are now depicted as history, something outside and apart, and the effect is nowhere more striking than in television documentaries where you are suddenly brought face to face with how people looked and what they said in ye olden days of, say, 1987. BBC4 is showing a trilogy of documentaries made by Vanessa Engle with the overall title of 'Lefties'. According to the programme notes, the films 'look back at a time when left-wing ideas occupied the moral and political high ground of our intellectual lives . . . revisiting a passionate and turbulent era when the extreme Left believed it could change the world for the better and many people lived out their profound commitment to a political cause'.

When was this − 1926, 1931, 1945? No, more or less twenty years ago. The first film tells the story of a Marxist squat in Brixton in the late 1970s, the second of a feminist collective in Leeds in the early 1980s, the third of the short-lived 'left-wing' tabloid *News on Sunday* in 1987. On the evidence of the last, the only one I've seen, they promise to be good and interesting films. The shock, perhaps, is the hammer-blow of realisation that these ways of thinking and living have walked out of the door, and yet they were there, somewhere at the edge of the room with their coat on, only a moment ago.

Another shock is to see how people were once imbued with such idealism and rash hope. The *News on Sunday* was inspired by Alan Hayling, the leading light in a leftist sect called Big Flame, who was also the only Ford production-line worker with a double first from Cambridge. Trade unions and local authority pension funds put £6.5 million into the project. Things went wrong almost immediately. The paper decided to be anti-metropolitan and, though many of the staff came from London, based itself in Manchester. The editor-in-chief, John Pilger, fell out with the editor, Keith Sutton, and quit. Very few of the senior staff had ever done their jobs before. A controlling interest in the paper's management was given to a group of outsiders, mainly trade unionists, who held a 'golden share'. There were conflicts over content and political approach. The journalism was abysmal. The paper needed weekly sales of 800,000 to stay afloat, soon declined to 200,000, and went bankrupt after eight weeks, to be rescued briefly by the eccentric estate-agent tycoon Owen Oyston before it closed for good.

As well as several survivors filmed looking rueful in their sitting rooms, two modern, adaptive figures emerge from Engle's account. The first is Alan Hayling, who is now head of BBC Documentaries. The second is John Hegarty of Bartle, Bogle and Hegarty, the advertising agency hired for the launch campaign. It was Hegarty who went up to Manchester with the slogan 'No tits but a lot of balls' – the paper was meant as a radical reply to the *Sun* – only to have it rejected by a staff who had serious concerns about sexism. I don't blame them and would have voted the same way, but it was Hegarty rather than the personnel manager (whose concern for disability led to a post room staffed by deaf people) who was linked to the future in a way that socialist idealism was not.

It happened only sixteen years ago. The year I last saw Mr Gemmill may have been 1961. Sixteen from 1961 = 1945, the year the war ended, Hiroshima, Clement Attlee, Stafford Cripps, a year well beyond my memory though not my life. What would I have made of a documentary about, say, Sir Stafford in 1961? It would have seemed then as it does to me now: as history and its persuasive sepia narratives – outside and apart.

Ghost Town

February 2006

When I last looked at the ruins of the old Co-operative Society store in Randolph Street, Dunfermline, I never imagined they might have a role to play in the fate of the nation. Now we are invited to believe that they had. In some political version of chaos theory – the butterfly flapping its wings in Amazonia leading to avalanche in the Alps – Labour's loss of the Dunfermline by-election was ascribed to 'local issues' including higher tolls on the Forth road bridge and Dunfermline's 'ailing town centre.' Hence Dunfermline's sad High Street may be the beginning of the end of Gordon Brown.

Who knows? But the ruins of the Co-op were certainly strong evidence of the ailment. Through the 1990s they stood tall, shuttered and abandoned on both sides of the street, the kind of buildings you might find near a closed railroad depot in a small American town. Nobody knew what to do with them. And yet they had once been so busy, so central to this town (as other Co-ops were to other towns) that the Co-op was known simply as 'the Store', again like something out of the American West. In the tearoom on the top floor my grandparents celebrated their golden wedding with 'store' steak pie. For years I remembered my mother's 'store' dividend number. The Scottish Co-operative Wholesale Society, which had large and ornate headquarters in Glasgow, supplied ownbrand goods to local co-operative societies across the country. Store tinned rice pudding, store mops, store custard creams, store slicing sausage ('I love a sausage, a Co-operative sausage' was a street song, to the tune 'I love a Lassie'), all of them often delivered in store vans to the outlying villages.

A relative who worked as a store butcher in the Cowdenbeath Co-op naturally smoked store cigarettes; they were called Rocky Mount and the picture on the packet reminded me a little of the mural painted high on the outside wall of the Randolph Street building which showed two 1930s hikers in hilly country, pointing a walking stick towards a bright horizon labelled 'the Co-op'.

But the Co-op is only one small part in the story of Dunfermline's decline and the disappearing purpose of so many similar towns and high streets throughout Britain. The fact that it has happened to Dunfermline is proof that nowhere is immune to the onward march of Wal-Mart and Tesco and new patterns of human behaviour, because Dunfermline is an old town and was once a handsome one, and not the kind of thrown-together product of Victorian industrialism that looked shameful and disposable to the town planners of forty years ago. Its roots are medieval. King Malcolm III, who defeated Macbeth, had his home in Dunfermline. Robert the Bruce is buried in its abbey. Charles I was born in its palace. This part of town, the royal-religious quarter, has buildings dating in part from the twelfth century. In later centuries the settlement spread out from here along a ridge that runs west to east. Coal was discovered early – mined on church land long before the industrial revolution – but that lay on the outskirts. At the heart of the town lay the cottages, and later the steam-driven factories, which produced the finest table linen in Britain. By the nineteenth century it had a nickname: 'the Auld Grey Toon'.

I was educated here, at a school that boasted origins in the fifteenth century and the poet Robert Henryson (then known as a 'Scottish Chaucerian') as one of its first masters. From the classrooms on the north side you looked up to the ridge and its horizons of factory chimneys, church spires, and the French-baronial tower of the City Chambers. To the west lay the Glen, a private estate that had been prettified in the early twentieth century into a public park. To the east lay the original Victorian public park, laid out by Joseph Paxton, and behind it the smoke of the locomotive sheds just over the hill. Between these two stretches of green, and invisible to the eye, ran the High Street, where almost everything happened.

It is worth remembering what the centres of small and medium-sized towns actually provided and how hard it would have been to live without them. Until the 1970s, Dunfermline's town centre held banks, the law court, the local newspaper office, four cinemas, a dance hall, the centre of local government, hotels and inns, a grand post office, two bus stations (the two railway stations were further off), several newspaper cryers (Edinburgh's *Evening News* and its *Dispatch*, Dundee's *Telegraph*), magnificently appointed public toilets and libraries, large churches, cafés, public baths. As to shops: a bookseller, various tailors, greengrocers, licensed grocers (the poshest, Bruce and Glen, smelled of newly ground coffee and stale wine), haberdashers, confectioners, butchers, bakers, milliners, electricians, ironmongers. All of these had loyal clienteles – people who would, say, favour the mutton pies of Allen's over those of Stephen's. On a Saturday the High Street was filled with people and it was tedious to frown into shop windows as your parents chatted (again, again!) to couples they'd met by chance, and who might not have been seen since 1948.

As a teenager, I privately disparaged the High Street as 'provincial'. Now I see how much I owed it; my first long-trousered suit from Burton's, a prized jacket in black corduroy from Russell's, afternoons in Joe Maloco's drinking coffee and looking at girls. Scott's Electricals had a record department with listening booths, like the one where Vic works in *A Kind of Loving* (or the adulterous wife in *Strangers on a Train*), and it was there that I first heard and bought the Everly Brothers. The bookshop, Macpherson's, lay down the Regal Close next to the town's biggest cinema and rambled over several rooms. Shelves outside held the second-hand stock; I once picked up a leather-bound collection of Rupert Brooke for £1.

It would be easy to say that what ended this life was the exhaustion of the mines, the collapse of the linen industry, the closure of the nearby dockyard. But it wouldn't be true. What ended it wasn't poverty but rootless wealth. In the 1980s the shopping and entertainments habits of Dunfermlinites moved east with their cars, to the multiplex and superstores that were built just off the M90. The High Street filled up with charity shops, its decent Georgian and Victorian architecture largely demolished and replaced with what the Penguin series *The Buildings of Scotland* describes as 'developers' shanty town'.

Today, out near the motorway, you can stand in the car park of Tesco's and look back across the housing estates to Dunfermline's remaining spires, remembering that beneath your feet was the place of Sunday walks: high farmland and curlews now replaced by a cornucopia of imports – and an empty, dead town on the horizon in the west.

Cousin Walter

March 2006

In some of John Profumo's obituaries last week a name appeared which was familiar to me long before those of Christine Keeler or Stephen Ward. This was Walter Birmingham, the warden of Toynbee Hall who gave Profumo his redemptive job as a social worker in the east end of London, which made Profumo famously obscure for more than forty years. Walter Birmingham was my father's cousin and long before we knew of his connection with Profumo – that information may have taken us until the 1970s to discover – he was celebrated in our family as the Relative Who Had Written A Book.

As a teenager I found it in the paperback section of Thin's in Edinburgh, then the city's best bookshop – now defunct, latterly celebrated as the supplier of notebooks to Muriel Spark. It was a Penguin, a slim volume in their special series for Africa, and titled *An Introduction to Economics*. There was no denying that this Walter was our Walter; the mugshot above the author's blurb showed some familial characteristics, though it was side-on rather than full-front. I bought it and at home we read the author's biography and studied his picture and sometimes showed off the book to visitors. We didn't, of course, read it – not because we weren't great readers (the opposite: my father's remarking that someone or other had 'no books in the house' was a severely unfavourable judgment of them) but because we had no great interest in reading a summary of Keynesian economics adapted for an African audience.

These days you can hardly spit without hitting an author, especially if you live in London or Edinburgh, or at certain times of year in Cheltenham, Bath, Oxford, Hay and a dozen other places that have literary festivals. Authorship, sometimes more than the books authored, is acclaimed everywhere. And there are more books and more authors; even the village that I took Walter's book home to now has a well-known writer, Iain Banks, living just through the railway bridge at the bottom of the street where we used to live. But not so long ago an author was a rare, shy bird. To have one in the family was a prize, even though Walter had never crossed our doorstep (and never did).

I met an author for the first time after I left school and got a job as a library assistant. It was such a big occasion that I still remember his surname: Douglas. He was sitting in the reference room late on a summer's evening, alone apart from me, his fetcher of documents, with a big writing pad and a roll of Rowntree's Fruit Pastilles on his table. 'Do have one,' he said, and as there was nobody else about (damp sugar on fingers = marks on the rare documents in the local history collection) I did. He was writing a book on the history of the Forth Bridge. I don't think it was a very good book – not enough time had been spent in the reference room – but when it was eventually published I had that odd pleasure of saying 'I met the author', the same pleasure that you see among the audiences at literary festivals and signing queues in bookshops.

After I moved to the big city, Glasgow, author sightings were only slightly more frequent. Authorship was not then a Glaswegian occupation. Today there are shelves and shelves marked 'Glasgow' in Borders in Buchanan Street, but in 1964, so far as I could tell, there were only three books in print about the city. One was the pre-war razor-gang novel *No Mean City* by Alexander McArthur and his London rewrite man, H. Kingsley Long; another was Cliff Hanley's lovely *Dancing in the Streets*, which now would be called a memoir; the third was a popular history by Jack House, who had a column in the *Evening Times* and a radio programme, *This Old House*, in which he reminded his listeners of Glasgow events such as the Empire Exhibition of 1938. McArthur was no longer available to be seen – he'd jumped into the Clyde to kill himself during the war – but it was possible to spot House, easily recognisable by his buck teeth, leaving his newspaper office, and a couple of us once saw the small and bearded Hanley on a street near the BBC. 'What a *wee* man,' we said, as though books needed to be written by giants.

It seemed then to me that only a certain kind of person could write and publish a book – a person with qualities beyond some literary ability. Boldness, perhaps, or eccentricity and bohemianism. In this way, it wasn't a shock that Walter Birmingham had written one: the Birminghams were the side of the family most likely to because so many things about them were dramatic and mysterious. My great grandfather Birmingham was an Irishman (nobody knew from where, or of what religion) who joined the Royal Artillery and went to India, where most of his children were born, including my father's mother and her brother, who followed his father's footsteps to become an artillery sergeant major in the Indian army. His son Walter was born in the army cantonment in Ferozepur, Punjab, in 1913.

Despite or because of this military tradition, Walter was a Quaker and pacifist by the 1930s – also a one-eyed Quaker and pacifist (he lost the other in an accident when he was sixteen, which probably accounts for the side-portrait in his book). He went to night school for a degree at the LSE; he became an economics lecturer; he taught for many years in West Africa. He married twice and had five children. And then he became warden of Toynbee Hall, where one day Lady Reading rang to ask him if he took on volunteers, in which case she had someone in mind called Jack Profumo. This kind of thing – this kind of life – never happened to the other sides of my family. A historian might look at us and see two sides of an imperial story: one side that stayed at home and made things, another that went abroad and had adventures.

He died in 2004 and is buried in an old Quaker graveyard in Dorset, in land that belongs to Madonna. We'd exchanged a letter or two, but I never met him. As for his book, his son, the historian David Birmingham, told me: 'Walter was a very gifted teacher but he wasn't a writer. Writing it nearly killed him.'

Klever Kaff

January 2002

1. A voice is a person

The town of Blackburn is built in a trough in the Lancashire moors. Streets pour downhill from all sides into its centre, where some noble reminders of its golden century still remain: the town hall, the concert hall, the library, the railway station, the museum, all of them Victorian or Edwardian and now stranded among the slapdash new primitivism of shopping malls and car parks that was thrown up in Blackburn, and many other northern manufacturing towns, in the 1960s and 1970s. The good end of town – the best end, the West End, the Mayfair of Blackburn – lies on the north-western slope, along and above Preston New Road, probably because (a common theory about the layout of Victorian towns and cities) richer people took care to live upwind of the mill smoke, and the prevailing wind in Britain is from the south-west. Lynwood Road is one of these streets that run steeply down the hill from the moorland. At the top of the street is the Dog Inn and, beyond that, the crest of the hill and fine views northwards that stretch across the green valley of the Ribble to the hills of north Lancashire. Lynwood Road itself faces south; not a poor street – the terraced houses have bay windows; but not a rich one either – two rooms upstairs and two down, the kind of place that a mill foreman or a shopkeeper or a schoolmaster might have paid rent on a hundred years ago. Migrant families from the Indian subcontinent, mainly Muslims from Pakistan, their children and grandchildren, live here now. On this September evening, they come and go from each other's houses, women in loose folds of white, small boys in prayer caps carrying green velvet cases which may contain the Koran. *'Salaam-alaikum'*, one bearded man says to another, as they pass on the slope.

Number 57 is on the steepest stretch, an end-of-terrace with a satellite dish fixed to its gable wall. The curtains are drawn in the bay. A pennant for the town's football team, Blackburn Rovers, hangs in one window. Beside the door there is a plaque which says that from 1913 to 1933 this was 'the home of Kathleen Ferrier, contralto singer'; a small plaque, modestly phrased – a Mr Mujib ur-Rehman has a larger and shinier nameplate just across the street. Standing on the pavement outside, I looked at the view Kathleen Ferrier would have had, from age one to age twenty-one, as she was jiggled up and down on her father's shoulder, or ran to school, or set off every morning to work as a switchboard girl at the Blackburn telephone exchange. A view of a street, then a town in a valley, both under drizzle and dark, and on the horizon, standing out sharp and patched with wet sunlight, the southern moors.

This would have been her view, and yet not quite her view: Blackburn in the years she lived there was a different place, more sharply defined in character and more blurred atmospherically. A cotton-weaving town with many mill chimneys between Lynwood Road and the southern horizon, and an atmosphere that cleared of smoke only one week in the year when the mills closed for the summer holiday – 'wakes week' – and their workers went to the seaside. She would have been lucky to see the hills.

Standing there, I remembered that I had first come to Blackburn when it was like this. We took the train from Bolton, where our home then was, came through the cuttings in the hills that can be seen from Lynwood Road and changed in Blackburn to a different train that took us up into the Yorkshire Fells. Blackburn's station, I remember, was filled with crowds hurrying up and down the subways between platforms, rather like the first scene in *Monsieur Hulot's Holiday*, and on our platform there was a model of a two-funnelled steamer inside a glass case, placed there by the shipping company that took holiday-makers from Fleetwood and Liverpool to the Isle of Man. That would be the summer of 1951. I would be six. Kathleen Ferrier would have had her first operation for cancer that spring, though very few people would know that then. She was a voice on the radio, singing British

folk songs ('Blow the Wind Southerly') or the aria in English translation from Gluck's *Orfeo* ('What is life to me without thee?'). Four
years later, my elder brother brought home our first gramophone –
or rather that new thing, a record player, portable, with three speeds
– and two 78 rpm records which had to be slipped carefully from
their paper sleeves. They had these two Ferrier songs on their A-sides.
My brother, who had charge of this delicate machinery, would wait
for the deck to stop spinning, turn the discs over with his fingertips,
and we would hear 'Weel May the Keel Row' and Handel's 'Art Thou
Troubled' on their reverse. Now, to hear Ferrier, the family need no
longer wait on the caprice of the BBC Light Programme's record
selection.

'She has such a lovely voice,' my mother said in the present tense,
though by then Kathleen Ferrier was two years dead. We agreed – it
was deep, it was thrilling, it was singular. But there were also two
things which then I would have found hard to put into words (and
it may be no easier now). First, I think we felt that Ferrier's was the
opposite of a 'disembodied voice'; a personality housed in flesh and
blood was singing, and directly, it seemed, to us. Second, the voice
made us respectful and contemplative – even to a ten-year-old it could
do this. I suppose we were in the presence of beauty – often a grave
beauty; even the jauntiest folksong, 'The Keel Row', had something
sad inside it. Well, it made you want to cry. But was that the composer's
notes, or the way they were sung, or the words in the lyrics and the
way they were sung, or something you knew or sensed about the
history of the person who sang them?

The answer to the last question, should it have been asked in our
house in 1955, would have become almost immediately complicated.
That same year, a few months after the record player arrived, my
brother gave our mother as a Christmas present a newly published
biography of Ferrier by her sister, Winifred. It had (still has – though
often read, it has been carefully preserved) a pink dust jacket with a
Cecil Beaton portrait on the front showing Ferrier apparently in mid-
song: erect, strong-necked, hair glinting in the photographer's lights,
teeth shining, eyes resolute, her wide mouth open (a mouth, as the
critic Neville Cardus wrote, that 'you could dive into'). This was the
singer at her zenith in 1951, a lovely and celebrated woman who had
sung often at Glyndebourne and the Edinburgh Festival, and in the

New York Carnegie Hall, Salzburg, Chicago, Paris, Amsterdam, Montreal. But inside the book was a different kind of picture; snapshots of a girl who, in her clothes, her hair, her smile, her locations on municipal park benches and North Country beaches, was as ordinary (and by extension as interesting) as ourselves. For us, and many people like us, it may have been the first moment of appeal in the Ferrier story – that such a voice could come from such a place: 57 Lynwood Road, Blackburn, Lancashire. What this provenance implied – and what the biography reinforced – was that Kathleen was a 'Lancashire lass' and therefore ungrand and unsnobbish, a 'good sort' and true to her orgins, with 'never a trace of swank'. People knew her by affectionate nicknames: to the conductor Sir John Barbirolli she was 'Katie', to Gerald Moore, her frequent accompanist on the piano, she was 'Kath', and to herself she was 'Klever Kaff' or 'Klever Question Mark Kaff' or 'Not-so-Klever Kaff', and sometimes at the end of her letters simply 'KK'.

The biography by her sister told the story of this last name. In her pre-war obscurity as a young housewife – Mrs Kathleen Wilson, wife to Mr Bert Wilson, bank manager – she had once sewn a button to a coat as a favour to a friend. The friend was Wyn Hetherington. The coat belonged to her husband, Jack Hetherington, who needed it in a hurry; the Wilsons and the Hetheringtons were about to set out for a picnic, which Mrs Hetherington was preparing in the kitchen. So, watched by the Hetheringtons' three-year-old son, Kathleen sewed quickly and with a nice final flourish, at which point the boy remarked ('with respect and surprise in his voice' writes Winifred Ferrier): 'Clever Kaff!' Perhaps because this is a childish story, it appealed to me as a child when I first skipped through the book. What the book did not disclose, however, was the fate of Mr Hetherington or Mrs Hetherington or Kathleen's husband, Mr Wilson. Jack Hetherington died a few years later. Kathleen divorced Bert Wilson, who eventually married Wyn Hetherington. His first marriage didn't produce children. His second one did.

All of this took place in Silloth, a small and declining little port town on the Cumberland coast, and all of it is interesting, and some of it may even be pertinent to the question of Ferrier's voice and career. But it is also after the fact of her triumph. When she was alive, her audience knew very little about her life, even when she was losing it ('arthritis' was the public explanation of her absences from the opera stage and concert platform). In the years she sang, the fully fledged notion of 'celebrity' had still to be invented. She gave very few newspaper interviews. She never appeared on television or in cinema newsreels. There is, so far as I can tell, no film footage of her outside a few silent and fleeting seconds that are now in the hands of a devout enthusiast. As for her speaking voice, it can be heard on CDs briefly and twice, on a tape made at a post-concert New York party and in a small speech she made for the BBC at the Edinburgh Festival (and a wonderfully modulated and enunciated voice it is too, without a trace of Lancashire; as a young woman in Blackburn, she had elocution lessons). In any case, who among the crowd that filled the Carnegie Hall in 1948 to hear her sing Mahler's *Das Lied von der Erde*, Bruno Walter conducting, could have cared about her original place in the echelons of British social class and geography? They had come to hear her sing. Already in Britain she had achieved a remarkable and – a safe prediction – unrepeatable thing. For a few months in 1946–7, her recording of the aria 'What is Life' (Christoph Willibald Gluck, 1714–87) outsold any other record in any musical category. Well, it made you want to cry, or at least think a bit. As an anonymous listener is quoted as saying in another and quickly forgotten biography, by Charles Rigby: her singing 'made you wish you had led a better life'.

Whether Ferrier was the *finest* singer of serious music to have come out of Britain in the twentieth century is a futile discussion; some would wonder if she was even the best contralto. Her vocal range and interpretation were limited and not every critic cared for her ('this goitrous singer with the contralto hoot' – *New Statesman*). Neville Cardus, the *Manchester Guardian*'s music writer, a fellow Lancastrian and a great supporter, conceded, for example, that it was no accident that her only two attempts at opera, the name parts in *Orfeo* and Benjamin Britten's *Rape of Lucretia*, were in roles that required statuesque nobility and no flirtatious movement: 'There was no surface glamour in her art and little exhibition of sex.' Then again, how wide a repertoire does a singer need to have? Ferrier knew what, and what not, her self-conscious body and voice were suited to. Verdi was out, even the *Requiem* – her voice wasn't hard enough. Wagner was a temptation resisted, even when the invitation came ultimately from Herbert von Karajan and the Bayreuth festival, though by then she was also too ill to accept. She sang mainly Handel,

Bach, Schubert, Schumann, Brahms, Elgar and Mahler – God, love and death – plus a selection of plainly arranged British folk songs which brought her a popular audience. On the one hand, 'Ye Banks and Braes'; on the other, Mahler's *Kindertotenlieder*, his 'Songs for Dead Children'. She and her greatest mentor, Bruno Walter, established Mahler's vocal music in the British repertoire with a performance of *Das Lied von der Erde* at the first Edinburgh Festival in 1947. Walter had been pupil and friend, had in fact conducted the first performance of *Das Lied von der Erde* in 1911 in Vienna in the year of the composer's death (he didn't live to hear it). After Ferrier died, Walter said that the two greatest musical experiences of his life had been the privilege of knowing Ferrier and Mahler, 'in that order'.

He loved her, and, according to the suggestion of Ferrier's third and most recent biographer, Maurice Leonard, for more than her voice. Most of her mentors did. Sir John Barbirolli, conductor of the Hallé in Manchester, and previously, like Walter, of the New York Philharmonic; Sir Malcolm Sargent, of the London Symphony; Walter Legge, the artistic director of the Columbia Gramophone Company and Elisabeth Schwarzkopf's husband: all loved her in one way or another. For Barbirolli, it was a matter of deep and familial friendship, playing and singing for fun, cooking and eating together, his wife and his mother usually present as well. But Legge tried it on in a taxi – Ferrier moved to the Decca company soon after – and Sargent is said to have gone rather further. Both were rebuffed.

Gerald Moore, her accompanist, wrote that one of her friends had told him: 'Any man who does not acknowledge that Kathleen Ferrier is the most wonderful woman in the world has something wrong with him.' Moore added that it was 'not a case of a hundred men and a girl, for though we men loved her, our wives loved her themselves'. And they did. Women who were not always wives began to follow her from concert to concert during her second North American tour in 1949. From Chicago, she wrote to Winifred: 'I've made some wonderful friends here – all women o' course. I've had women following me from one concert to the next 200 miles apart – and they are the nicest pets . . . I could ever wish to meet.' Three years on, there were groupies in the modern and less engaging sense. On 28 October 1952, the *Daily Mail* reported that, on the same evening that Ferrier was to perform the *Messiah* in the Albert Hall, eight chauffeur-driven cars had arrived outside her Hampstead flat. They had not been ordered. There had also been anonymous telephone calls and other japes; Gerald Moore later wrote that he had arrived home with her after a concert one night to find her door barricaded with dustbins. Ferrier told the *Daily Mail*: 'A number of young girls have been following me around concerts in London and the provinces – they have even been present when I sang in Edinburgh, Newcastle and Dublin. They sit up all night in the queue and then get rather noisy, screaming at the ends of performances. I can only assume that the people who perpetrate the hoaxes belong to the same group.' Then a typical Ferrier touch: 'I do not mind so much for myself, but I am sorry for the firms who suffer the expense and inconvenience.' Though her fans were not to know this, she was gravely ill.

So *finest* British singer of the century? Who can say. But *best-loved* is beyond doubt. Who else could make a girl scream at the end of Handel? By the time she died in Coronation Year, age forty-one, she was probably the most celebrated woman in Britain after the Queen; and also, to most of her audience, the majority who heard her on the radio and on records, and who never set foot in a concert hall, an invisible one. But then, though the voice is an instrument, it is also not a thing of brass or wood like a trumpet or a violin. As the tenor Peter Pears once said, in the context of Ferrier, with whom he had often sung: 'A voice is a person.' What kind of person did we at home detect? Somebody sympathetic and simple and direct – all three words occur often in descriptions from her friends – but also someone who had grieved, or who knew what grieving was, our time here being short and not always a bowl of cherries. Bruno Walter wrote: 'She was very simple and natural; one could seem to read her mind like an open book, but only her singing revealed the abundant wealth of her inner life . . . to hear her meant to feel her innermost affectionate, rich and lofty self. She was not enigmatic, not problematic, but a rare combination of profundity and clarity, of abundance and simplicity.'

Reading her letters in the archive at Blackburn's museum, I began to see how easy it would have been to love her.

2. Accidents

It is a cold-blooded observation, but Ferrier's life was made to film. The arc and incident of it are dramatically perfect. Since 1953, several people have had the idea, including Lewis Gilbert, who directed *Reach for the Sky*, the story of the legless Second World War pilot Douglas Bader and his triumph over adversity. But their projects always fell on the stony ground of Winifred Ferrier, who refused to cooperate on the basis that she did not want her sister's life turned into a weepie; triumph was fine, adversity, and particularly the final adversity, not. By the account of everyone who knew her, Winifred was, right up until her death in 1995, a formidable woman and a most zealous keeper of the Ferrier reputation, and her fingermarks are all over most of what has so far been published about Kathleen's private history. In life, they were close.

The singer was born on 22 April 1912, in the Lancashire mill village of Higher Walton, near Preston, where her father, William Ferrier, was the headmaster of the primary school; he moved the family the next year to Blackburn when he was given charge of a larger primary school there. She was the youngest of three children, and a late child – her mother was forty and her father forty-five when she was born. The family were on the lower rungs of middle-class respectability, but only a generation away from a harder way of living: clogs and shawls, and steam whistles rather than school bells announcing the start of the working day. Her father's father was a guard on the railways, her mother's father went to work in a mill at the age of nine. Win was the eldest child, and then came brother George, who vanishes from the story at an early stage. He had, in Winifred's words, 'always caused the family anxiety' and ran away from home three times. Eventually, showing no inclination to work and earn in Blackburn, he was packed off to Canada under an emigrant scheme funded by the Salvation Army. According to Maurice Leonard, who was a friend of Winifred's, Kathleen in later life was always 'terrified that he would turn up out of the blue and touch her for money'. George was a large youth; aged fourteen he stood at 6 feet 8 inches. All the Ferrier children were large, 'big-boned' as people used to say. Kathleen herself grew to 5 feet 9½ inches and, in the years of her success, often weighed more than twelve stone. Neither she nor her siblings were particularly pretty children and Kathleen's later beauty came unexpectedly. Her mother used to tease her for her plain looks, a cruel habit on the face of it, though as Neville Cardus observed: 'It is a Lancashire custom to lock endearment up in the heart except at weddings, Christmas and at funerals.'

Music was then one of the main recreations of northern England. People sang for pleasure, in front parlours, concert parties and churches, with the *Messiah* once every Christmas at the town hall. The Ferriers were no exceptions to this tradition, though Kathleen's particular skill was at the piano. At school, as at the keyboard, she was an able student and her teachers expected her to stay on for the examinations that would get her into university; her sister was already at college and training to be a teacher. Then the Ferrier family hit a money crisis. Her father was about to retire; brother George continued to be a worry; her sister had still to earn. At fourteen, Kathleen left school and went to work as a switchboard girl at the Blackburn telephone exchange for eight shillings and threepence (41p) a week. For the next nine years she answered callers and put them through. In 1933, she entered the contest to find the recorded voice which would automatically announce the time to anyone who dialled the letters TIM – a new device called the 'speaking clock'. Along with hundreds of other young women entrants, she had to say 'At the third stroke it will be ten forty-five and thirty seconds', but she failed to get past the local heats. Her voice remained untrained – her first serious singing lessons began only in 1939, when she was twenty-seven. Musically, her reward was still the piano. She won competitions and accompanied prominent local and visiting singers. When she got married in 1935, the *Blackburn Times* felt able to announce 'MISS K FERRIER MARRIED: BRILLIANT BLACKBURN MUSICIAN'.

Her husband, Albert Wilson, came from over the hill in Chorley and worked at a bank on the outskirts of Blackpool. His family was well-to-do and – in Chorley – prominent; his father, a businessman, chaired the local council and sat on the magistrates' bench. The wedding, therefore, took place at a Methodist church in the bridegroom's parish rather than the bride's and, by the standards of that time, was quite grand. The *Blackburn Times* recorded the details of the event under a photograph four columns wide. The presents included an oak standard lamp from Kathleen's fellow telephonists and a walnut clock from the bridegroom's colleagues at the bank. After the reception, Mr and Mrs Wilson left 'for a touring honeymoon in the South'.

Kathleen had to give up her job; in 1935, married women could not be employed in telephone exchanges or any other department of the Post Office. The Wilsons first set up house in Warton, just west of Preston at the beginnings of the Lancashire holiday coast, and then, when Bert was promoted to the rank of manager the next year, moved a hundred miles north to Silloth in Cumberland. There Kathleen lived the life that fitted a small-town bank manager's wife. She learned to play golf well and tennis moderately, she swam, she got up gallantly on stage in amateur theatricals, she gave piano lessons, she shopped, she cooked. It began to be noticed that the Wilsons produced no children, though Kathleen was by now in her mid-twenties and in ruddy health. It was also noticed, by her friends the Hetheringtons among others, that she could sing. There were musical evenings at her flat over the bank. In 1937, her husband wagered a shilling that she wouldn't dare complete at the annual music festival in Carlisle, the nearest large town, as a singer as well as a pianist. Kathleen took on the bet and won the silver rose bowl for the festival's best singer, a judge recording that 'Mrs Wilson, of Silloth, had a very, very beautiful voice indeed'. For the next two years, she sang at local concerts, sometimes for nothing and sometimes for trivial fees and often with crowd-pleasers such as 'The End of a Perfect Day' and 'Curly Headed Babby'. In 1938, she appeared with acrobats and comics at the Workington Opera House in a variety show called 'Artists You Might Never Have Heard'. The next year she sang a couple of songs ('The End of a Perfect Day' again) on a regional radio show from Newcastle. She was becoming known – 'Mrs Kathleen Wilson, the Silloth contralto' – but it would be hard to detect from her engagement book any sign of onwards-and-upwards progress, any suggestion that her future lay otherwise than in being a woman with a 'natural' but untrained voice, who, because she was a childless wife-at-home supported by her husband, could afford the time to sing. Professional classical singers need seven or eight years' coaching – breathing, vocal technique, lyric interpretation, musicianship, foreign languages – which, ideally, they should start in their teens.

And then the war happened and everything changed. Her husband was called up to the army. Her father, now a widower, came to live with her (as it turned out permanently, until his death in 1951). She turned her back on her marriage, hired one of the best teachers in northern Engand (Dr J. E. Hutchinson, of Newcastle), and relaunched herself as Miss Kathleen Ferrier. The war unleashed a new supply of work in the form of uplifting entertainment – this at a time when 'uplifting' and 'entertainment' were less divisible – which was brought direct to the factory floor in lunchtime concerts, or in the evenings to country barns and working men's clubs. Kathleen got a contract from a government body called the Council for the Encouragement of Music and the Arts, CEMA, and took Handel and Bach and Purcell to men and women who had just finished a morning shift making rubber dinghies for the Royal Air Force or a day digging coal. By the end of 1942, she had a comprehensive knowledge of the geography of industrial England, its railway junctions, cold lodging houses, sparse food, tinny upright pianos and blacked-out streets. She sang for CEMA in places that are difficult to find on a medium-scale map. Between 25 November and 12 December 1942, for example, in Stanley, Holmes Chapel, Winsford, Great Saughall, Runswick Bay, Crook and Hackness, as well as in Cockermouth, Crewe, Chester, Newcastle, Durham and Sunderland. But by then she knew her destination was London. Earlier that year, Malcolm Sargent had met her in Manchester and encouraged her to move south, and there had been an encouraging notice of one her lunchtime performances in the *Manchester Guardian*, her first review in a national newspaper, which began with the words 'Miss Kathleen Ferrier, a new singer of remarkable talent'.

She was now earning eighteen guineas a week. She determined that she would rise to a new level as a performer. On Christmas Eve 1942, she and Winifred and their father moved into a rented, £150-a-year flat in Hampstead, number 2 Frognal Mansions. She acquired an influential agent, John Tillett, of the Ibbs and Tillett concert agency, and a new teacher, Professor Roy Henderson, who taught at the Royal Academy of Music. Kathleen was thirty. Henderson thought she had come to him ten years too late, but what lay inside her mouth amazed him – a 'wonderful cavity at the back of her throat'. Later he wrote: 'In the course of my teaching I have looked into hundreds of throats, but with the exception of a coloured bass with a rich voice, I have seen nothing to equal it . . . one could have shot a fair-sized apple right to the back of her throat without meeting obstruction. This space gave her that depth and roundness of tone which were distinctive. The voice rolled out because there was nothing to stop it.'

Henderson worked with her for the rest of her career. This wasn't easy. Ferrier grew to be in such demand – seventeen *Messiahs* in seventeen different towns, for example, in the month of December 1945

– that the time for private coaching had always to be fitted around her public performances. Musicianship was not a problem; as an excellent pianist Ferrier understood scores. But she and Henderson had to work hard on her unreliable top notes, her interpretation, her memory (no sight-reading of scores on stage), her awkward platform stance and her breathing. He would make her lean with her back against a wall and kick hard with her diaphragm against the force of his fist (Enrico Caruso could kick his diaphragm against a grand piano, and move it several inches). In the end, Henderson wrote, 'she played her voice as she willed'.

Her career at this national and international level – finally, a diva – lasted barely ten years. She first entered the musical consciousness of London – as opposed to Silloth or Workington – in May 1943, when she sang the *Messiah* at Westminster Abbey. After that, the milestones came regularly: 1944, Elgar's *Dream of Gerontius* in Leeds, and her first recordings; 1946, the first Lucretia in Benjamin Britten's new opera at Glyndebourne, and her first overseas performances, in Holland; 1947, the first of her six Edinburgh Festivals and her first Mahler; 1948, the first of her three North American tours, and at the Edinburgh Festival of that year a programme which gives her equal prominence with Yehudi Menuhin, Jean-Louis Barrault, Artur Schnabel, Margot Fonteyn, Andres Segovia and John Gielgud; 1949, New York again, Havana, Holland for the premier of Britten's *Spring Symphony*, Salzburg, Copenhagen, Oslo; 1950, New York for the last time, Nebraska, Wisconsin, Illinois, Missouri, New Mexico, California, Montreal and Bach's B Minor Mass with von Karajan and Schwarzkopf at La Scala, Milan; 1952, to Vienna to record *Das Lied von der Erde* with Walter, in England a private recital for Britain's new Queen; 1953, 6 February, at Covent Garden as Orpheus, a new English translation of Gluck, her last public appearance.

Accidents: what if her marriage had been happy? If her marriage, unhappy or happy, had led to children? If there had been no war? Wonderful throat cavity or not, it seems unlikely that these ten years would have unfolded for her in the way they did. Neville Cardus wrote that he doubted that she would have turned away from a more loving and rewarding domesticity 'to embark on the wandering life of a concert singer'; that 'disappointment in marriage probably canalised her emotional impulses . . . and [her] aim and purpose were consciously or subconsciously crystallised'.

Still, there was a price. In November 1952, Cardus heard her sing
Schumann's *Frauenliebe und -leben* cycle – 'A Woman's Life and Love'
– at the Royal Festival Hall. He thought she had made too many
gestures, that she'd overstressed the lyrics with too much theatrical
'business' with her face and hands. After the concert, he walked up
and down the Embankment 'battling with his conscience' over the
duties of friendship and honest criticism, and then, criticism winning,
had committed his thoughts to the pages of the *Manchester Guardian*.
He wrote to Ferrier explaining his reasons, and Ferrier replied
graciously. The fact was, she wrote, that she hadn't been consciously
'acting' – she couldn't help singing these songs about love, marriage
and children this way: 'If someone I adored had just proposed to me,
I should be breathless with excitement and unable to keep still; and
if I had a child, I should hug it till it yelled . . .'

3. Tears

She liked to laugh. All her friends attest to that. She liked to laugh,
and cook, and paint, and garden. Also, she liked to smoke. Passing
Clouds was her favourite brand; expensive, oval cigarettes with a King
Charles cavalier on the packet, lying back and smoking with his boots
on. Untipped, of course. During her tours, she would ration herself
to one after each concert, but when she was ill and at home in bed
she could smoke to her heart's content; a silver lining – she never
neglected those. Neither was she averse to a drink. The phrase 'a dirty
big pint' appears in one of her letters, and when Barbirolli delivered
good vintage wine and port to her flat for celebrations, the bottles
were emptied. Above all, perhaps, she liked to eat. After seven years
of British rationing, she found a cornucopia in North America, and
on the way there. Her letters delight in the details of ships' menus,
and never mind the swell. Rarely can the food of Cunard liners have
slipped down a more appreciative throat, or one so wide and free of
obstruction.

A woman of hearty appetites, then, a good woman for men to be
with. She liked their company. Sex? We may never know. Romantic
love? We'll come to that.

There are apparent paradoxes, but only to those of us who expect
other people to be all of a piece, and chained to their upbringing.
For a woman who left school at fourteen, she showed fine instincts

for eighteenth-century furniture and glass. For a woman of great and almost Victorian personal probity – incontestable on the evidence – she took enormous pleasure, again incontestably, from what was then known as filth. She loved double entendres, limericks, swearing, all kinds of bawdiness and ribaldry. Barbirolli, Benjamin Britten and Peter Pears called her 'Rabelaisian'. Cardus said that she could 'lend to a sequence of swear-words the rhythm of hexameters'. A couple of her more harmless favourites are quoted in Maurice Leonard's biography. She liked to recite:

> *I wish I were a fascinating bitch,*
> *I'd never be poor, I'd always be rich.*
> *I'd live in a house with a little red light,*
> *And sleep all day, and work all night.*

And:

> *Here's a toast to the girl on the hill,*
> *She won't, but her sister will.*
> *Here's to her sister.*

Probity and ribaldry may be the complementary sides of the same old northern English coin. The paradox that is harder to reconcile is her determination to make zestful light of everything – even her music, even (and especially) her illness – with her musical ability to move an audience to the point of tears. In her letters, almost to the end, Ferrier is a writer marked by a multiple exclamation mark (*Whoopee!!!*). Life is a great adventure for 'lucky, lucky Kaff', this 'lucky old twerp' who is 'tickled pink' and sometimes 'pickled tink': nothing is sacred, and nothing numinous. Brahms' Alto Rhapsody becomes his Alto Raspberry. Saint-Saëns has composed 'Softly Awakes My Tart'. Purcell didn't write 'Mad Bess of Bedlam' but Bad Mess of the same.

Her mastectomy becomes 'a lump off mi busto'.

Well, you have to smile. Listen to Brahms' Raspberry on a CD, however, to the point where the previously silent chorus joins Ferrier in the final stanza, the one that asks God to save Goethe's bereft young wanderer; and is that or is it not a pricking behind the eyes? No cause for shame. Hardened conductors and orchestra players have also cried.

According to Elisabeth Schwarzkopf, Herbert von Karajan burst into tears when Ferrier began to sing the 'Agnus Dei' in Bach's B Minor Mass at La Scala, though he had heard it often enough before and he was conducting her (and Schwarzkopf) at the time. The following year, 1952, she did *Das Lied von der Erde* with Josef Krips conducting the London Symphony at the Festival Hall, and at the end, according to Krips, 'we all, the orchestra and myself, were in tears'.

Only when she was singing did Ferrier herself cry in front of other people. It often gave her difficulty. As Peter Pears told a BBC programme in 1978: 'If anything, Kath felt things almost too strongly. She often had to fight to control her tears.' In 1944, Winifred watched her practising Brahms's *Four Serious Songs*, which are set to verses from the biblical books of Ecclesiastes and Corinthians, and noticed how one of them, 'Oh Death, How Bitter Art Thou', regularly made her cry. But Mahler, after she was introduced to his music by Bruno Walter, gave her the fiercest struggle. There had been so much death in Gustav Mahler's life – his siblings, his four-year-old daughter – and when he sat down to compose *Das Lied von der Erde*, 'The Song of the Earth', a heart ailment already gave intimations of his own. The music has parts for a tenor and a contralto, who sing alternately, with lyrics which are translated from a collection of Chinese poetry. The last song, the '*Abschied*', or 'Farewell', is given to the contralto and lasts, with orchestral punctuation, for twenty-eight minutes. The message is: our lives are brief, but the beauties of the world go on:

> *Allüberal und ewig blauen licht die Fernen!*
> *Ewig . . . ewig . . . ewig . . . ewig*
>
> *Everywhere and for ever, the blue distance shines!*
> *For ever . . . [and] ever . . . [and] ever . . . [and] ever*

Rehearsing these final lines with Walter before her first performance of *Das Lied* in Edinburgh in September 1947, Ferrier sometimes choked and could not finish. At the performance itself, she could barely get the final two '*ewigs*' out. Her face was running with tears. Nobody complained. In Britain, nobody had heard Mahler so brilliantly sung before. The critic in *Punch* wrote: 'Days afterwards I still seem to hear that haunting heartbreaking farewell and Kathleen Ferrier's

glorious voice singing "*Ewig . . . ewig . . . ewig*" across time and space.'
Cardus wrote: 'Such experiences cannot be written of in terms of
musical criticism.' Afterwards, he went round to the artists' room to
congratulate her – they had never met before. She greeted him 'as
though she had known me for a lifetime' and said: 'What a fool I've
made of myself. And what will Dr Walter think of me?' And Cardus
told her that she shouldn't worry, for he was sure that Walter would
take both her hands in his and reply: 'My dear child, if we had all
been artists as great as you we should all have wept – myself, orchestra,
audience, everybody.'

What was it in her that responded so fully, so rawly, to music that,
as Walter later said, 'men wrote in moments of solemnity and devotion'? A few people, though not her intimates, saw her jollity as a
disguise. Ronald Duncan, who wrote the libretto for Britten's *Rape
of Lucretia*, met her several times during production meetings in 1946
and said that he thought tears were never far from her eyes, caused
'not only by her unfortunate marriage but a need for love which life
itself could not fulfil'. But there was also a more general morbidity.
According to Winifred, both in her book and in conversations with
Maurice Leonard, Kathleen had feared cancer ever since childhood,
when she saw a woman neighbour in Blackburn die of it. An underlying reason for the move to London in 1942 had been access to
better doctors and hospitals. Though her cancer wasn't diagnosed until
1951, she had gone through the 1940s worrying intermittently about
pains in her breast. According to Winifred, the soreness had started
soon after she was married in 1935, when someone had 'accidently
caught her a blow with his elbow'.

According to Winifred, the someone was Kathleen's husband, Bert
Wilson.

4. Winifred

A modern question, which nobody would have asked in 1953: was
Ferrier gay? A few women, too young to have known her or that
time, like to think so. A lesbian colleague of a friend of mine, hearing
that I was interested in the singer, said: 'She spent only one night
with a man, and that put her off it for life.' But we know that, or
think we know it, because of Winifred's opinion, as it is indirectly
quoted in Leonard's biography: 'Years later Kathleen confessed to

Winifred that she had dreaded every night of her honeymoon.' In Winifred's own biography, there is a passage which, considering the period and the fact that Bert Wilson was still alive (he died in 1966), is remarkable for its intimacy and implication. During the rehearsals for *The Rape of Lucretia*, Ferrier found that she could not reach the climactic top A that she had to ring out while stabbing herself. Britten rescored the piece to replace the A with an F sharp. Then, at one of the last Glyndebourne performances, Britten was startled to hear her hit the original higher note – 'the first she had ever sung in public, I think I remember her saying'. Winifred Ferrier makes a great deal of the event. She reproduces Ronald Duncan's libretto and Britten's music – the only place that musical notation occurs in her biography's narrative.

> *Last night Tarquinius ravished me*
> *And took his peace from me . . .*
> *Even love's too frail to bear the weight of shadows,*
> *Now* [she stabs herself] *I'll be for ever chaste,*
> *With only death to ravish me.*

Winifred's commentary runs underneath: 'In this opera to sing these words demands a high order of emotional control, but when their meaning has personal significance, the strain can be almost intolerable. Perhaps the real explanation of that top A lies in its symbolic revelation of how she dealt with the deep problems of her life.'

It is hard to be completely certain where Winifred is pointing her readers with these words: rape seems the likeliest destination, on the other hand it could be the line about a life of chastity, with or without rape to set it off. But if rape was in Winifred's mind, then the consequence of her vindictiveness towards another Ferrier biography that was published in the same year sits at odds with it. While Winifred was writing her book for Hamish Hamilton (who was a friend of Kathleen), a journalist, Charles Rigby, was finishing a rival biography for the publisher Robert Hale. Rigby's book appeared first, though the author died before its publication. Winifred read it and insisted – she was indeed a formidable woman – that it was republished to include a page that would correct, in the publisher's words, 'errors of fact and and expressions of opinion which are clearly wrong'. There were nine of them, and none of them serious (page 166: 'This Swiss tour was, in fact, cancelled due to ill health') apart from the marriage question. Rigby had dealt with it perfectly decently as a private matter. Kathleen and her husband had 'just gone their separate ways'; the divorce had not been reported in the press and Kathleen never talked of it. Winifred, however, wanted things more public and more plain. The note published at her request reads: 'The author has clearly formed a misleading impression of one important aspect of Kathleen Ferrier's marriage. This was dissolved by reason of her husband's incapacity to consummate it.'

Not rape then, but the opposite of rape, or rape successfully denied, or – the common thing – some want of desire in the chemistry between two people. But Winifred always remained keen on the idea of non-consummation as the husband's fault. Among Kathleen's papers in the archive at Blackburn's museum, there is one of Winifred's own: a type-written sheet which reads like a memo to herself, reminding her of the facts she would disclose to any future biographer or enquiring journalist:

KATHLEEN FERRIER'S MARRIAGE

While she was married to Albert Wilson, Kathleen never talked about it. I did not question her although I was surprised that they had no children.

After the Annulment she told me that, even before the wedding she realised that it was a mistake but she had got so involved with his family and with the people in the village that she could not face the prospect of upsetting them all by breaking it off. She said that her future father-in-law would have had a stroke if she had!

She tried to be a good wife to Albert and said to him once, 'I do wish that you would make a bit of a fuss of me,' and he replied, 'You don't run after a bus when you have caught it.'

In the War it was Albert's call-up and Kathleen's growing reputation as a singer which set her free. Eventually she applied for an Annulment of the marriage and this is an extract from the Divorce Registry in the High Court of Justice. [*31 March 1947*]

Kathleen Mary Wilson, (orse – *original surname*) Ferrier, Petitioner Albert Wilson, Respondent.
The marriage at Brinscoll Methodist Chapel, Chorley,

to be pronounced and declared to be absolutely null
and void to all intents and purposes in the law by reason
of the incapacity of the Respondent to consummate
the marriage

According to Maurice Leonard, Winifred was simply so peeved at
the idea of anyone writing a book about her sister other than herself
that she would have done anything to spoil its chance of success, even
to the extent of breaching Bert Wilson's privacy in her need to correct
its 'mistakes'. But there may be more to it – resentment towards the
man who had taken Kathleen from her. Winifred was, even for a big
sister, unusually devoted to Kathleen. The 'touring honeymoon in the
South' reported in the *Blackburn Times* was in fact spent in Winifred's
flat in Edgware, north London, where Winifred had a job as a teacher.
When Bert was called up in 1940, she took another teaching job in
Carlisle, so that she could live again with her sister and her father. And
in London the same *ménage à trois* continued for several years. She never
married. She was her sister's biggest supporter. She became headmistress
of a school in Chiswick, west London, and then, thanks to a connection made through Kathleen, went to work as a fashion buyer for Marks
& Spencer. For the forty-two years she lived after 1953 her emotional
life was gathered around her sister's memory and the medical charities
and musical scholarships which served it.

As for Kathleen's 'gayness', projection is the obvious explanation; the
young women who screamed at her concerts in 1952 liked the idea of
it. At that time, she represented the lesbian ideal; or perhaps what lesbians
were supposed to be like. She was a tall, beautiful woman with a deep
voice and no apparent ties to men. Very few people knew she had been
married. Several of the songs she sang were originally written for the
male voice. Her most famous dramatic role, as Orfeo, required her to
act as a man (the part was written by Gluck for a castrato). The private
truth, however, is that she loved men and was involved with them. One
of the boxes in the museum at Blackburn contains her pocket diaries,
which start early in the war and after Bert had left for the army. They
are touching in the brevity and simplicity of their entries, and by what
they show of her ability to pick herself up and get on with life. A man
called John appears in 1942.

May 16 Sunderland. Up at 5 a.m.!! John met me in Newcastle. Had breakfast in station. Went to Station Hotel to pass the time till lunch and train for Sunderland. Concert went off very well. Tea in Station Hotel all together. Home at 8.20 after salmon mayonnaise in Eldon Grill! Walked home. Two heart-to-heart talks today. What a strain.

June 8 Letter from John.

June 10 Bert coming home.

July 7 London. Met John. Went to [unclear] and punted.

July 11 John rang up from Bedford.

July 23 Telegram from John.

August 4 Letters from John and Bert.

August 13 Gateshead Miners Welfare Hall Whickham. Stay at Mrs Cooke's [in ink – then in pencil:] Letter from John. Rang him up. Final break. Concert not bad.

August 14 Came home. Depressed. Went to flix [the cinema] with Mrs Simpson. Shopped.

So much for John. Rick arrived in 1944.

May 4 L'pool. Dinner dance with Rick Davies. Gorgeous time.
February 15 [1945] Rick rang from Liverpool!!

Rick Davies, who was a Liverpool antique dealer, appears regularly in her diaries until December 1951. He wanted to marry her, but by that stage Ferrier had decided she was 'a lone she-wolf' whose dedication to singing was absolute. In June 1950, Davies had flown to Zurich to spend some time with her. Kathleen wrote to Winifred: 'I don't mind him for a buddy for two days, then I've had enough and want to retire behind an iron curtain and not have to listen and make conversation. Fickle, that's me.'

5. A lucky ole twerp

How else did Ferrier see herself? If private correspondence is any key to a person's character, then as blessed and mustn't complain and lucky, oh so very lucky. In 1978, Tennessee Williams heard a recording of Ferrier for the first time and was so moved by her voice that he immediately wrote a mournful and not very good poem about her ('the string of the violins / Are a thousand knives in her breast'). But there is no self-mourning in Ferrier, or none that she wants to let on about. Alan Bennett might have confected her. The letters at the Blackburn archive almost dance out of their boxes with good humour.

America was her great discovery. On her way there for the first time, on the *Mauretania*, she wrote to her sister.

Tuesday 6th Jan/48

Dearest Win,

Hello love! Here I am, propped up in bed, having had a gorgeous breakfast & feeling the complete diva!

Heavens! I never expected to enjoy this trip so much. We've had sunshine, gales—heavy swells and I've never turned a hair—even when I've seen other folk in distress! Bless Dr Morton for his littul pills.

I don't know where to start, but our main conversation is the food! I have never ever seen such dishes, and we are being very spoiled by the chief steward, who thinks up meals for us, so that we start with tomato juice, caviar with all the trimmings, soup, fish, lobster or salmon, beef, steaks, joints of all descriptions, and the most amazing sweets ever. Baked ice cream—that is ice cream with cherries in brandy & the brandy lit with a match till there are blue flames all over it. Mr Tillett [her agent] has a liver, but if he *will* have two eggs for breakfast—! True he only asked for one, but they always double the order!

I have a cabin to myself with my own shower & lav, and everything is sheer luxury. We have deckchairs on the Promenade deck, and as soon as we arrive in the morning our feet are tucked up in warm rugs & we get chicken soup & a dry biscuit!

We share a dining table with James Mason's mother-in-law, and an Australian lady,—Mrs Stilwell, whom I always have to arrive at her name by steps—such as 'Quite good' 'Getting better' and 'Very well'!! Also on ship are Zoltan Korda (film man who made Sanders of the River), Viscountess Rothermere and Ernest Ansermet [her conductor at Glyndebourne in 1946] and wife! But otherwise nobody startling. We have been invited to cocktails with the Chief Steward & the Captain, and altogether have had a wonderful time & a grand rest. I won 10/- on the horse racing & lost it all the next night!!

There are people on board who haven't had more than a couple of meals the whole trip they have been so ill, so I'm feeling elated at my seaworthiness! Mr Tillett's a good sailor—it's just his liver wot gets him down! He's grand and good company and very anxious as to my welfare, and we're getting on fine.

Have seen about four films & the time has just flown! My earrings are lovely & I'm taking great care of them—will write again after we arrive tomorrow. Loads of love to you both and I hope all's well with you. Klever Kaff!

In New York, she wrote to her father and her personal assistant and secretary, Paddy Jewett. In conversation, she always used 'me' for 'my' – 'me face, me breakfast' – which in her letters becomes 'mi'.

Hotel Weylin, New York City
Sunday 20th March

Dearest Pop & Paddy,

. . . I now have six concerts off mi chest, and they have all gone very well, Pittsburg was a huge success, thank goodness!

Sandor [Arpad Sandor, her accompanist] continues to annoy me almost more than I can bear – he played so softly in the Ash Grove the other night I could hardly hear him, & I had to say 'LOUDER' out of the corner of my mouth in between verses, but of course he didn't hear me! He's the only thing that makes me nervous for my recital here—I never know what he'll do next. At Pittsburg we did Heidenröslein as an encore, unrehearsed, and he put in trills where there weren't any—I stood with my mouth open—the audience would think it was peculiar interpretation!! Twice, he's put in a major chord where there's only an octave in the Erl King & when I asked him to play it & Röslein again at a rehearsal the other day, he played them both just as written! I think he'll go ga-ga one day very soon!

I think mi pitcher's good in the Evening News—it flatters me. I can hardly wear that hat now cos Ann chopped mi hair off the other day & now I'm like this—s'rather fetching!!

Yesterday I bought myself a girdle for mi spare tyre—it's a beauty & comes right above mi waistline. Instead of oozing at mi waistline I just ooze top & bottom—it's beautiful! I also got a brassière-top petticoat—no bra needed—in nylon & 3 prs of pants—all needing *no ironing*!! And it works too, cos I've washed a pair of pants to make sure! I think even John would be proud of my waist now.

Bruno Walter is going to play for me in a New York recital next year as well as Edinburgh & London (Sep 28th) Isn't that marvellous? He's given me 8 new songs to learn, but I do it gladly for him! . . . Loads of love to you all . . . Kaff

She went alone on her second tour of North America. Her agent, John Tillett, had died. For sixteen weeks she criss-crossed the USA and Canada by train, and on her own. She wrote to her father that at Granville, Ohio, 'the concert was about a quarter filled, and some of them knitting!! I could have spat at them'. From Saint John, New Brunswick, she wrote to Tillett's widow, Emmie, who now ran the agency.

12th March 1949

My dear Emmie,

I am enclosing a few criticisms I have collected on my travels, Los Angeles, San Francisco, New York and Montreal, and I would like—if you agree—to have an insertion in the Times and Telegraph with a few quotations just to let people know I've been working hard—and not disappeared for three months!

Aren't they lovely ones? I'm being very spoiled and just lapping it up!

The two poppets in Montreal—Mrs Langdon and Mrs Russell-Smith—send kind greetings to you.

Just shooting off for yet another train! but wanted you to see that I've been behaving myself!

All goes well here—it's been a lovely tour—and I still haven't signed owt! Klever Kaff!

Hope you are well, darling, and your Momma too. Won't be long now until I arrive in my new hat and the white flour [scarce in Britain] under mi arm! O boy!

Tell Miss Lereculey [in Paris] my French grows apace—I'm learning some Chausson—and she'll have to look for competition! I can say 'Darling, je vous aime beaucoup—passepartout—cul-de-sac—Vouley vous coucher avec—oh no! that's the rude one!

Heigh ho quelle vie! Ain't I a lucky ole budder!
Much love to you all
KATHLEEN

Later the same month, after a concert in New York Town Hall, she wrote to her sister from the Hotel Weylin.

Dearest Win,

Well, that's over, thank goodness! It was a complete sell-out with about 100 people sitting on the platform!!

I've never known such applause—I couldn't start for about 5 mins! Must have been mi red frock. Bruno Walter and Eliz Schumann were in the audience and the clapping became almost a nuisance. I was a bit dry about my throat, and so wet about my torso, I had to keep my frock from sticking to my legs by holding it out in the front of me when I walked. People shouted and stamped, but the critics this morning are only luke-warm. I can't get away with the budders here, but it's the audience that are the final judges, and they couldn't have been more marvellous. Whattastrain.

Bruno Walter rang me up—he said the loveliest things and that he was really proud of me. The afternoon papers are better. But I am told these are the most wonderful notices and that I've had the greatest success ever, and, quite honestly, I'm past caring. They were the most lovely audience and they're the ones who've paid for their seats.

Am just dashing to catch train to Canada and am in the midst of packing. Eee! if mi mother could see me now!!

Well, poppet mine, look after yourself—love to Pop and Paddy . . . Loads of love.

Klever Question mark Kaff

She went to Havana ('Oh! So luxurious & oozing rich, fat women,' she told to Winifred) and wrote to her sister again from the Hotel Weylin in New York.

18th May/49

Dearest Win'fred,

Back 'home' again & they were all thrilled to see me at this ole pub. Also, all my letters were here from March 28th!! 56 of them! I played hell in Columbia [Columbia Concerts, her US agents] this morning! I'm just beginning to enjoy playing hell . . . I never stopped! I didn't cry either, Klever Kaff, and think I've made 'em think. I pointed out they hadn't put up my fee for next year, and got it put up on the instant! My! but isn't it hard work! Only 50 dollars a concert but better than nowt. Actually I wouldn't have missed this tour for anything, especially Miami & Cuba, but I don't like being put on!

To give me courage I bought a new hat, bag, shoes, stockings & summer nylon pantie girdle and could have coped with a whole blinking board of directors. I have only sagged a little now having discovered that the tab on my dress had been sticking out at the back of my neck all the time. I thought people were looking at me, I thought it was admiration!! That'll larn me! I bought a navy blue & white spotted pure silk dress for £4 in Miami, so I bought a little white hat, blue & white shoes, white bag & gloves & felt real dandy. The white hat has a navy blue veil—I gave my black one to a negro porter in a rushed moment when I hadn't a hand free!

Thank you for all your letters love,—you *would* think I wasn't appreciative of them—but I'd just not had them, the twerps!

I'm so glad you had a good weekend when Rick [Davies, Kathleen's boyfriend] was down—he'd be thrilled to bits to take two bonny lasses out, the old sheik!

. . . Oooooh! I'd love a black paint box for mi birthday—yes please!

Will get on with the other 54 letters now! Ta ta for now love. Shall be at Brown Hotel, Louisville, Kentucky 22–25 leave N.Y. 27th midnight. Whoopee!

Loads of love . . .

Kaff

In 1950, she was in the USA for what turned out to her last tour there. Bruno Walter gave her the use of his house in Beverly Hills – the Walters were away – and from there she used his typewriter to write to Emmie Tillett.

c/o Dr Bruno Walter,
608 N Bedford Drive,
Beverly Hills,
Calif
3rd Feb

My dear Emmie,

Thank you so much for your letters love . . . I am so glad your back is better again, and your Momma well—much love to her, and I am looking forward to seeing her when I get back. I heard Dame Myra [Hess] is ill and has cancelled her tour here—I *do* hope it isn't serious??

Oooooooooo, boy . . . Orpheus with Dr Bruno ?????? YES PLEASE—would forgo all my holiday for that.

The Halle and Orpheus? I think as it was my suggestion that they do it, I must do the Sheffield date, tho I feel rather sadly about the Passion if Dr Jacques has asked for me—but I couldn't travel overnight to do it, as you say.

Gee whiz//// all this work// aren't I a lucky ole twerp/ (I have no exclam. marks on this machine – it does limit me).

Yes, I can do the Apostles for Hanley—it is the Music Makers that gets me doon. Lovely to do Gerontius for the Royal Choral on May 24th—whooppee . . .

All is going so well here. The concerts have been a great success— we've been to some lovely places—and now I am installed here, and have the house to myself with man and wife [servants] to look after me. It is just wonderful. Dr Bruno and his daughter and [her] husband are in New York so I shan't see them until March. The sun is shining—this place is just amazing—the palms and the houses and the glamour pussies, and the luxury of it all. I am being ruined here—I have the use of two superb cars at anytime—my bathroom plumbing is an hourly—well nearly— delight, and, oh, it's so warm. I have so many dates with new-found friends that it is almost embarrassing, but today I have started on my real holiday—ten days before going to North Calif., so I am as happy as a lark, and feel very grateful for this wonderful opportunity to see so much . . .

The concerts are much better this year—smaller halls, and altogether different, and I should say I have one of the best accompanists in the world . . . honest . . . so we enjoy our music making and make the most of opportunities to study new things, so it is grand for me.

Here is where I am going to be, so that you can write me direct—

leave here Mon 13th
Feb 14th Hotel Senator	Sacramento, Calif.
16th, 17th, 18th, 19th	Hotel Whitcomb, San Francisco
21st	Hotel Morek, ABERDEEN, Washington
24th, 25th	c/o Mrs Cress, 2005 King St, La Crosse, Wisconsin
27th	Hotel Tivoli, Downers Grove, Illinois

I think that is all love—I hope I have not forgotten anything.

Much love to you and thank you for all your endeavours on my behalf—I *am* a lucky twerp.

Look after yourself,

Love

Kathleen

During her first American tour, Kathleen had sung at La Crosse, Wisconsin, and made friends with one of the concert's organisers, Benita (aka Bonnie) Cress, and her husband, Bill. When she went back to La Crosse in 1950, she stayed with them. The Cresses became two of her closest friends. Ferrier wrote to them regularly until she was too ill to write.

[2 Frognal Mansions, Hampstead]
8.4.50

Dearest Bill and Benita,

Well, loves, home at last, and the Spring is here to welcome me with blossom, bulbs and sticky horsechestnut buds. It all looks green and lovely. I had a wonderful voyage [home] with the [Benno] Moiseiwitschs, Danny Kaye & Rex Harrison—we did have fun & I have never had so many late nights. Benno M. won the lottery on the ship's run—£755!!—so we had to celebrate!

. . . The flat looked lovely—Paddy's mother had colour-washed the walls of all the rooms & I had new curtains & carpet in my room—very swish! And everybody was well & happy, so it was a good home-coming after the most wonderful time & tour ever. Lucky Kaff!

Eggs are off the ration too & somebody brought us a pound of real farm butter this morning so we're in clover.

I'm seeing Mr Mertens [Andre Mertens, her US agent] next week & if I ask him to send you a cheque for $100 could you send us a few things occasionally? Our greatest miss at the moment is sugar—not cubes—and soap—toilet and flakes—& if it were possible to pack some white flour for baking cakes I should be top of the class with my manager here! The grocery stores—I think—will do it all for you, rather than you having the bother of finding boxes, paper & string. I *hope* this isn't asking too much of you love. Don't trouble for *one* minute if it is.

Mr Anderson in Chicago sends us Peacock Sliced Dried Beef (Cudahy? Wisconsin) & Paddy & her mother have thought of every way of cooking, steaming, baking & grilling it—with no success. Do you know anything about it—it comes from your part of the world. They've even tried soaking it overnight, but it still baffles.

It's been wonderful to be with you lot—I have such constant reminders of you—if I needed any—: my lovely housecoat & blouse & perfume—you are so generous in every way, I am at a loss to thank you enough for all you have done for me. But I do thank you with all my heart a thousand times, and shall remember this tour a thousand times as one of the happiest times I ever had—bless you both for your great share in it . . .

Roll on 1951—I'm looking forward to seeing you all again then, I hope. Much love to you both & thank you again for all your wonderful & many kindnesses.

God bless you & keep you,

Yours till hell freezes

Love

Kathleen

Three weeks later, on 1 May 1950, she wrote again with 'a naughty limerick'.

> *There was a young lady of Nantes*
> *Tres chic, jolie et elegante,*
> *Her hole was so small*
> *She was no good at all*
> *Except for la plume de ma tante!*

In July, Ferrier went to see a doctor about pain in her breast. Her teacher, Roy Henderson, went with her and waited outside the surgery. 'Look, Prof!' she said when she came out, 'he's given me a clean bill of health!'

The Cresses, meanwhile, sent two food parcels. Kathleen replied on 10 August.

Dearest Bill and Benita,

A wondrous parcel arrived yesterday, full of just all the right things!! Bless you for a 1000 times—we haven't seen such salmon for 10 years so we're going to have a feast one of these days. Thank you so very much for all your trouble. It couldn't be lovelier. Yes love the 2nd June box arrived safely and in wonderful order—food seems to get here without difficulty—fingers Xd!—we are getting a good store now—but as you say it's a jolly good idea with the world situation looking menacing! Isn't it a bluidy shame for young boys and their parents to be suffering five years after the last holocaust! Whattaworld!

. . . Going back to your letter. Coffee has always been easy here, because we are a tea drinking nation—so there is no difficulty there. Paddy still gloating over the cake mixtures—they really are a blessing in a hurry particularly! We can get Fab here now too and soon soap should be off the ration altogether so we shan't need any more—it will be gorgeous to go into a shop and buy soap without coughing up a niggly bit of printed paper!

Schwarzkopf is a fine musician and she does a terrific amount of work—some things absolutely superb and others, I think, Unsuitable—but all the Viennese singers work themselves to a standstill—I just daudle in comparison! Klever me—I've been home nearly two months—having sometimes two lessons a day and a real rest from concert giving—and I think it has done me a world of good. I've been going a bit gay too, and going to theatres and dinners. Tonight I am going to the Promenade concert—a Beethoven night—and dining afterwards with Malcom Sargent and a friend—M.S. is conducting. I've been spending a lot of money too,—bought a fur coat—dyed Russian ermine (very unpatriotic!) but very beautiful—ordered three cupboards to fit in my room for all my odds and sods—and ordered a Beau Decca— longplaying, shortplaying and radio—so now I'm broke, but tickled pink, so what the heck!!!!

My first concert is Aug 28th at Edinburgh with the Brahms Alto Rhap, with Fritz Busch—and it will be lovely when that is over, because I shall be able to relax and enjoy the rest of the festival.

Now I must get ready to go to a lesson before my night out, so thank you again for everything and God bless.

Much love to you both,
Kaff

She was working hard, she was tired.

13th November 1950

Dearest Bonnie,

I am 'all behind' mit my letters to you, but have been dashing madly round, now that the season is in full swing again.

The records should really be out now in the States—if they're not soon, I really will get a hat pin to Decca—they said Sept. the bar stewards [bastards]!

The boxes you sent sound just wonderful—all your others have been perfect, and it is nice to be a bit extravagant sometimes and not wonder if the rations will run out before the weekend!—and such lovely things too. The canned chicken was gorgeous and fell to bits with tenderness, the pore littul budder! The cookies were a treat too—but they are off for me now, cos I'm getting too fat— so I'm cutting all starches (when I'm strong enough) and trying to get my bulges a bit less rotund. I had some new photies taken the other day, and I look like the bull at the other end of the Toreador!!—*fraightful!!* But, otherwise, all is well, and we're all full of beans—and hope you are too. You are lucky still having nice weather—ours is terrible—cold and wet—am hating the thought of flying to Holland on Saturday. Shall be at the American Hotel

Amsterdam until the 13th December—just in case you have a minute to spare!

Dashing off to the north tomorrow—Manchester, Bolton, Huddersfield and Grimsby. Thank you for everything, bless you, and look after yourselves.

Much love from us all,

Kaff

In 1951, her assistant, Paddy Jewett, left to get married. Ferrier hired as her replacement a young New Zealand woman, Bernie Hammond, who also happened to be a trained nurse. In March, Ferrier asked her: 'Have a look at this bump will you?'

28.3.51

Dearest Benita,

I have neglected you I fear—but things have been happening with such rapidity, I haven't written any personal letters for ages.

First I have got a 'jewel' to look after me & to keep Paddy company until the latter marries. She's a New Zealand girl called Bernie and a trained nurse—but wanting a job where she can be independent. She nursed my manager's mother when she died—and I knew her well, but never thought she'd consider such a mundane job. But she seems in her element, has a wonderful sense of humour & is altogether a pearl. She hasn't got out of her nursing as she thought, as I have to go into hospital any day now for a rather formidable op for a 'bump on mi busto'. But having Bernie here has lightened the load enormously & I am in the finest radiologists & surgeons hands in the country. I have had to cancel a month's tour in Scandinavia & everything until the middle of May—but I am glad of a rest—I feel better now that everything is getting done. I should have gone earlier but haven't been home for months. The X-ray yesterday was better than they thought.

So don't worry, love, & I'll ask Paddy to send you a line. We are fine for everything in the food line and don't want for *anything*—thanks to you. And I'm smoking with abandon being as 'ow I've not to sing for 6 weeks!

I hope you & Bill are both flourishing & much, much love to you—

Yours till hell freezes over,
Kaff

18th April 1951

Dearest Bonnie,

Thank you for my lovely birthday present—they arrived yesterday—and are *so* lovely—thank you very, very much.

I am writing my first letters for a bit & feeling real cocky—just waiting for the doctor to come—and being glad it isn't this time last week—when I threw up four times all down Bernie's front—poor, sweet Bernie—she's been an absolutely bluidy marvel—and I just don't know what I should have done without her.

I don't know about my itinerary yet love—it's at home & I'm not even thinking about singing yet—but I'll let you know in a bit. I shall be here another week or ten days yet—then have to have some rays [radium treatment] for a few weeks—then a holiday—so I'm really enjoying a rest— & gee! I *was* ready for it. I seem to have startled all the staff here with my quick recovery, and I'm being spoiled to death and thoroughly enjoying myself!!

I hope your arm is much better love—you just be a good honey-chile now and have a good rest—and thank you again for the gorgeous present and lovely card. I am not telling any of my buddies in N.Y. about my op. as such exaggerated rumours get round—you'se the only one wot knows! Much love to you both.
    Kaff

17.5.51

Dearest Benita,

Thank you so much for all your letters—I am so sorry we have neglected you lately . . . I'm feeling better each day & my anaemia, which was rather low, is almost normal again. I have been going each morning to the hospital for rays, and should have only another two weeks to do—perhaps even less. The budder of it is, I haven't to wash my neck and it's about an inch deep in dust—but, I suppose, one of these days, I'll be a clean girl again!

I haven't had a bath for over six weeks!—I don't 'arf pong!

The doctors are enormously pleased with me—and I'm in wonderful hands—I couldn't have been better cared for—and I've loved the rest, and don't ever want to start again!! My dr says I have to go easy for 2 yrs that is why I have had to cancel the first month of America—but I shall be doing Chicago so hope to see you there. Bernie is coming with me & is pickled tink.

Between you and me, I'm very lop-sided at the top but am camouflaging with great taste & delicacy!! And what the heck, as long as I feel well & can sing a bit, eh?

. . . We're all right for parcels for the moment, love—and I'm not short of a single thing—I'm just spoiled to death!

Much love to you both—will write again

Kaff

She began to sing again. She toured Holland and appeared at the Edinburgh Festival in September. But she cancelled the American tour that was scheduled for later that year. Her disease and her frequent radium therapy were exhausting her.

7th August 1951

Dearest Bonnie,

. . . I have been dashing about a bit since Holland, and have just been hibernating on my bed in between concerts to be ready for the next one. Bernie has been doing everything!! Keeping me in control, the housework, shopping (quite a long job here with queues!) endless letters and the cooking—and she's still bright and cheerful. You'll have to see her—she's every jewel rolled in one. Lucky Kaff!

Here it comes love! I have to cancel my American trip—not because I'm any worse—I hasten to tell you—but because Holland took it out of me a bit, and the doctor feels that so heavy a tour would be asking for trouble so soon. If I needed treatment it can really only be given here, as it is such an intricate business that only a doctor who knows the case could cope. HELL! HELL! HELL! My tour started off with a recital every other day and travelling in between, and it just makes me tired to think of it, but I am grieved to the core to miss my buddies there, and especially La Crosse, but I think it is wise, and it will be the first long rest I have had in ten years! I know you will understand and try not to be too disappointed, because by this time next year I hope to be bouncing with health.

. . . I do hope you are well and happy and forgive me for not writing sooner—the days go so quickly!

God bless and look after yourselves and much love from
Kaff

24th Sept. 1951

Dearest Bonnie,

. . . Edinburgh went well—Bruno was 'pickled tink' and said it was a privelge to work with me, which made music in my heart! The hall was full and sitting on the platform and it was broadcast all over the place so it was quite a strain—and I've felt better ever since!

Had another X-ray last week and the doctor is very pleased and I have finished my treatment at the hospital which is a lovely thought—pets though they are! I hope it's for good. I'm putting on weight and getting so perky there's no holding me—but it's a lovely thought that I can have a complete rest until the New Year, even though it means not seeing my buddies in La Crosse. I'm even catching up on letters as you can see—have tidied my drawers—the first time in ten years!!! and have even had a bit of decorating done to cheer up the place. We're looking *fraightfully* posh now old girl!

. . . Much love to you and Bill and God bless, and thankyou for everything

Kathleen

27. 10.51

Dearest Bonnie,

Just a word in your ear of real thanks for the heavenly soap which arrived this morning—bless you—it's a very special treat and a real luxury. You are a poppet of the first rank!

All well's here—I'm having a complete rest from singing and going gay a bit—to Covent Garden & theatres—first time in 10 yrs!

I hear there are all sorts of rumours about me there—originated from of Edinburgh—Mr Mertens says. Between you & me, love, I think some of it comes from Ethel Bartlett—I may be wrong—but will you keep your pretty pink ears open—or perhaps just ask for news of me if given the chance—& tell me what she says? I'd like to be proved wrong, but have mi suspicions! There are malicious rumours going around—so don't let on you know me. Okeydoke. And don't believe any of the rumours—I'll let you know the truth, first thing—and at this moment—I'm jes full o' beans! God bless, darlings—

I'll write again soon.

Much love to you both

Kaff

29th Dec. 1951—Saturday

Dearest Bonnie and Bill,

The MARVELLOUS wallet has just this minute arrived, and I can't tell you what pleasure it has given me already. It IS beautiful and I am proud of it, and will treasure it for many years to come—thankyou, thankyou, thankyou for all your sweet kindness and generosity. I am thrilled with it, and think it is most beautifully made and arranged. I SHALL swank with it, bless you! Various, wondrous parcels have arrived too, and I just have no words to thank you for all the trouble you have taken to pick out sich luscious items—our store cupboard is well filled, and I am putting on weight all the time, much to everyone's delight! Thankyou for everything, loves—you are 'woody blunders'—I am just wordless at your faithful, generous friendship. Thankyou, thankyou a thousand times.

We have had a grand Christmas. Bernie, Win (sister) and I went to Mrs Tillett's on Xmas day—opened presents and gave some— and painted a pheasant as being in the Xmas spirit! Had a light lunch and we went across to my doctors for tea—played Lexicon with them and the daughter and friends and the first word I achieved was 'urine'! Klever Kaff!! Couldn't miss putting that down however polite the company! Back to our painting and dinner of turkey and plum pudd!—a bit of orl rite!

I start again on Jan 7th with the Four Serious Songs in the Albert Hall with Malcolm Sargent conducting—and from then on, I am very busy. But I have had a wonderful rest and it has been heavenly to be at home for so long. Sir John Barbirolli came up the other night and brought his cello—he was a prodigy before he started conducting—and we went through several

sonatas and pieces and had a wonderful time. I adore accompanying and he loves playing so we were very pleased with
ourselves! And now, darlings, thank you again for everything—
God bless you—and so much love & luck for the New Year,
from a very grateful

    KAFF

She spent 1952 in pain – backache, referred to publicly as 'mi rheutam-
ics' or 'screwmatics'. Often she was cold. Hotels in provincial Britain
had to be told to bank up the coal fires in her bedrooms. Recording
Das Lied with Walter in Vienna, she at one point collapsed. Her itinerary that year included Aldeburgh and Edinburgh. She consulted a
leading oncologist, Sir Stanford Cade, who suggested a 'bilateral adrenalectomy', though this was not at the time pursued. Radium therapy was
renewed. After Ferrier had performed for the Queen at a country-house
party that summer, the monarch sat with her and asked how she was.
Her reply, as given in Leonard's biography: 'Just the odd ache, Ma'am.
You have to expect these things.'

In February 1953, she was scheduled for four performances of the
new *Orpheus* with John Barbirolli at Covent Garden. Four was thought
to be the most she could manage. During the second performance, on
6 February, the femur in her left leg partly disintegrated. She vomited
through pain – but in the wings – and continued to sing till the close.
After a morphine injection, she took several curtain calls and received
well-wishers in her dressing room. She never sang in public again.

27th February 1953

Dearest Benita,

    I am so sorry I have not written for such an age, but I have
been terribly busy rehearsing 'Orpheus', and then at the second
performance I snipped a bit of bone off in my leg, so here I am
once again, reposing in University College Hospital! I am having
treatment every day and it is already much better, but I shall probably be here for another month at least. I don't feel a bit poorly,
but am not allowed as yet to stand up on my legs, but hope I'll
be all right for some more performances of 'Orpheus' in May.

    Your wonderful, amazing, delicious, heavenly, gorgeous choc-
olates arrived a couple of days ago, and I haven't tasted anything

like them for ages. They are so pretty, too. Thank you so very much—you do spoil me terribly . . . and how I lap it up!!

I had to miss going to Buckingham Palace [she had been awarded the CBE], but have heard a whisper that I may be pushed in to one of the summer Investitures. I do hope so, because I've got a new hat and coat!

The first night of 'Orpheus' was absolutely thrilling, with a very distinguished audience shouting their heads off at the end. Everyone was thrilled and the notices were all splendid, which makes it all the more disappointing that I could not carry on.

I have your face towels here with me—that you sent for Christmas—so have a constant reminder of you both. Bernie is here nursing me most of the day, not that I need it much, so that makes it very pleasant.

I do hope you are both full of beans and thank you again with all my heart for innumerable kindnesses. Much love to you both and God bless.

Kathleen

3rd April 1953

Dearest Benita,

Thank you so much for your sweet Easter card & handker-chief—it brightened my day considerably, and it's *such* a lovely hanky. I'm still in hospital, but leaving in the morning—whoopee, whoopee—& going to a new home at 40 Hamilton Terrace, which Bernie tells me is looking lovely. I should have gone three days ago but caught a bug from somewhere & a temperature & a very queasy stomach, so had to stay—I was furious! But I'm quite all right now & looking forward to the morning. My legs are much better & I can take a few steps, but not too many & for the moment will be whizzing round in a wheel chair.

We had 48 steps to my old flat & it meant that once up them and I should be a prisoner there, so Bernie & Win had to rush round & find something else. We've been *very* fortunate and got a maisonette (half an old house) with a bedroom & bathroom downstairs for me & a lovely garden, which is something I have always yearned for. We've had the house papered & painted (to hell with the expense!) so I can hardly wait to see it.

I am going to have a complete rest this summer & work quietly for Edinburgh. Will write again when I'm home & tell you all about it.

Much love to you both
from
Kathleen

Diary entry, 22 May: 'Dr Eccles – must have mi ovaries removed'. They were removed the next month. On 27 July, she had Sir Stanford's 'double adrenalectomy'. Earlier, she had worried about the operation's effect on her voice. There was no point worrying about that now.

15th Oct. 1953

Dear Mrs Cress,

I am so sorry that I did not send you a cable or let you know about Kath, it must have been an awful shock to you – we were just snowed under with the Press and millions of other things and I just did not manage to do it. But I would like you to know that Kath was perfect to the end, the last few days she had injections and slept most of the time and just went very quietly in her sleep as I had hoped and prayed she would.

If this had to be in the first place, one just must accept it and make the necessary adjustments, Kath would expect that of us. She had so much to bear these last few months, if she was not going to get out of bed then it is much better thus and I am convinced that the essential part of Kath is never very far from those who loved her – so don't grive too much sweetie, be thankful that now nothing can hurt her or cause her pain and *know* that she is happy somewhere. Do keep on writing to me.

All my love
Bernie [Hammond]

Kathleen Ferrier died on the morning of 8 October 1953. She was forty-one. Barbirolli said that it was 'one of the great tragedies of our time'. Bruno Walter wrote that 'whoever listened to her or met her personally felt enriched and uplifted'. But her nurse, Bernie Hammond, said the simplest thing: 'She was an extraordinary person, and an ordinary one.'

Coming to London

April 2006

Perhaps the best Sunday morning of my life happened in June 1970, when I walked across Hampstead Heath from an interview with Harold Evans which closed with his saying that I'd got a job on his newspaper. It was sunny, warm enough for the *Sunday Times*'s editor to wear nothing more than a dressing gown (he'd told me to be early, but he was in bed when I got there) as he conducted the conversation over his breakfast orange juice at a table in his back garden. His house was a pre-war Tudorbethan detached on the Holly Lodge Estate in Highgate. I remember he said, in the context of where I could afford to live, that a house like this would cost around £14,000, but that flats could be had for £5,000 or £6,000. My salary as a subeditor would be £3,000. All these amounts seemed large.

I walked across the Heath to the Tube at Hampstead in a daze of excitement. The sun sparkled on the ponds, couples walked dogs or kissed each other on the grass, the dome of St Paul's shivered far away in the haze, a kite bobbed up on the horizon. Glasgow, where I lived, was rarely so Mediterranean. Soon I would be part of all this, a single atom trying to join with others, because I knew nobody here other than an aunt who lived in Banstead, in the Surrey suburbs. I'd been to London before – there had been a few trips in the 1960s when I'd eaten in Lyons Corner Houses and seen the King's Road – but now I would discover it properly for myself as a resident.

Two Penguin paperbacks came with me in the suitcase. The first, *Nairn's London*, was an eccentric architectural guide by Ian Nairn, who wrote for the *Sunday Times* and whom I soon came to know as a big, shy man in a shiny black suit who smoked Senior Service and drank several pints of Guinness every lunchtime, and in the afternoon would sometimes bark ('woof! woof!') into any telephone he was answering rather than saying 'Hello, *Sunday Times* travel department. Can I help?' Ian died many years ago and in several moves, bedsits to flats to houses, I lost his good book.

The second I still have and still sometimes read. *Len Deighton's London Dossier* appeared, price 7s 6d, in 1967 to take advantage of the city's new reputation: 'the most exciting city in the world – the place where the action really is', as the back-cover blurb says. The front cover is plain black with a keyhole shape cut into it. Through the keyhole you can see an eye. Turn back the outer cover and you can see the full face on the inner cover: Twiggy's. It was an early, perhaps the first, example of a new kind of guidebook – 'an altogether new way of taking a city apart' – with accounts of the city by 'insiders' who are informal, knowing and opinionated, and write as much about the present as the past. Deighton, fresh from his success with *The Ipcress File* and *Funeral in Berlin*, pulled it together as the editor. His contributors included Drusilla Beyfus, Daniel Farson, Milton Shulman, Godfrey Smith, Nick Tomalin and Frank Norman.

What kind of city was it, the London I came to, the London of nearly forty years ago? Different, of course. Telephone numbers had letters and numbers, EUS 8833, KEN 5641; a taxi from Heathrow into town cost £1 15s. But even the weather was different. 'Rain is accepted by the Londoner as an inescapable fact of life, like shaving, contraception and income tax,' wrote Deighton, 'so come equipped with a raincoat or buy one here.' (A raincoat? When did I last have one of those?) Manners were different. Tourists wondering which bus to take should always consult a bus conductor rather than Londoners in the queue: 'A lot of bus conductors are Jamaican, and very sunny fellows they are.' Hotels were different. 'British hotels prefer you to write Mr and Mrs [in the register] even if you are sinning.' The restaurants were different. Where is the Kenco coffee house now, or the Trattoria Terrazza, or the Indian vegetarian Saruna hotel, or Lyons? Behaviour was different. How touching to read that in Soho after the pubs close 'there is the slim possibility that you will see a couple of drunks trying to fight and stay upright and managing to do neither'. By implication, the least well-regarded figure was the 'advertising executive' in his pink shirt. City brokers in their bowler hats were merely part of a colourful tradition, like Beefeaters.

Not least, nomenclature was different: how we talked of our fellow Londoners. According to the *Dossier*, Indian restaurants are mainly run by 'Pakistanis' – this was before East Pakistan became Bangladesh – and 'Negroes have moved on now to the Flamingo in Wardour Street, home of Georgie Fame and the Blue Flames'. In barbers' shops, Italian barbers spend their morning shaving themselves 'for like many Southern Europeans they see no reason to waste their pristine chins on a morning of work'.

As to slang, the book reprints Frank Norman's essay first published in *Encounter* in 1958. Example: 'I had a *fair bird* (good girl) when I got *nicked* (caught) . . . but she went off with some *schfatzer* (Negro) and the last I heard he had *stuck her up the spout* (made her pregnant).' It reads like Dick Van Dyke in *Mary Poppins* and as remote from the street patois of modern London ('da bitch is cool' and so on) as Chaucer.

But for all the differences between then and now, the *London Dossier*, with its attention to consumption and fun, clubs, restaurants and immigrants, does have an embryonic sense of what the city was to become. None of its authors could have guessed that the changes would be so swift – in 1967, for instance, it was still one of the world's great seaports – or that the city would grow so rich and turbulent, or that managing racial difference (multiculturalism wasn't yet invented) would mean more than being pleasant to bus conductors.

I certainly didn't as I walked that morning into Hampstead. Nick Tomalin, in the best essay in the book, writes about the different bohemians of Hampstead and Chelsea, and how the former had escaped Auschwitz and the latter Tunbridge Wells: 'The tyrant they defied was Daddy, not Hitler.' I remembered his description and for a very brief time I wondered which would be the better place to live, until I discovered that I could afford to live in neither.

Sundays

May 2006

A reading of my pocket diary for 1959 tells me very little about my fourteen-year-old self. As with the diaries for the previous six years (sweetly preserved by my parents) very few words are written in it, and hardly any at all after February, the month the recording instinct always died. Pepys I was not. 'Same as usual' is a frequent entry. Trips to the cinema are always noted – 'Saw *The Fly* in Alhambra (X cert)' – but how I felt about anything is unknown, with one exception: Sundays.

'Usual depressing day' is the entry for most of my Sundays in January and February, with the gloomy addition of 'Developed a sty' on Sunday 25 January. I was prone to sties. The word recalls a long medical process: first a rubbing with my mother's gold wedding ring, which rarely worked, then damp lint and oilcloth held in place over the eye with a bandage to 'draw it out'. But Sundays? Did I really feel as John Osborne's Jimmy Porter did when he first appeared on the Royal Court's stage three years earlier? 'God, how I hate Sundays! It's always so depressing . . . Always the same ritual. Reading the papers, drinking tea, ironing. A few more hours, and another week gone.'

The ritual aspect was certainly present. My brother and I would get out of bed late and eat a fried breakfast in our pyjamas. The radio would be switched on for *Family Favourites*, the Manchester Girls' Choir singing 'Nymphs and Shepherds' for Tom in BAOR Mönchengladbach, and then switched off again as soon as the vulgar (and worse, Cockney) Billy Cotton shouted 'Wakey, Wakkehh-y!' at the opening of his *Band Show*. High tea appeared on the table at five, sometimes with aunts and uncles present. Then there was homework, and more music from the radio when Max Jaffa and his orchestra struck up with their signature tune (Strauss's 'Roses from the South', according to my brother's memory) and we were invited into the Palm Court of the Grand Hotel, which now I come to think of it must have been a plain BBC studio rather than an ornate room with potted plants and waltzing couples behaving in an unsabbatarian way.

On fine days, we went out as a family for long walks or rode our bikes past hatted church-goers in stilled villages. Apart from the occasional newsagent, no shops were open, nor cinemas, nor pubs. Railway stations were closed and the signals on the many lines stood all day disappointingly at red. Sometimes you might encounter an ice-cream van tinkling 'The Happy Wanderer' or, in the early evening, a busful of men heading towards a hotel which sold drink to 'bona fide travellers' after they had signed a book which declared they'd travelled at least three miles. Neighbours chatted over the hedge as they dug their gardens, church bells sometimes tolled. Otherwise, a great external quietness meant to encourage reflection in our inner selves. Perhaps this was what I meant by 'usual depressing day'. Nobody knew then that it would be exchanged forty years later for arduous trips to Ikea and jams on the motorways.

The slow collapse of Christianity and the advent in 1994 of the Sunday Trading Act have abolished the difference of Sunday. Secular progressives in Britain used to dream of 'a Continental Sunday', but now the fact is that Sundays in most European countries, still constrained by shopping laws and more enduring traditions of family behaviour, look high-minded and decorous compared with our own. In Britain, only the long Hebridean island comprising Lewis and Harris has defied the tide. Calvinism still holds sway. Games aren't played, shops do not open, and the churches are filled with the sound of unaccompanied psalms. Ferries sail to the rest of the Hebrides on Sundays but not yet to Stornoway or Tarbert, thanks to Caledonian MacBrayne's care for 'moral' or 'community' concerns. This is the old Sunday's last redoubt, and I give it no more than a couple of years; first there will be a flanking attack in the shape of the little ferry that connects Harris to North Uist (a petition is already calling for Sunday runs) and then in Stornoway the containers will start rolling off direct from the mainland despite the protests of Free Kirk congregations.

Despite nearly two hundred years of struggling vainly against the swell of commerce and fun, the Lord's Day Observance Society still exists, and at an address which suggests how workaday Sundays have become: Units 7 and 8, Southern Avenue Industrial Estate, Leominster, Herefordshire. Its general secretary, John Roberts, is surprisingly (and I surprise myself by adding hearteningly) gung-ho about the prospect of returning British Sundays to their previous state. When I called him, he said, 'I still believe passionately that the vast majority of people still value a day that's different. The pressure of the rat race, a society where everything's about profit – people need a break from that. Things come in cycles and I think Sunday's turn will come again.'

The Lord's Day Observance Society has done its best to catch up with the present by operating under the title 'Day One' (in defiance of Genesis 2:3 which clearly states Day Seven). It was founded in 1831 and quickly began to lobby against the running of Sunday trains and the opening of public parks. According to Mr Roberts, its first leading light was the Reverend Daniel Wilson, vicar of St Mary's parish church, Islington, and later bishop of Calcutta.

St Mary's is close to where I live. Last Sunday afternoon I walked past it to count the number of things I could do or buy within a couple of hundred yards of its clock tower. How the Reverend Wilson would grieve; there was so much sin. Tapas, kebabs, pizzas, furniture and flowers for sale, organic juice bars, pubs, estate agents, a Sainsbury's and a cinema with queues at their tills. The only two social institutions with locked doors were the Northern District Post Office and the Reverend Wilson's church.

The scene didn't look like any other day – it looked busier than any other day and perhaps also happier. Only those of us who remember homework with fountain pens and the violins of Max Jaffa would have thought there was anything wrong.

See, the Workers Move!

January 2005

Recently, I was lucky enough to sit in a small cinema at the British Film Institute in London and for a couple of hours watch a series of short films, none more than a few minutes long and all of them about one hundred years old. Only one of them contained people who might have been actors. Most of them showed the industrial working class of northern England, with occasional forays north to Scotland, west to Wales and Ireland, and south to the Midlands. This was working Britain at its apogee as the world's supreme imperial and industrial power, brought alive in black-and-white pictures that were wonderfully clear and sharp, unscratched and unfogged. Watching them was to see generations of people, previously known to us mainly through still and stiff family photographs, become more fully human. They walked, they ran, they clowned at the camera or self-consciously ignored it. There was a lot of humour and confidence in them. Some of these animated people – the old woman weaver, a white-bearded mechanic – must have been born before 1850. They might remember the Crimean War. Now they were walking towards me, sometimes staring boldly at me, on a screen in central London in late 2004.

These pictures were moving in another sense. It is quite hard to put a finger on why, though when a selection of them is shown later this month on BBC2 and at the National Film Theatre I am certain that their audience will be as affected as everyone else who has seen them so far. It isn't as though we don't know that our Victorian and Edwardian ancestors walked and ran and laughed, or worked in mills, or took the tram, or bled when pricked. Some of us thought we knew these things quite vividly. In my own case, I briefly shared a bedroom (and, come to think of it, a bed) with a grandfather who was born in 1874 and could recall the storm in Glasgow that, further east, blew down the Tay Bridge; I remember his long underwear and his pipe, which was tapped out only before he made the decision to sleep. But even though I knew this man, and as a child literally rubbed up against him, he was for me a relic. In one of these films, he would be different: a young man among other young men and women, a lively part of the age that shaped him, working in a bleachworks, stepping out into the twentieth century, innocent of all the wonder and horror it would eventually contain. Sitting in the BFI's cinema, I felt that history had suddenly been enlarged and one of its divisions abolished, that between the living and the long dead.

Why has this feeling been so delayed? Where have the films been until now? Why haven't we seen them before? The answers lie in a remarkable story of preservation, discovery and restoration that to British film history is a near equivalent to the finding of the Dead Sea Scrolls. In 1994, workmen stripping out an empty shop at 40 Northgate, Blackburn, Lancashire, went down to the cellar and discovered three large metal drums, like big rusting milk-churns, which turned out to contain more than eight hundred rolls of nitrate film. A cinephile and film historian, Peter Worden, knew of the site as the old studios of two Blackburn men, Sagar Mitchell and James Kenyon, who had made and processed films there until 1913. Worden had kept a watchful eye on the shop in case anything was discovered inside it. He arranged for the metal drums to be delivered to him – the alternative destination was the skip – and transferred their contents to seventeen plastic food containers, the size of family ice-cream tubs, and stored them in a chest freezer. To preserve and restore the films proved beyond Worden's means. The British Film Institute took them over as the Mitchel and Kenyon Collection in 2000 and then began their painstaking restoration at its laboratories in Berkhamsted.

Most were made between 1900 and 1907, but the age of the films is not in itself the most significant thing. The Lumière brothers, gener-ally accepted as the founders of cinema, showed their first film to a paying audience in Paris in 1895 and in London the next year. By the late 1890s several British film-makers were at work and several of their films survive – short bursts of sea breaking on rocks, trains at speed, the procession at Queen Victoria's Diamond Jubilee in 1898. Nor, when their hoard was discovered in 1994, were Sagar Mitchell and James Kenyon unknown. Their films of the Boer War, depicting British bravery and Boer depravity, had a minor celebrity as early examples of cinematic propaganda and fakery (they were shot entirely in the Lancashire countryside). To the film historian, what was exciting about the discovery was its size – translated to DVD or video the films take up twenty-eight hours of viewing time – and its technical quality. The reels were the original negatives, kept in good condition for most of the century in the cool of the cellar. Their positives, the film actually projected on to the screen, would have been damaged by the wear and tear of machinery, the heat of the electrics, the carelessness of the operator.

The images, then, have a freshness and clarity, but that (to the film historian or otherwise) is only part of their appeal. What they show is a world now lost to us: the busy world of north Britain in its manufacturing, mining heyday. Not until the 1930s and the British documentary movement did film-makers pay it so much attention again, this time as a subject for moral concern because it had then begun its slow collapse. In Mitchell and Kenyon's films you can see it as an independent civilisation, glorying in its new easements and enjoyments such as electric trams, professional sport, street parades and pageants and seaside holidays. There are films of thirty-two northern soccer matches, and of eighteen rugby games played by professional teams in the newly founded Northern Union (later the Rugby League), which broke from the amateur Rugby Football Union in 1895. You can see the new electric trams in Halifax, Lytham and Accrington, Catholic and temperance processions in the streets of Manchester, a flotilla of destroyers moving up the Manchester Ship Canal, the crowded piers at Blackpool and Morecambe. You see horses pulling people and goods – stables in British towns then contained 1.7 million of them. You see many factory chimneys, smoking.

Most of all, you see people. Very few of them, no matter how poor, are bareheaded: the men wear flat caps, bowlers, straw boaters, trilbies, toppers; the women, shawls or floral hats. Waistcoats are everywhere, as are moustaches and mufflers, pipes and cigarettes. Tobacco smoke drifts close to the camera, coal smoke further off. Nobody is fat. Many have bad teeth; people have a way of smiling that manages not to reveal them. Perhaps this technique has been forgotten; a particular male stance afforded by the waistcoat – the thumbs in its pockets – has also disappeared.

The streets of Lancashire look impossibly crowded and surging, and probably they were much more so then than now. But there is another reason for this vibrancy: the filmmaker's presence. Mitchell and Kenyon were businessmen and only by accident social documentarists. They made three kinds of film: the fake (as in their Boer War films), the fictional (as in *Diving Lucy* of 1903, billed in the USA, improbably for a film made in a Lancashire public park, as 'the hit British comedy of the year') and 'actualities'. The last, also known as 'local topicals', were their bread and butter, and worked on the principle then (and still) well-known to local newspapers: the more names of local citizens that appeared in the paper – as prize-winning scholars, Sunday school excursionists, speech-making councillors – the more the paper sold to people who liked to see they had been noticed.

So it was with the local topicals, which were mainly commissioned from Mitchell and Kenyon by showmen and fairground owners who had begun to see the potential of cinema shows in tents and civic halls (there were as yet no cinemas). People would come to watch the huge novelty of their appearance on film; the more people Mitchell and Kenyon could capture in the frame, the larger the showman's audience, the more handsome the profit. The countryside and the market town were no good for this. A large and dense population such as industrial Lancashire's was ideal. But where could the largest press of people be found – people moving quickly, one face replaced by another, streaming through a space no wider than the lens on a fixed camera could accommodate, as many people within a one-minute film as would, with their friends and relations, make a decent audience at the screening a few nights later? The solution was the factory gate, but not the factory gate at clocking-on time, when workers arrived too randomly and at the wrong angle, but when their shift was over and they surged out, free and quick, and straight towards a camera being hand-turned by a man behind a tripod, against which a sign might be mounted: 'Come and see yourself as others see you, seven o'clock p.m. at the Drill Hall in Jessop Street'. And there they would go and, according to contemporary accounts, point to themselves on the screen and shout out, tickled by the strangeness of it all.

See, the Workers Move!

Mitchell and Kenyon didn't invent this genre, 'the factory-gate film', which is as old as film itself. The film shown by the Lumière brothers to their first paying audience in 1895 was called *La Sortie de l'Usine*, one of three shot outside factory gates in Lyon, not to make money from their workforce but to demonstrate to a Paris audience how a film could capture human movement. Nor were Mitchell and Kenyon its only British practitioners. In southern England, the pioneering film-maker Cecil Hepworth, announced in his promotional literature that 'a film showing workers leaving a factory will gain far greater popularity in the town where it was taken than the most exciting picture ever produced. The workers come in hundreds, with all their friends and relations, and the film more than pays for itself the first night.' The Blackburn men, however, were in the right place at the right time. In 1900, Lancashire employed 600,000 men, women and children in its cotton-spinning and weaving factories and another 100,000 in the cloth-finishing trades. More than sixty per cent of cotton goods traded internationally was made in Lancashire, and accounted for a quarter of British exports by value. Blackburn's own speciality was the dhoti, the traditional Indian loincloth, many millions of which were shipped to Bombay and Calcutta.

The mills were on the film-makers' doorstep, and if these mills were ever exhausted as audience providers, then it was easy to move on to collieries, engineering shops and ironworks, or to take the train across to the worsted factories of Yorkshire, or further afield to the great ship-yards on the Tyne, or in Barrow or Greenock. In an office at the BFI they have a map of Britain on the wall, with pins to mark the hundreds of Mitchell and Kenyon's known locations; a very few pins south of Birmingham and then a dense spread across the Pennines to the north: Darwen, Chorley, Ormerod's Mill in Bolton, Pendlebury Colliery, Parkgate Ironworks, Platt's of Oldham, Haslam's Limited of Colne. In the Parkgate film, a young man does a rather modern thing and gives a V-sign to the cameraman. In another film titled *20,000 Employees Entering Lord Armstrong's Elswick Works* made on Tyneside in 1900, we see a grave crowd of men moving steadily down a slope towards the camera, ready to begin a day's work in the yard that built battleships for the Japanese. It lasts for two minutes and thirty-four seconds, the camera angle unchanged: a sea of faces moving forward, replenished from behind, like something out of Eisenstein. Many other films have the crowd controller in shot, sometimes James Kenyon and some-times the showman who commissioned the film. Their good suits separate them from the crowd and they can be seen gesticulating, urging their subjects to move past the camera rather than stand and stare at it, or staging a mock fight or teasing a woman – anything to give the film animation and interest. In this way, and unlike many documentaries since, their version of reality is strikingly honest. You can see the human intervention in it.

The people leaving their factories in these films look happy enough and yet, despite the wealth they created, many of them lived in scan-dalous ill-health and poverty – a scandal that was beginning to rumble through Britain in the same years that the films were made. The Boer War had brought certain facts to light. Four out of ten young men offering themselves as recruits to the British army had to be rejected because their bodies weren't up to the job. They had bad teeth, weak hearts, poor sight and hearing, physical deformities of all kinds. Most obviously, they were too short: in 1901, the infantry had to reduce the minimum height for recruits to 5 feet from 5 feet 3 inches (it had already been lowered from 5 feet 6 inches in 1883). A government committee (the frankly named Inter-Departmental Committee on Physical Deterioration) was set up and reported in 1904. It found that boys of ten to twelve at council schools were on average five inches shorter than those at private schools; that working-class girls, according to the evidence of a factory inspector, exhibited 'the same shortness of stature, the same miserable development, the same sallow cheeks and carious teeth'. It was established that breastfeeding was rapidly declining, partly because increasing numbers of new mothers went out to work in the factories, but also because many mothers were simply not healthy enough to provide milk. Chronic digestive troubles, bad teeth, anaemia, and 'general debility' were almost universal among working-class women. Instead of milk from the breast, mothers gave their infants the cheapest food they could buy, which was usually sweetened condensed skimmed milk – high in sugar and devoid of fats and thus an excellent diet to promote rickets. The very poorest mothers substituted a mixture of flour and water, which was milk-like only in appearance. In the County of London – and the same was surely true in the northern cities – more than one in every five children did not live beyond infancy.

All this began to change well before the First World War, but too late for the boys and girls leaving Ormerod's Mill in 1900. Think of them when you see these films and of what that war held for them. Think also of the fate of Blackburn and its dependence on the export of dhotis to India, which imposed cotton tariffs in the early 1920s. J. B. Priestley visited Blackburn early in the next decade, and wrote: 'The tragic word around [Blackburn], I soon discovered, is *dhootie*. It is the forgotten Open Sesame . . . This fabric was manufactured in the town and the surrounding district on a scale equal to the needs of the gigantic Indian population. So colossal was the output that Blackburn was the greatest weaving town in the world. It clothed the whole vast mad peninsula. Millions and millions of yards of *dhootie* cloth went streaming out of this valley. That trade is almost finished.'

The terms of international trade were to blame. Lancashire, Priestley concluded, was 'learning a lot about this queer interdependence of things'. Every factory town in the Mitchell and Kenyon films has since learned the same lesson. The people who appear in them, however poor and unhealthy, held the key to Britain's industrial importance in the world. Which among them could have realised that that superb position was as temporary as life itself?

Chimneys

May 2006

The words 'dream' and 'imagination' are often confused, but one of the interesting things about dreams, the proper dreams induced by sleep, is how unimaginative they are. Strange and disturbing events occur in them, but their cast of characters and their settings are usually drawn from life. Monsters never appear in my dreams, but my mother often does; while the imagination can create pasts and futures, James Ivory on the one hand and George Lucas on the other, dreams tend to be furnished by the materials to hand. And so, in the history of dreams, each generation must dream differently according to its surroundings when awake: dreams featuring crinolines in the nineteenth century being replaced by dreams about miniskirts a hundred years later, and so on. Given that our minds are now infused by all kinds of artificial imagery from the past and supposed future, this may be changing. It may be that people can now fall asleep and easily dream of themselves as Roman gladiators, but so far it hasn't happened to me. Perhaps I'm too prosaic a dreamer.

It was passing the Horlicks factory at Slough last week on the Oxford train that caused me to recall the earliest dream I can remember. The Horlicks factory is an old brick building with a chimney. My childhood dream placed me on top of a similar chimney, running dizzyingly around the rim several hundred feet up with someone in pursuit. Peas – the dried kind that you soaked – also came into it. I was five or six years old and feverish – measles perhaps – and I remember that when I came to in bed I heard the late-afternoon sound of children playing in the street; oddly distanced noises, as though they belonged to the faraway land of the healthy and well.

The dream's location made perfect sense. From the corner of our street you could see the twin chimneys of the Bolton Textile Company and further off the single one of Cross's spinning mill, where my father worked. Later, in Scotland, I passed tall chimneys every day on the bus to school, those of the paper mill, the brickworks, and the linen factory of Erskine Beveridge, where my father also worked. Tall chimneys made of brick or stone were a key part of many British landscapes and of our mental furniture. In textile towns such as Oldham, Halifax and Dundee they rose in priapic forests. Today they are rare enough to have preservation orders slapped on them.

Their purpose is interesting. The primary reason for their great height wasn't to remove noxious fumes from industrial processes and spew them high and relatively harmlessly above people's heads. They were high because steam power needed something called 'natural draught'. As James Douet explains in a monograph for the Victorian Society, 'Air inside the enclosed shaft of the chimney becomes rarefied by being heated, thereby creating a pressure differential between it and the cooler air outside the furnace . . . The effect of the differential is to draw fresh air through the furnace, and boost the combustion of the fire.' The principle was first described in Germany in the seventeenth century. By the late eighteenth century its practical application could be seen everywhere in Britain from Cornish copper mines to the coal pits of central Scotland. Improved steam engines needed more steam, which meant hotter fires, which needed stronger draughts; and the higher the chimney and the more light air inside it, the stronger the draught.

Technical tables were published for builders to consult: a boiler raising ten steam horse-power would need a chimney of 60 feet; for 250 horse-power, 180 feet. As chimneys grew taller, they needed deeper foundations and became free-standing, apart from the workshops. They tapered. They changed in cross-section from square to octangle and to round. Sills appeared at their tops to prevent smoke drifting down their sides. Their numbers and increasing heights became, as Douet writes, a barometer of Britain's economic growth and the most potent symbols of its industrialisation. By the nineteenth century, architects were employed to give them Italianate and Gothic tops. Two at the Tower Works in Leeds were modelled on Giotto's Florentine campanile and the Lamberti Tower in Verona.

Size mattered, and not only for technical reasons. In 1842, the Glasgow alkali firm of Tennant and Company completed a chimney of 436 feet, which for a time was the world's tallest. Not to be outdone, their Glasgow rivals in the alkali trade, Townsend's of Port Dundas, built one reaching 468 feet and opened it to the public for a fortnight, proclaiming to the crowd who clambered up the ladders inside the shaft that it was the fourth tallest building in the word (the three taller were probably the Gothic cathedral spires of Cologne, Ulm and Beauvais).

At sea, the marine chimney also grew taller and more numerous to meet the demand for greater steam pressure. The public saw four-funnelled liners (a fashion begun by the Germans in the 1890s) as especially powerful and speedy, so that even when there was no engineering need for so much funnelling, shipping lines added dummies, a fourth to the *Titanic* and a third to the *Queen Mary*. According to the maritime historian John Maxtone-Graham, the dummies 'existed primarily to reassure steerage passengers who tended naively to choose ships by the numbers of funnels they sported'.

The last great brick chimney to be built in Britain was that designed by Sir Giles Gilbert Scott for the Bankside Power Station: 325 feet high, finished in 1960, and now the crowning glory of the Tate Modern. Long before then, and other than in power stations, most of the non-environmental reasons for tall chimneys had gone. Diesel and electric engines had replaced steam as a source of factory power, and where steam boilers still existed furnace draughts were fan-assisted.

I doubt that they appear in the dreams of five-year-olds. Today when I spot one of the few that remain I think of them both sentimentally and sinisterly: of the heat shimmering from their tops at Bolton Textile on a sunny day, and of their role as the first great instruments of global warming, changing much more than they knew in the dream-territory high above.

The Seaside

July 2006

Last weekend, the weather being fine, we went to Broadstairs. There was the usual discussion beforehand: which is the nearest seaside to London? Followed by: which is the nearest seaside to London reachable by train? Followed by: which is the nearest seaside to London reachable by train which isn't mud and doesn't make you want to kill yourself? That ruled out Southend. Brighton was vetoed on the grounds of a pebble beach. The children shrugged at the mention of Eastbourne. The case for Frinton was put, but though I like Frinton for several reasons (the interesting change of trains at Thorpe-le-Soken, its teetotal gentility, its good fish and chip shop, the town map that until recently advertised its main shopping street as 'the Bond Street of south-east England', as though the real Bond Street was in Rome), I ruled against Frinton on the grounds that it was too regular: a straight esplanade, straight cliffs hiding a straight beach, a straight sea all the way to the sky. The best seaside has curves and punctuation: a bay, rocks, a lighthouse, boats, a pier. Broadstairs has those.

The trouble with Broadstairs is that the trains are slow. A hundred years ago, a train could fetch you from London to Broadstairs in just over two hours, and the time now is not much shorter. We slipped quickly through the tangle of junctions in the southern suburbs and then began to stop. Rochester, Chatham, Gillingham, Faversham: places that remind you that London is different from England. A big Russian woman who should really have been in charge of a samovar pushed her trolley up and down the train. Outside, the flag of St George hung like sun-dried washing from the windows of terraces and flats.

We reached green orchards and glimpsed the blue sea. Fields of mobile homes appeared. Herne Bay, Birchington, Margate: places that were once advertised by railway posters in which women wore cloche hats and the bandstand had a firm silhouette.

Broadstairs is just round the headland – North Foreland – from Margate and faces east rather than north. It is 'nicer'. According to one of my favourite reference books, the guide to 'Seaside Watering Places' for 1902, Broadstairs did not 'present overpowering attractions' but was at least free (unlike Margate) from 'the obtrusive German band and the irrepressible "nigger" [minstrel]'. My parents would have seen the sense in that. One crude way to slice up the old working class was to note where they spent their holidays. All over Britain, smaller resorts drew the kind of people who were offended by too much noisy vulgarity and alcohol, and therefore preferred Millport over Rothesay, Aberdour over Burntisland, Southport over Blackpool, Tynemouth over Whitley Bay, Mablethorpe over Skegness. I think of their preferences as towns marked by an improving hush, with dads bending over rock pools and mums knitting nearby on the promenade, and the welcome prospect of the WEA's evening classes resuming in the autumn.

Every resort needed to boast of a particularity – a special attraction for the visitor. Minute and often imaginary differences in climate are prominent in my 1902 guide. Margate had the endorsement of the Astronomer Royal: 'From meteorological observations, I find that Margate has a larger number of hours of sunshine, a less[er] rainfall, and a more even temperature than any other seaside town in the three kingdoms.' Birchington-on-Sea, four miles to the west, had 'considerably less rainfall than in other places (about five inches less than London)'. According to the Registrar General, Herne Bay was 'one of the healthiest places in the kingdom; indeed, for those requiring a bracing air it is unequalled'. Broadstairs, meanwhile, had air that was 'especially suitable for children', a fact amply testified by the number of convalescent homes that had recently been erected.

Dickens was a big fan of Broadstairs, rented houses and wrote here, including chapters of *David Copperfield*. His last summer house, a pseudo-fort now called Bleak House, stands prominently above the harbour. There are pubs with Dickens, Copperfield and Trotwood in their titles. Down the hill from the station, we bought sweets measured from jars in a shop called Sweet Yesterdays. Then we undressed on warm sand and walked straight into the sea.

Two things about this experience at the British seaside never change. The first is the inclination to turn back when your feet touch the water's edge: impossible that you could immerse yourself in such coldness. The second comes when you are on your way out, having swum around for half an hour in deeper and even colder water: the sea in the shallows now seems the temperature of a warm bath – how could you ever have imagined it to be, as you exclaimed at the time, 'bloody freezing'?

Swimming has always been the only part of my life where I can think of myself as physically brave. Not that I'm a good swimmer, but learning to swim in the Firth of Forth (it was the glorious summer of 1955) perhaps taught me that you need to face and overcome the initial shock to win a few minutes of pleasure. Last year I even managed it off the sands of Barra and Harris in the Outer Hebrides. I notice, though, that while British beaches many be enjoying a renaissance, with their Blue Flags and litter patrols, there seem to be fewer people up to their necks in the sea. (Two or three years ago, Bute's local newspaper reported that the police had been alerted when a man was seen swimming in Rothesay Bay, only to be stood down when the man was discovered to be 'a visitor' eccentric enough to be swimming for fun.)

And so at Broadstairs we swam out until we were nearly abreast of a dinghy race. It wasn't perfect. The water was cloudy with mud and the depth rose and fell with the sandbanks. But there was a yellow-funnelled ferry on the horizon making for Ramsgate, and when you looked back to land you could see how pretty a town Broadstairs is, with its hotels perched above a bay of yellow sand, now scattered with deckchairs and picnics. I thought of my mother and all those women of her generation who never swam or owned a bathing suit, for reasons of bodily inhibition and perhaps money, and how sad that was. Sometimes my mother would say when I came out of the water on a hot day, 'I envied you swimming. It looked fine and cool.'

Ashore again, we lay on deckchairs and ate cherries. Come December, it will be hard to imagine that such things ever happened in England.

FARNWORTH

Hippodrome

S.W. Corner of Egerton St. & Cawdor St.

No upstairs.

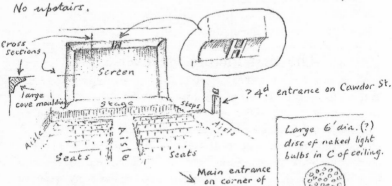

cross sections

large cove moulding

Screen

Stage

Steps

Aisle

Aisle

Seats

Aisle

Seats

? 4ᵈ entrance on Cawdor St.

Main entrance on corner of streets.

Large 6' dia. (?) disc of naked light bulbs in C of ceiling.

Dimmed out before start of show. <u>Bulbs</u> in centre dimmed first.

This was watched for, then a cheer went up. (Kids' Saturday P.M. matinee.)

Records played before show started.
ALWAYS Victor Silvester. (aargh!)

Common to many cinemas — but the Hip. was always like this :—
Irritating habit : gauzy curtains kept closed until the film actually started. Trying to read the MS handwriting on the BBFC certificate through the wavy curtains. Is it the big film? Or what?

(Plan) →

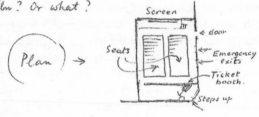

Screen

Seats

door

Emergency exits

Ticket booth.

Steps up

The Best Picture He Ever Saw

July 2004

1. Going back

One afternoon in the autumn of 1933 the writer J. B. Priestley drove north from Manchester towards Preston and Blackpool. Priestley was then England's most successful young novelist. Not yet forty, with five novels and the internationals success of *The Good Companions* behind him, he had decided, as many novelists do, to take a break from his desk, forsake fiction for a bit and become an enquiring traveller, so that (in this case) he might describe the condition of England. The book that he made from the experience is called *English Journey* and in it he wrote of that particular afternoon's travels in Lancashire: 'We went through Bolton. Between Manchester and Bolton the ugliness is so complete that it is almost exhilarating. It challenges you to live there.'

What did he mean by 'ugliness'? The answer from my own memory is: two dark rivers, the Irwell and its tributary the Croal, their surfaces crowded with little icebergs of industrial foam; a railway line and an abandoned canal along the valley; a power station and various bleach works, chemical factories and sewage beds beside the rivers; a coal mine or two on the valley's western edge; many cotton mills, some five storeys high, with even taller chimneys; streets of small Victorian houses with doors that opened straight on to the pavement; meat-pie, fish-and-chip and tripe shops; a few people who still wore clogs; smoke.

My father moved from Scotland to the centre of this landscape in 1930, shortly before he married my mother. He was a fitter, a mechanic, and he'd found a job in a Farnworth textile factory that made belting and canvas for housepipes. Unemployment was severe in Scotland at the time, though in Lancashire it was hardly much better ('We were going through the country of the dole,' Priestley wrote). He lived in digs for some months, and then returned to Fife for his wedding – Christmas Day 1930, when the minister came to the house for the ceremony. Husband and wife were back in Farnworth by the turn of the year. Had Priestley gone by train rather than by car, by might have looked out of the window at Farnworth and seen their first proper home, 139 Cemetery Road. The street ran over the railway and down the hill towards an old pottery, the black junction of the Croal and the Irwell, the discused canal – and the cemetery. Their house was one of the last in a terrace which came just before you reached the cemetery's entrance lodge and the monumental home of the dead. Later, when they moved away, my parents used to speak wryly of this location.

Unless it was a Saturday or a Sunday afternoon, Priestley would not have seen my father, who would be repairing looms or crankshafts inside the weaving-sheds of George Banham and Company. But he might have seen my mother, a twenty-six-year-old woman of fair Scottish complexion, out shopping for that night's tea. A crowd, a face; thousands of people and things that cross the eye's threshold every day, most of them ignored and lost to mind and memory. The eye may be a lens, but the mind, with its random fixative, is not a film. In the autumn of 1933, she would be 'getting over' the death that spring of her first son, George, aged ten months, and seized with the happiness that she was pregnant again (and with another son, though she was yet to know that).

All four of her and my father's sons were born there, in this complete, almost exhilarating ugliness. Two of us survive. Earlier this year, in March, my elder brother Harry and I got off the stopping train at Farnworth, a place we left in 1952. We were searching for cinemas. What did we look like? Like a man of fifty-nine and man of seventy, greying or grey, a little lost, walking up the slope from the empty platform and into empty streets, looking for things that were no longer there. We might as well have been the ghosts of old Trojans, coming back a thousand years later to walk on the soil that buried old Troy. Our childhoods had been here somewhere.

Harry, as usual, pulled out the maps. He loves maps; he used to draw them for a living, and he rarely travels without them. Here was Cemetery Road, now crossed by the Manchester to Bolton expressway. Here was Railway Street, where he remembered Sally Malley the abortionist (truly, a backstreet abortionist) had lived. We found the steps that had once led to Banham's factory and the house in Lime Street that was once home to Nurse Grant: Nurse Grant, the town's 'nitty nurse', who combed children's hair for lice, Scottish, from Grantown-on-Spey, a family friend, her friendship enshrined in my parents' gift of 'Grant' as my middle name. What do I remember of her? That she had long hairs above her upper lip and lived with another old woman, Mrs Haydock, plump and black-shawled and infirm, who never stirred from her chair beside the fire.

How small this world had been, and how convenient. The factory, the railway station, Nurse Grant, the pub, the market, Mum and Dad's house – all only a few minutes' walk from each other. Not much of this survived. The factory and the pub had gone; the station buildings had been demolished; many streets of straight terraces had been replaced by new houses and gardens built in less regular and more spacious layouts. It was no longer a dense Lowry townscape, but it was not country or a suburb either. Really, the only way to look at it was as an ex-town, a place shorn of its dynamic ugliness, but also of its newspaper (the *Farnworth Journal*), its school (Farnworth Grammar), its five cinemas (the Ritz, the Savoy, the Empire, the Hippodrome, the Palace). Cotton-spinning in more than thirty mills had made all this possible. Cotton was no longer spun here, or anywhere else in Lancashire. Farnworth had become a place of absences.

Harry looked at the map again. Where the devil was Peel Street? Where was our first cinema, the Ritz?

2. The Ritz

My father first visited the Ritz in 1930, my brother in 1938 or 1939 (to see the Three Stooges in *Back to the Woods!*), myself in the late 1940s. Had any of us of heard of Cesar Ritz and his grand hotels when we first went through its doors? No, of course not, and not for a long time after. Cinema names seemed independent of any history. They may have been intended to suggest luxury, romance, good birth and breeding, foreign parts, ancient history, and therefore to be fitting vehicles for the films shown inside them; escapist images within escapist architecture. But how many among their audiences could have connected the Hippodrome to horse racing in ancient Greece, or the Rialto to Venice, the Alhambra, Granada and Toledo to Spain, the Lido to Mediterranean bathing, the Colosseum to Rome, the Savoy to the Strand, the Odeon to Paris, the Regal to majestic behaviour? Not me, certainly. Before they were anything else, they were the names of cinemas. Cinemas were what they described.

When my father came to Farnworth, the Ritz had been known by that name for only three years. Before 1927, it was the Queen's Theatre, a Victorian palace of varieties which continued as a venue for live stage acts after its screen was installed – films one week and hoofers the next. It was in this way that my father encountered the Glen Louise Girls, who were appearing at the Ritz in a variety bill which also included a snake charmer and the Three Aberdonians ('Too Mean To Tell You What They Do!'). The troupe and my father stayed in the same lodgings, at a Mrs Walker's in Church Road. He was a twenty-eight-year-old bachelor; the situation might have been fun – just as it is in *The Good Companions*, when the working class hero of Priestley's novel falls in with a group of touring theatricals, the eponymous Good Companions, and his view of life is thrillingly challenged and expanded. That didn't seem to have happened to my father. Many years later he would some-times entertain us with stories of late-night card playing, of the surprise of discovering sloughed snakeskins inside sideboard drawers, of actors who turned up unexpectedly from late-night trains and were found the next morning bedded down in the bath. But at the time he must have wearied of it, because quite soon he moved on to less chaotic lodg-ings. He was, after all, a man who needed to rise early to get off to the factory and his chisels and files, unlike Glen and her girls and The Three Aberdonians, and their evening shifts at the Ritz.

Glen must have liked my father though, because she gave him or sent him half a dozen postcards of herself and her girls, and he must have liked her, because he kept them. She wrote on each of them – 'To our Scottie' or 'Choose your girl, Jack!' or 'Knees up XXXXX'.

'What do you reckon Mum made of those cards?' I said to Harry as we turned into the bit of Peel Street that survived.

'We'll never know now,' Harry said. 'But she might have thought it was a funny business.'

Of course, the Ritz wasn't there. At first we thought it must have occupied a gap site next to the Farnworth Christian Spiritualist Church, and then Harry looked at the map again and decided no, it had been further down the street where there were some new houses and a parking bay. He remembered the building had a fancy red-brick exterior and a sign with the letters R I T Z arranged vertically, one over the other. Later, at our hotel in Bolton, he drew a sketch of its proscenium arch and quick pictures of other Farnworth cinemas, one of which prefaces this essay.

What did he see at the Ritz? '*The Wizard of Oz, Bambi*, and *The Four Feathers* twice in one week – or maybe more than three times if you add on the bits we sat through again.' What had I seen here? *Captain Kidd* (Charles Laughton and Randolph Scott, 1945), *Oh, Mr Porter!* (Will Hay, 1937), *Annie Get Your Gun* (Betty Hutton, Howard Keel, 1950). From each I remember one scene. From *Captain Kidd*, a sailing ship becalmed; from *Oh, Mr Porter!* some washing hung over a railway line and getting entangled with a train; from *Annie Get Your Gun*, either a silver gun or a piece of bright jewellery on a bed of dark velvet – and a song about there being no business like show business, whatever that was. Mum took me to see the last one in the afternoon. It was bright when we came out – sunshine bright, a different kind of brightness from the film.

3. The Savoy

A British audience saw a moving picture for the first time in 1896. Early shows were in fairgrounds, music halls, shops, railway arches, anywhere that a projector and a white sheet could be set up and chairs arranged. Fires were a problem; nitrate film was highly combustible. In 1909, Parliament passed the Cinematograph Act, which imposed fire-safety regulations on venues. That was the real beginning of the purpose-built cinema and the architecture of escape. By 1914, London alone had four hundred cinemas. By 1927, 20 million cinema tickets were sold every week. By 1940, there were 4.2 million cinema seats. By 1946, nearly one out of every seven British adults went to the cinema twice a week or more. Then, between 1945 and 1960, cinema admissions fell by more than two-thirds, and a third of the 1945 total of 4,700 cinemas closed. An article by Sue Harper and Vincent Porter in the *Journal of Popular British Cinema* (volume two, 1999) refines some of these statistics by gender and class. In 1946, sixty-two per cent of the adult audience had been women. By 1960, they were only forty-seven per cent. The number of sixteen- to twenty-four-year-olds in the audience doubled between 1946 and 1950. In 1939, the skilled working class and the classes below comprised sixty-nine per cent of the audience.

By 1954, that proportion had risen to eighty-two per cent. That was a peak year for the cinema as a British working-class entertainment. Television culled audiences thereafter, though our family didn't get a set until 1961 and so 'the pictures' remained a big part of our lives for longer.

We were, in any case, cinephiles. Dad was born in a small Scottish town in 1902, seven years after the Lumière brothers showed their first film in Paris and six years after they brought their box of tricks to Britain. He watched his first moving pictures, one-reelers, on screens set up in public halls before the First World War. He loved Chaplin – had anyone *ever* been so funny? – and Mary Pickford and Pearl White. Later, when I knew him, historical pictures were his thing: *Ben-Hur, Spartacus, The Robe, Alexander the Great, Cleopatra, The Vikings*. Not musicals – perhaps this was why Mum snuck me into *Annie Get Your Gun* on her own. Not comedies, unless by visual comedians who had perfected their acts on stage (Chaplin, the Marx Brothers and, for a brief time, Norman Wisdom). As a late child, I had missed his middle period. Harry said: 'I think Dad's taste in films remained in the silent era. The first talkies he saw were just all static-camera yak-yak-yak. I think that must have been an awful let-down after some of those well-made so-called artistic silents. He had his favourite performers, though – Paul Muni, Claude Rains, Will Rogers, Wallace Beery, Charles Laughton, Will Hay, Will Fyffe.' All men and too many Wills, though I remembered a coloured print of Greta Garbo he'd carefully preserved in his keepsake book, whereas the Glen Louise Girls were in a box.

Harry and I had turned out of Peel Street and were now walking down Market Street, which becomes Manchester Road. He was remembering things. He has a beautiful memory – photographic is the only word. Here was where the trams turned, here was the ice-cream shop, here the site of the hoarding that used to say 'Britain's Bread Hangs by Lancashire's Thread' and 'For a Secure Future, Join the Palestine Police'.

I thought about how much I owed him in terms of films and books when I was in my early teens and he in his twenties and we were living back again in Scotland, when Lancashire (in my case, though not in his) was no more than a smudge on the horizon behind me. Teaching himself about the cinema, he bought little blue Pelican paperbacks – Roger Manville's *Film*, Paul Rotha's *The Film Till Now* – and I would look at their black-and-white stills from *Intolerance, Battleship Potemkin*,

Drifters, The Cabinet of Dr Caligari. We shared a small bedroom. Lying
late in bed on Saturday or a Sunday morning, he'd tell me the stories
of the films he'd seen at screenings by the local film society or in stop-
gap bills at remote suburban cinemas or on trips to London. If you
lived in Fife in 1958, to see Eisenstein or Renoir or *All Quiet on the
Western Front* took character and strength of will.

'And then,' my brother might say, 'you see the meat that the crew have
to eat and it's crawling with maggots . . . And then the Cossack brings
his sabre down and this old woman's glasses are smashed and there's blood
in her eyes . . . And then he reaches out to catch this butterfly and you
hear a shot and he's dead . . . And then Mister Hulot tries to play tennis
like he thinks he was taught in the shop.' And then, and then.

And now we were in a street called Long Causeway and facing the
Savoy, once the Ritz's rival as Farnworth's most superior picture house
and now a 'Nine Ball Pool and Snooker Centre' with a Stars and Stripes
painted on its sign. It looked like a 1920s building; high on its red-
brick façade was a series of porthole windows. What did I see here? I
think *Oliver Twist* (Alec Guinness controversially as Fagin, 1948). What
do I remember of it? Only the first scene, as Oliver's mother struggles
to the workhouse, and then not for her but for the storm and the
bending trees, which were frightening. In fact I remember more of the
cinema itself than any film I saw there: the orange light behind its
translucent curtains, fading before the curtains drew apart; and the art
deco rising sun above the screen. Whenever I see or hear the word
Savoy, I think of the colour orange, and not of the hotel or a province
in France.

My brother saw many, many films at the Savoy. One in particular
was *Arabian Nights* (Jon Hall, Sabu, Maria Montez, 1942). He saw it on
the night of Monday 2 August 1943, with Mum and Dad and our
brother Gordon, two years before I was born. Gordon was seven and
Harry nine. The war was on, but the family seemed settled. Mum, Dad,
two little boys, a decent house with a bathroom and three bedrooms,
a big garden with an air-raid shelter, a tandem equipped with a sidecar
so that four of them could cycle off to the country on a Sunday, down
quiet roads emptied of cars by petrol rationing. Little George's death
had, as it were, been conquered. After the performance, Gordon said
that *Arabian Nights* was the best picture he'd ever seen.

Outside the Savoy, this was too sad to talk about. Harry pointed out the Sundeck Tanning Studio and said it used to be a shop that sold foreign stamps to schoolboy collectors, and jokes – joke dog turds, for instance, which could be put on a salad plate and cause domestic consternation, though only once ('Oh not that thing again, Harry, please!'). Then we turned right and began to walk down Albert Road. It was dusk. Occasionally the great square bulk of an abandoned mill stuck up above the houses and stood in silhouette against the sky. Down Kildare Street we saw one that still had its chimney attached. 'The Century Mill,' Harry said. 'Ring-spinning, whatever that was' – not needing to add that Dad would have known. That everybody in Farnworth would have known, once.

4. The Empire

It was difficult to find the exact site of the Empire, a cinema which had been cheaply converted from a tram depot. The story was that the tram rails still existed under the carpet in front of the stalls. According to the *Kinematograph Yearbook* for 1940, it was the cheapest cinema in Farnworth with a top price of ninepence. 'Cowboy films and a bit of a bug-house,' Harry said. I remembered the story of the last words of George V, or possibly Edward VII, and the debate of whether he said 'How goes the Empire?' or 'What's on at the Empire?' We walked on past the municipal park and thought of having a drink in a pub we both remembered called the Shakespeare, but it was shut.

5. The Hippodrome

At last, the Hippodrome. At the corner of Egerton and Cawdor Street we discovered a level rectangle of concrete where the Hippodrome had once been – perfectly level, perfectly matching the cinema's boundaries, as though it were a kind of minimalist monument to the cinema-going habit, the Tomb of the Unknown Audience. We went inside – that is, we left the pavement and walked over the concrete – and Harry began to describe what had been here. 'We're going down the aisle now,' he said. 'Up there on the ceiling' – he pointed at the sky – 'there was a big disc of naked light bulbs, which dimmed before the start of the show. The ones at the centre of the disc dimmed first, and we looked out for that, and when it happened a big cheer would go up. Some kids would ask the manager "Is the Three Stooges on, Mister?" and the manager would say "Wait and see, lads, wait and see."'

We paced around the square of concrete for another few minutes. The Hippodrome had been our local. Towards the end of 1933 our parents had moved across town, exchanging Cemetery Road for a council house on a new estate where all the streets were named after flowers: Lupin, Begonia, Pansy, Daffodil, and in our case Iris and then Lily avenues. The Hippodrome had matinees, and queues for matinees, and this is where both of us had seen Curly, Larry and Mo do cruel things to each other and never come to harm. On a Saturday afternoon we would sometimes walk to it, my hand in his, I imagine, across the playing fields and then between the twin smoking chimneys of Bolton Textile Mills, Numbers One and Two.

By now it was dark. Harry said: 'Farnworth never amounted to very much and now it amounts to nothing at all.' We found a mini-cab and asked the driver to take us to Bolton. 'You gents have been on a sort of sentimental journey then?' the driver said.

6. The Arabian Nights

Why, among so many inexact memories, am I so certain that the family of which I was not yet then a part saw *Arabian Nights* on Monday 2 August 1943? My father wrote the date down, not in a diary and not at the time, but in October that year and in his keepsake book. Looking at his writing now, in the purple ink of a fountain pen, I understand what he was trying to do. To record, obviously, but also to restore and bring to life, as a writer might doodle the name of some absent lover, as the next best thing to the lover's presence in the room.

Monday 2nd August 1943. Went to 'Savoy' and saw 'Arabian Nights'. Gordon told his Mummy it was the 'Best' picture he'd ever seen. I took his hand up Kildare Street on the way home. He was exceptionally cheerful and lively.

Tuesday 3rd August. Both complained of being ill. Gordon slipped back upstairs to bed but Harry went to school. He came home at dinner [lunch] time and went to bed. Gordon was very hot at night.

And then, and then. Events move quickly. On 4 August, his glands begin to swell. On 5 August, Dr Tinto comes and suspects diphtheria and an ambulance takes both boys to hospital. On 7 August, Gordon looks iller.

On 14 August, Gordon says he feels better. On 15 August, he is very low. On 16 August, at 12.15 a.m. in Hulton Lanes Hospital, Bolton, he dies.

On 11 October, my father writes: 'Life is very hard.' On 27 October, he writes: 'For the loving worm within its clod / Were diviner than a loveless God.' On Christmas Eve, he writes: 'My Dear Wee Gordon. How we miss him.'

When I asked Harry about *The Arabian Nights* on our trip to Farnworth, he said he hadn't thought it was up to much, hadn't been as taken with it as Gordon had. I have never seen it. No video or DVD version exists in Britain, though a video is available in the USA. The *Radio Times Guide to Films* (2004 edition) says of it: 'This piece of Hollywood exotica, made to cash in on the success of *The Thief of Baghdad*, stars Jon Hall as the Caliph, Sabu as his best buddy and Maria Montez as his suitor. The actors have their tongues firmly in their cheeks and the whole show is on the brink of send-up, which is exactly where it should be. Producer Walter Wanger was one of Tinseltown's more enterprising independents, though he was later brought to his knees by the crippling costs of *Cleopatra*.' The script is from stories by the Victorian orientalist Sir Richard Burton. The film is in colour and lasts eighty-six minutes.

I wondered if the British Film Institute's National Film and Television Archive had a copy, and at first they thought they had and then they said they hadn't. But I decided to take up the invitation to see the archive anyway – it's probably the largest and most comprehensive of its kind in the world. I took the train from London to Berkhamsted in Hertfordshire, and then a taxi up a hill to a cluster of farm buildings which are the archive's offices. Andrea Kalas, the senior preservation manager, showed me around.

The archive contains books, documents, letters, posters, stills, but its chief holding is its collection of about 475,000 separate cinema and television film titles – about a billion feet of film. We went to the various air-conditioned and dehumidified stores. The flammable nitrate stock was kept in small cells with heavy steel doors and water tanks above – much more of it is stored completely separately in Warwickshire. The newer and more fire-proof acetate and polyester films rose shelf by shelf to the ceilings of large warehouses, called vaults. Men and women in white coats worked in rooms that looked like laboratories. Here I began to see films in a different way. Projected, they were interesting images. In a can, they were only chemicals with a chemical history. Films were cellulose coated with emulsion. At first, and until about 1960, nitrate had collected the silver in the emulsion – silver refracted light. Then there was a switch to acetate. Since the 1980s, polyester has been the chosen substance. Nobody knows how durable this will be. All film, Andrea Kalas said, is inherently unstable. It decomposes.

The most valuable work of the archive is to restore deteriorating film and transfer the images to newer stock – film-to-film reproduction. In one room, a woman in a white coat demonstrated what happened to old films – I think the example may have been Shackleton's *South*. She opened a can and their contents looked like brown sugar crystals. Another can; yellow-ochre dust. A third can: acetate film that had bonded and yellowed like a large reel of flypaper and gave off a sharp smell – Andreas Kalas said that was known as vinegar syndrome.

I had come here with thoughts of injustice, of how I could never see Gordon and yet – somewhere – the best and last film he ever saw would be as lifelike as ever, filled with people talking and moving. But now I saw it differently. The truth is that every principal in the film is now dead, poor Sabu at the age of thirty-nine. As for their lively images, if they have an infinite future it will be thanks to technicians in white coats, tending the chemicals that contain them.

Always and everywhere, this unequal struggle to preserve and remember.

Mother in her kitchen, Fife, 1955

Images